A CALIFORNIA
LOVE STORY

A CALIFORNIA LOVE STORY

———

JOHN W. THILL

PACIFIC DREAM PUBLICATIONS

Copyright © 2023 by John Wilcox Thill
All rights reserved.

No part of this book may be reproduced, or stored in a retrieval system, or transmitted in any form or by any means, electronic, mechanical, photocopying, recording, or otherwise, without express written permission of the publisher. Excerpt from *The San Diego Union-Tribune* used with permission from *The San Diego Union-Tribune*.

Published by Pacific Dream Publications, Carlsbad, California
www.johnwthill.com

Cover design: Richard Ljoenes Design LLC
Project management: Reshma Kooner
Project editorial: Bethany Fred

Image credits: The Wilcox House Sketch © Eileen Roberts
Oceanside Pier photograph circa 1908 © Oceanside Historical Society used with permission from the Oceanside Historical Society. Full cover photo © Marcel Fuentes/ Shutterstock

ISBN (paperback): 979-8-9878493-0-9
ISBN (ebook): 979-8-9878493-1-6

First edition

For Annette and our family. I remember the day you asked for "the secret" from the wise hunter and fisherman while we walked on the beach. He might as well have written his answer in the sand, because it seems to disappear twice each day. "It's love . . . just love. Everything comes from it, and everything is connected to it."

All the knowledge I possess anyone can acquire, but my heart is all my own.
—J. W. von Goethe

CONTENTS

Acknowledgments	xi
Introduction	xvii
Dreams	1
You Should See California!!	9
1926: Longing, Land, and Leverage	49
Rings and Plans of a Home by the Sea	94
Reflections on Moments in Time	119
Fifty-Two Years, Six Months, and Twenty-Two Days	166
Roses, Romance, and Heaven in California	211
Time and Changes	258
Epilogue	263
About the Author	265

ACKNOWLEDGMENTS

The truth is I've been in a small fight with myself to complete this project. Thirty-six years seems like a ridiculously long amount of time to get something done. However, for many years it seemed inappropriate to publish the words that my grandparents wrote privately to each other, and the question of what they might think about it still nags at me a bit. So, I am going to credit myself with thirty years of uncertainty as a consolation prize for perseverance.

Another lingering item is the fact that I am a first-time author. Acknowledging this reality, I also find it a little reassuring that at this moment in time nearly a million new books are written every year. So, apparently anyone can do it, and they are doing it often.

Recently, two things became clear to me: we have a shortage of love stories, and this story should be published. It was also clear that I needed a lot of help to complete this project. Enter writer and editor Bob Yehling. He encouraged me, and we worked on ideas and plans for finding a way forward; I am grateful for him and our friendship.

This book would not have been completed without coaching and support from the talented editor Karalynn Ott. The skill set she brings to projects is a mixture of competence, positivity, and patience. She tolerated and nearly accepted my strange thoughts, ideas, and practices. She was generous and also direct enough to send me a website link that educated me about the purpose of a preface and what it should include. We also reached a critical moment where she "called me out" about my practice of writing sentences and whole paragraphs in a jumble of both past and present tenses. She said she was concerned the readers might get confused. I kept quiet but wanted to ask, "Well, considering there may only be six of them, is that really a problem?"

My marriage also got tangled up during the writing process. It became like a fishing hook-and-sinker outfit that got lodged in the rocks and tide pools in the shore break while I fished for something unknown and unseen in the ocean of life. It reached the point where my wife began asking me to go surfing more and more. She sent me out often on errands, usually to faraway places. Perhaps this was part of God's larger plan to locate and bring home additional plumeria trees to plant as memorials for our relatives who kept dying through the years.

I want to thank two of my daughter's dear friends, Shelby Grates and Emmie Leese, for proofreading and reviewing the original manuscript, sharing their thoughts about the letters, and uncovering some hidden themes. You both sparkle like sunlight on moving water and create inspiration and hope for the future.

I'm gonna ask for forgiveness right here, because I can't really be sure if the events in this book already happened or are still happening. Sixty years of living with the good fortune of being the grandson of Ray and Dora Wilcox was, and is, so rich that the past and present have merged into a sentimental state of appreciation. In fact, maybe that is the ultimate endgame—moving from California to the state of gratitude.

♦ ♦ ♦

At its heart, this book is a collection of my grandparents' love letters from the 1920s, when they were just two young people from the dusty, landlocked center of the country. They were dreaming of a life together in the still-small community of Oceanside, planted along the mostly raw and undeveloped coastline of California. I came to be the keeper of these letters, and their storyteller, decades later, after they'd passed.

The language and contents in Dora's and Ray's letters are intact, and they add glimpses into how things were done and said in their era. For example, it was common practice in the 1920s for both sexes to use the term "girl" to describe relatively young women, and both Ray and Dora did so often—but, interestingly, Ray also at least once used the word "bimbo" to describe a man (another of Dora's suitors, to be exact)! Their banter was far from dull and often entertaining.

ACKNOWLEDGMENTS xiii

Sometimes, it made me think I was reading the script of a screwball comedy film. Ray often tossed around modern-sounding and colorful phrases and terms like "burnt out," "fed up," and "zowie!" or jokes like "Will write better the next time—tear this misdemeanor up." And Dora was colorful in her word choice too, once referring to her financial situation as "not broke but badly bent" and describing something with the word "freaky."

This story begins during an era when much of North America was wide open and wild. In fact, my grandfather nearly didn't even get to start his life, as he was born prematurely in an open field after a horse-and-wagon accident on a cold December day in what is now Oklahoma but was then just called "Indian territory."

The process of organizing the letters and researching our family history to provide more context and details produced some new discoveries, like that of Ray's birth. This project also led me to explore today's Oceanside with fresh eyes and to revisit a few places Ray and Dora helped establish and once loved. It even spurred me to leave my own cozy coastal nest in Southern California and venture out to Kansas and Oklahoma to learn more about my grandparents' birthplaces and what made them who they were. Because who they were and what they did changed my hometown and changed my life.

◆ ◆ ◆

During my early upbringing I was fortunate to have two male heroes to guide and steer me: my grandfather, Ray Wilcox, and my father, Jack Thill. Now that I've gained more life experience and seen a few things, it's clear to me that in many matters, women are often more heroic than men.[1]

Women are the true wonders of the world and life givers to us all. And through the process of discovering and reexamining her letters,

---

1. Our surveys and research have demonstrated that the men's team produced a meager 8 percent of the scoring results for heroism, and these were in only two categories: (1) Gathering and eating food that had fallen to the ground, and (2) Trying hard to conceal tears and emotions while watching others complete the child-birthing process. These numbers are based on a mostly private research project spanning six decades and have not been reviewed by an independent survey firm.

my grandmother Dora Wilcox has emerged as my new "dark horse" influencer and sassy female hero. Family and friends were used to seeing her casually and expertly hosting events in her modern 1950s home. But many did not know the Dora whose letters as a nineteen- and twenty-year-old woman were filled with much competence and practicality—in them we learn about her decisions to work or go to business school instead of taking a vacation to visit Ray in California— and also peppered with a quick wit, tales of her own adventure-seeking outings, and strong, informed opinions.

Young Ray's letters were filled with a passion not only for Dora but for California. Recently I came across these words attributed to J. W. von Goethe: "A man sees in the world what he carries in his heart." Ray's life view, revealed in the words he composed to Dora, was reflective of this sentiment. Here was a man who had lost two brothers by the age of twenty-two and who also supported his remaining brother, who struggled with a brain injury. His parents were forced to leave their farm and home, and Ray had to forgo the education he deeply wanted to instead become a breadwinner in the family. Through all these challenges he never lost his confidence and clear vision for creating and leading a productive, meaningful, and successful life. Ray was a community builder, and for decades that was what he did in his beloved Oceanside, from 1925 until his death, in 1986.

I recall that, as a young person, I mostly wanted to be with the adults—that was where the action was and the good stuff could be learned. Sometimes on visits with my elders, I'd bring a tape recorder along to capture their stories. So, while I hadn't planned on formally writing or publishing a book, I may just be the right person to share this story.

In 1986 I began to compile a simple book for our family. I borrowed a bulky forty-eight-pound IBM Selectric machine to type up the handwritten letters Ray and Dora wrote to one another. This was during a vital period in their young lives—just before the Great Depression and Dust Bowl disasters hammered America. Somehow their love managed to sprout through the dry soil, dust, and poverty of the Midwest before Ray left Dora and his family to find work. First, he hustled by train to the East Coast and worked briefly in bustling Miami, Florida, only to be forced to turn around and race back across the country when his parents moved to the West Coast. This is where his train finally stopped and he found a new love interest. There waiting was a beguiling, sun-drenched, fertile, and ocean-kissed enchantress named CALIFORNIA.

It's a strange trip to try and navigate your way back in time nearly one hundred years when all you have is a map of scattered letters written by two young people trying to make something of themselves and find their way forward through life and love. The experience provided me with a deeper appreciation for the thinking, planning, and determined efforts of many of our forefathers and foremothers to improve their standing in life. It intrigues me to think of Dora and Ray using their precious time to patiently and vividly write about their literal and figurative dreams of one another and about the things they longed for in their relationship and future home in the Golden State. Their dreams were so big.

The letters remind me that life can be full of small but interesting events, subtle humor, and irony too. In one letter Ray (a Protestant) revealed his not-so-subtle thoughts about taking a "Catholic girl" out for a date in California. I'm not sure if he was "playing games" or "shooting straight" with Dora when he wrote that since she was Catholic, "there can be nothing serious ever with us." This makes me smile and wonder how he must have felt a few quick decades later when his firstborn daughter fell madly in love with a young Catholic boy who lived down the street. Young Bobbie Wilcox (my mom) admitted to using some bold tactics—including riding a bike around the neighborhood with her dress skirt flowing, trying to capture the attention of young Jack Thill. All their lives were about to get a little more interesting then! Forgive me . . . I'm now getting ahead of myself.

But time is an odd thing, especially when we dip back into history, whether it be larger or smaller events and more personal records. During the early 1980s, while still a young man, I read an editorial in the *San Diego Daily Transcript* that noted how the ultimate goal of Western civilization is the transcendence of space and time. I believe this to be mostly true. I now invite you to transcend our present fast-paced, "see it and have it now" culture and browse backward in time to experience a bit of what life was like for two young friends who fell in love and were determined to make a good life together. I believe they approached their lives with the thinking that if they remained positive and dreamed and planned, they could do some remarkable and romantic things together. Perhaps that alone is what's worth remembering.

Warm wishes and saltwater kisses,
John Wilcox Thill
Carlsbad, California

INTRODUCTION

Heritage Park is a small park in Oceanside, California. It features a number of historic buildings that trace back to the days of the city's founding in the late 1800s. The park includes several simple, aging wooden structures, along with metal machines and tools that were commonly used in that era. The accompanying exhibits attempt to present what life was like at the turn of the twentieth century.

When my grandmother died, in 1978, my mother planted a sycamore tree in the park and placed a small black marble monument at the base of the tree. The monument had the name "Dora Wilcox" etched into it, along with the years she lived. On a visit to the park, nearly four decades later, I noticed how remarkably tall the tree had grown. It was taller than anything else in the park. Then I looked down and was shocked to see that the trunk and roots of the tree had completely enveloped the black marble monument. It was gone. It was as if it had never existed. Time and nature have a way of reclaiming people and the things we have created.

In a quiet way, this moment served to encourage me that my grandparents' story—including the effort, love, hopes, and dreams found in their words to each other—*is* worth preserving. Within their love letters we find two dimensions of a California love story: their emerging passion for each other, which led to fifty-two years, six months, and twenty-two days of togetherness; and Ray's deep love for his new Oceanside home, for the Golden State, and for the possibilities he saw for the region's future. That vision is seen today in many of the places that make Oceanside attractive: the pier, harbor, reimagined beachfront, and community parks throughout the city.

As I visit these places, I'm reminded that the ongoing correspondence between my grandparents was not just words and messages. It was more like promises to each other, and they presented a future of something better, an inspiration and expression of what might be possible.

DREAMS

Some nights, I visit my grandparents' house and garden while I sleep. The paths to this place are familiar and full of wonder. The things I see and feel are vibrant and vivid. While these dreams are mine, they appear to be more like layered expressions of *their* hopes and dreams. Sometimes, it takes a while to understand these things.

Ray and Dora Wilcox's property included a simple ranch-style house perched on a hill in Oceanside, California. The views from their 160-acre spread were remarkable: for starters, the front yard overlooked the deep-blue Pacific Ocean just three miles to the west. This portion of the Wilcox property was unfenced and provided a sanctuary for all kinds of wildlife. I remember watching rabbits, pheasants, and coveys of quail gathering on their front lawn. The animals and birds would rush for cover when the coyotes hunted up the hillside.

To the south lay San Diego (and beyond that, Mexico), where Ray took some of his first trips as a Californian. And to the north were more rolling green hills, once part of the massive 133,000-acre Rancho Santa Margarita y Las Flores[2] that featured seventeen miles of Pacific coastline. (After the Pearl Harbor bombing and America's entry into

---

2. In 1821, following Mexico's independence from Spain, the Californios (a term used to designate Hispanic Californians) became the new ruling class of California, and many were first-generation descendants of Spain from the Gaspar de Portolá expedition. The Mexican governor was awarding land grants and ranchos to prominent businessmen, officials, and military leaders. In 1841, two brothers by the name of Pio and Andrés Pico became the first private owners of Rancho Santa Margarita. More land was later added to the grant, making the name Rancho Santa Margarita y Las Flores, and that name stayed with the ranch until the US Navy acquired it in 1942.

the Pacific theater for World War II, the federal government purchased these ranchlands for a new Marine Corps base and renamed it Camp Pendleton.)

And finally, a valley opened to the east, where the winding, historic El Camino Real led to Mission San Luis Rey, the former Spanish mission (and the largest of those in California), built in 1798. Here was also their backyard, which was designed as a half-acre formal garden, with some small grassy areas joined by flowering plants and citrus trees, all tied together with ribbons of concrete and brick walkways edged by boxwood shrubs as borders. A main feature of the garden was a gazebo, used for card games or as a play area for unruly grandchildren. Grandad handcrafted a sign that read "Attitude Adjustment Center" and carefully nailed it above the entrance of the structure. None of us kids ever wanted to be sent there, but in reality, it was a pretty nice spot for detention. Nearly one hundred rosebushes graced the yard, along with sweet gardenias and orange blossoms; the scents in the backyard were as intoxicating and unforgettable as the smell of the bourbon in Grandad's favorite cocktail.

As a child, I experienced only a bit of what Ray and Dora Wilcox accomplished, and most of that was through the lens of them simply being my grandparents, decades into their relationship and business success. Yet, as I dug into the record of their early lives many years later, I saw how young Ray's dream for their future was ready to bloom like their rosebushes in the warm California sunlight. Their future together was like a garden he had planted many times in his mind. He first shared that garden with Dora through written words . . . and then brought it into their lives, one piece at a time.

Life lessons—and a wonderful slice of Southern California as she existed a century ago—lay within these letters, which shared their efforts to grow and sustain their relationship as first Ray and then Dora traveled there from the Midwest to build a life together. Their success stemmed from a mixture of optimism, love, and determination. Ray possessed the latter quality in abundance, and for good reason: as a young man, he had experienced the many hardships and disappointments of the early Dust Bowl era and how it impacted members of his own family, along with large swaths of the population. However, he didn't let these events crush his enthusiasm for his own destiny.

Within his written words, he envisioned creating a happy life for them in the small town of Oceanside, then made a commitment to his future wife, Dora, that he would make good on that promise.[3]

⋯

Following my grandparents' deaths, my parents decided to sell the Wilcox property. I helped them pack up Ray and Dora's books, business- and community-related records, and correspondence. There were boxes and boxes of newspapers, files, documents, press clippings, property appraisals, and random photographs. Ray had been extraordinarily busy during his decades in California. He established a land and insurance company, founded a national bank, co-founded a Presbyterian church, and presided over two memorial parks—one in Oceanside, the other in Riverside, seventy-two miles northeast of his home and office. He was chairman of the first governing board of the Armed Services YMCA in '43 and '44, served on the Oceanside City Council, and became mayor in 1946.

The deteriorating items in the storage boxes were rich and diverse. Among them were agendas, notes, and plans for establishing the Oceanside Small Craft Harbor (for which the planning alone went on from 1946 to 1961), the Oceanside Boys Club in 1952, and the Eternal Hills Memorial Park in 1947. They also included Ray's 1942 contract with the US Navy, when he was hired to survey and appraise the Rancho Santa Margarita y Las Flores land before it was purchased and became Camp Pendleton. The project was massive in scale, and some of the land was so mountainous and rugged that it couldn't be reached by vehicle, so Ray covered a great deal of it on horseback and on foot.

Ray had also saved hand-typed documents that showed the comparable pricing of nearby properties, with numbers that would boggle the mind of anyone who's familiar with today's Southern California real-estate market: 40,793 acres of Vail Ranch in Temecula at $34 per acre, and 2,500 acres of Ida Dawson's Rancho Agua Hedionda in

---

3. In the early 1900s the census was completed every ten years. The historical records for Oceanside, California, in 1920 list the population as 1,116 in 1920 and 3,508 in 1930. Ray Wilcox estimated that in 1925 the population was 2,200.

Carlsbad at $55 per acre. Today? You can barely buy two simple three-bedroom houses on Vail Ranch for that $1.38 million listing price. As for Rancho Agua Hedionda? The $137,500 total listing price for all those acres back then would hardly cover a down payment for an average three-bedroom home in Carlsbad today.

All these documents filled me with a sense of wonder as I realized how long ago Ray was convinced about California's future expansion and the impending dramatic growth, development, and creation of new opportunities here. His vision soon came true, and suddenly he was swept up in and part of it all. He was thriving in this new and exciting, sun-kissed country.

Yet for all those great historical finds, my most interesting discovery while rummaging through their belongings was something far more personal: a lady's hatbox full of Ray and Dora's love letters, written between 1925 and 1927, as they courted via the US Postal Service and telegrams. The words within gave me a window into their youthful dreams, daily lives, and emotions back then. For instance, in April 1927, when Ray was twenty-three and still building the foundation for a life in California, he wrote to Dora, who was still living in Wichita, Kansas:

> *All this week, I have been thinking and dreaming of you. If it was not for your picture above the fireplace on the mantle, I could not stand it as well as I do. Some nights, when everyone is in bed, I sit down by the fireplace and hold your picture before me and wonder and think of you—and the future. Darling, I am not worthy of such a person as you. I feel like I am getting so much and have so little to offer. But dearest of all, somehow I feel that I can make you supremely happy when we are married. I know that I can and will do my best and that's all any man can do. One thing that I have that I want to keep and that is ambition. With you to work for and to love and to cherish, I know that I can succeed. Success in a material way, too. It may be that I will never know what it means to be rich, with money. But real riches of life are not always found in computing the amount of any*

man's money. Good friends and neighbors, a happy wife and children, and a clean life count for more than mere dollars. The west is a good place to test out this, because here they measure a man by what he is instead of what he has.

The letters were captivating. As I read them, I found Ray and Dora's cross-country communications filled with mutual encouragement, appreciation, love, and respect—as well as healthy doses of sly humor and, at their base, true friendship. They made promises and then confirmed and reconfirmed their commitment to one another, even during the moments of doubt each felt—not a surprise, considering they did not see each other for *almost two years*, the period of their letter writing. They developed plans to marry and begin a family together. And my grandfather shared his boundless optimism amid the joyful experience of living in the beauty of Southern California long before it grew more densely populated.

Ray's experience provided a gleaming contrast to the less-inspiring reality of Dora's life during their courtship, when she was an office worker at the Mentholatum Company in Wichita, the town where she'd grown up. While she appeared to like her job and was a good sport, at one point she simply told Ray, "I hope that nothing happens so you will have to come back so soon, because you are doing nicely, and you had better stick and do better. There isn't anything here to do."

The letters reveal how Ray planned and persevered after his parents and siblings were forced to leave the Midwest. They also spell out how he considered Dora's boldness, wit, and independence a gift, making him even more determined to create success and happiness for both of them.

They both faced the God-awful reality of the emerging Dust Bowl in their native states of Oklahoma and Kansas, the winds and dust and lack of rain killing livestock and crops alike. (These losses reached $25 million per day by 1936, equivalent to $526 million per day in 2022 dollars.) The Dust Bowl eventually forced tens of thousands of families to abandon their farms, as they were unable to pay mortgages or grow crops. Cities filled with people going hungry from the scarcity of work—during the heart of the Depression. The people were withering, just like their crops and the opportunities to work. The drought affected more than one hundred million acres across Oklahoma, Texas, and parts of New Mexico, Colorado, and Kansas.

According to historical records, the brutal Dust Bowl drought and farming crisis took place from 1930 to 1936, with the worst dust storms peaking in 1935. But it began well before then, as this foreboding letter from Dora to Ray on May 10, 1927, indicates:

> *Speaking of fresh air. I would like to breathe a little right now. The air is so full of dust and sand that it nearly chokes one. It was this way yesterday, too.*

Many of these displaced families were referred to as "Okies" because so many came from Oklahoma. Those who did not resettle in midwestern cities migrated to California and other states to seek work and a new start. Writer John Steinbeck memorialized this exodus and hardship in his novel *The Grapes of Wrath*, which was later made into a film featuring actor Henry Fonda. (And in a coincidental twist, Ray later sold Fonda a large parcel of land in Fallbrook, California; the pair also became friends.)

Whether it was luck or foresight, or a little bit of both, Ray and Dora got out before the mass Dust Bowl migration. By the late '20s, Ray had already made his way to California, which he viewed with young and opportunistic eyes and a vision colored by his own long-time ties to land. On November 17, 1926, he wrote to Dora:

> *I have a new dream to tell you now. It's about our home in California. I want an orange or lemon orchard and some kind of fruit crop to have as our own. I think that we could be very happy along the Southern Coast. I want to work in the land business and real estate. I love the soil and would have been a farmer if I had stayed in Oklahoma. All my ancestors have been either farmers or merchants, so it's in me to make my living that way, only I want to sell the land and have a little left to call our home. But dreams mean nothing, not even much pleasure, when they don't work out unless they can be*

fulfilled by hard work and effort. I am trying and feel that I can make good.

Their tender, practical correspondence reveals how Ray and Dora collaborated on that dream together, even before they finally reunited in Oceanside. When Ray, who was working in the grocery business at the time, became discouraged with his progress, Dora sent him this important message:

> *In my life, I have only had a very few disappointments, and I know how hard they are to take. You have had more than your share of troubles, but things won't be that way always; already things are looking brighter, aren't they? Everything is for the best—perhaps this does mean that you should change your business. I don't think, Ray, that you will ever be satisfied until you have gotten into the real estate business, do you? For deep down in your heart, you like the real estate business better than any other—always you are dreaming of it. It must have been born into you.*
>
> *Remember you will always succeed better at anything you like than at any other trade. I know that you will succeed in the grocery business, for you are that kind—you will do good in any business—but will you ever be satisfied to stay with it? Why don't you try the real estate business? You can win in it, and the sooner you start, the better.*

Two years later, in 1929, on his twenty-sixth birthday, with Dora finally at his side on the land he had also fallen deeply in love with, Ray wrote this personal tribute to Southern California:

LAND OF SUNSHINE AND HEART'S DESIRE

To one who has lived on the Southern Coast of California, there is no other place on earth which means so much in beauty, in comfort and enjoyment. One may travel to the far away corners of the world to seek pleasure or happiness and livelihood, but sooner or later his mind will wander back to the romance and magic of California's South Coast. No other spot in all the world offers so much and holds such great enchantment.

Wonderful cities, towering mountains, marvelous sunsets share but part of the glory of soft moonlight nights, the languorous roll of the Pacific and the fragrant perfume of orange blossoms. Dreamy, sunny afternoons melt into charming eventide when one can forget the cares of the world and stroll through moon-lit gardens under a canopy of shining stars. What a place to rear children, to carry on business, to enjoy yourself, to really live. With the charms of the desert away but a few hours by motor and snow-clad mountains within sight, with palm-lined highways beckoning to be tried, is it no wonder that people love to live here? . . .

It is futile to try and describe the charm or the spell that the Southland has upon the hearts of its people but it has to do with the one thing without which life would be dull indeed . . . romance.

YOU SHOULD SEE CALIFORNIA!!

I recently drove up the California coast from my home to visit my daughter and son-in-law. A simple highlight of these trips is getting outdoors for walks with their beautiful Australian shepherd. The dog's luxurious coat and kaleidoscopic eyes literally stop people on the street.

During a late-summer weekend, the dog and I were strolling around her neighborhood when a middle-aged man approached us. He wore sandals, shorts, and an attractive long-sleeved shirt. He walked toward us with a sense of attitude and importance, as if he were the mayor of Driftwood Drive. As we got closer to one another, he swung out wide of us and into the street, then paused to admire the dog.

"He is gorgeous! Is he a border collie or an Aussie?" he asked.

"Aussie," I said with a bit of fatherly pride.

"Do you have a groomer?"

"Are you referring to me or the dog?" I joked.

After a brief laugh, we shared our gratitude for the beautiful morning and for living in California. Looking up the street, I noticed well-tended white roses and orange canna lilies peeking out and glowing in the early light. We took it all in.

During our conversation, I learned that the man's grandfather was from Poland and had suffered in a German concentration camp for six years. His grandfather was a carpenter and eventually made it to Italy and then the United States, where he worked for the Thrifty company building cabinets and store-related fixtures all across the country.

In turn, I mentioned several of my own grandparents' achievements, to which he said, "Wow. Our grandparents were interesting, and they did interesting and remarkable things. I'm convinced our generation is less interesting, and now our children are even less interesting than us."

As if to prove his point, the next most interesting thing he said was to suggest the grand idea of hosting a dog parade on this small street. We agreed that there aren't enough dog parades in the world. I am presently reworking my short list of life's burning ambitions to include becoming the grand marshal of the Driftwood Drive Dog Parade.

◆◆◆

The trail and journey that Ray Wilcox and Dora Kullmann undertook to reach California and build their dream home and life together there wasn't always clear to me. But by digging through records and remembering snippets of conversations with the adults in my family, and later by reading their letters, I learned more. Neither Ray nor Dora kept a daily journal of their early life events, but the hatbox full of letters, plus items and documents stored in my parents' files left clues as to what was important to them and what they decided was worth saving.

Through the years, and as I prepared this manuscript, "bread crumbs" from Dora and Ray's trail would magically appear. For example, while I rummaged through my parents' boxes of files and other things, I found an unfiled fourteen-page typed document held together with a rusting staple. It had no date, no note, and no explanation connected to it. Its contents included eight mini-stories recounting important Wilcox family events from 1869 to 1903. I figured it had been written by Ray and Dora. Then, twenty years after this discovery—while I was finishing the final draft of this book—my cousin, Kevin Bender, reached out to me and asked if he had given me a copy of a fourteen-page document of ancestral history that he had created for our family. I was thrilled to learn it was this same document. It originated in 1980 from an oral interview that Kevin conducted with our grandparents, Ray and Dora. One little mystery solved, and one more cache of information verified.

It is a fact that Ray was born in 1903 in a wild and wide-open place, and four years later this territory would be certified by President Teddy Roosevelt as the forty-sixth US state: Oklahoma. Ray's father was a farmer and one of many European American settlers who ventured to the Midwest. Their farmhouse was eight miles from Quinlan (an unincorporated section of Woodward County) in the northwestern region of the state. This was just a tiny part of the much larger region where Indigenous peoples—including the Kiowa, Comanche, Cheyenne, and Arapaho tribes—had thrived for centuries. Woodward was a small but growing county benefiting from the railroad's expansion, which created the ability to export cattle.

The first story in the Wilcox family history describes the dramatic events surrounding Ray's premature birth near present-day Quinlan. The details include a wagon accident and how his father, William Homer ("WH") Wilcox, rushed off to find a country doctor to try and fix another son's crushed leg *and* help his wife deliver baby Ray.

> **On the afternoon of December 6, 1903, my father, William Homer Wilcox, was engaged in hauling sand from a creek bed in the country below the farmhouse eight miles from Quinlan, Oklahoma. He was hauling sand to mix with gypsum to chink up the cracks in the Wilcox homestead. The wagon was double-sided, and was drawn by two horses. My brother Orville was riding on the wagon and was standing on the brake bin. About halfway up the steep hillside, my father stopped for the purpose of letting the horses "blow," that is, to rest a bit from their exertions.**
>
> **As soon as the team was ready to start up again, my father released the brake, and this caused Orville to fall off the wagon into the path of the rear wheels. The wagon of great weight passed over his right leg and broke it.**
>
> **Of course, everything became serious in the family. We were eight miles from the nearest doctor. The boy Orville was in tremendous pain and no one could be sure how serious it was, whether an**

amputation would be needed or what other damage to him would occur.

Dad rode a horse to Quinlan in a great hurry and found a doctor who came out as soon as possible. At that time my mother was in shock. This led to my premature birth—about six weeks early.

The doctor had his hands full: trying to repair and set the brother's leg, giving attention to my mother who was very ill, and trying to see if I could make it. My mother was deeply concerned, as was my father, because I only weighed three and one-half pounds—which is pretty tiny.

My father said that when they got me cleaned up, they put me in a shoe box and laid me near the fireplace. It was December and quite cold. Dad was chopping wood for the next six weeks to keep the fireplace going and the house heated.

My mother told me a little story about what happened when the doctor was examining me close up. He got his head down there with a stethoscope right close peering into my shoe box, and I let him have it. I urinated right in his face. The comment he made to my mother was: "I am afraid now this little boy is going to make it!"

Mother made a recovery in the next few weeks and my brother Orville's leg was not much of a burden. He walked with a very slight limp. He weighed about 195 to 200 pounds when he was twenty years old and was always active and strong. And that's how I came to be six weeks early.

◆ ◆ ◆

Ray indeed made it, and grew up in Woodward with his three older brothers and younger sister, Bernice. He graduated from Woodward

High School in 1922, and in the summer his family relocated to Wichita, Kansas.

Ray and Dora likely met in 1923 when they attended night-school classes in Towanda, Kansas, twenty-five miles outside Wichita. Dora, then seventeen, was an excellent student and musician with a clever sense of humor. She had a progressive outlook on life and was confident and bold. Ray and Dora shared many friends, and they both participated in Christian Endeavor youth ministry and church groups; they also both led Sunday-school classes.

There were other interesting tales as well, some of which revealed more about Ray's early years. In 1982, when I was twenty-one years old and Ray was seventy-nine, I drove him to his younger sister's home. My grandaunt Bernice (by then twice widowed) lived on Sunny Creek Road in Carlsbad, an eight-mile drive south along the coast from Ray's house. Most of the route was on pavement by then, but the last mile we bounced along together on a remaining dirt road. My plan was to use a small tape recorder to capture memories and stories while they still had the ability to share them.

Bernice's house, built in the 1970s, was designed and constructed by her son, Rusty Wilcox Grosse, a successful business owner and "land man" in his own right. The single-story rambler, built with functionality in mind, worked well for her (she lived on her own at that point). The kitchen and dining area—complete with breakfast nook and oversized sliding glass door—led to an outdoor patio and her prized garden. Bernice's gardening and baking skills were top-notch, and her place carried the scents of new and old things combined: fresh-cut flowers, fresh vegetables, and fresh-baked food along with old furniture, old spices, and old tobacco.

Bernice had remarkable eyes. They reminded me of sparkling stars in the night sky, or moving water reflecting the sunlight. They were a fascinating mixture of light blue and light gray, with silver flecks of what seemed to be stardust (very different from her brother Ray's brown eyes). The closest match I have ever seen to Bernice Wilcox's eyes was in a photograph in a museum in Woodward, Oklahoma. They belonged to Mr. Temple Houston, the son of Sam Houston, who served as the president of the short-lived Republic of Texas. Temple was a

Great Plains pioneer and is remembered as a gifted orator. He spoke French, Spanish, and seven Indian languages. He was a successful and brilliant frontier attorney, a politician, and a gunfighter. A 1960s television series, *Temple Houston*, was also created about his legendary life. Learning about this intriguing man was one of the highlights of my visit to Oklahoma. It somehow seems fitting that he and Bernice shared something in common. Even as a young man, I knew there was something special and daring lurking behind those eyes of hers. She was a straight shooter from the frontier herself, but she also had a wide, mischievous smile and was known to kick up her heels and dance a jig now and then.

Being in my elders' company, sitting around Bernice's kitchen table, was comfortable and enjoyable. Once I pressed the Play and Record buttons on my tape recorder, however, things shifted slightly. It was mostly pleasant as we talked about their lives and many different things. There was no agenda. They were free to ramble about their lives.

The siblings fell into a steady banter, reminiscing about life in Oklahoma and Kansas, farming, horses, and family. Ray said things like "We had a horse named Rocket. He was twenty-nine years old but always looked like he was a hundred." Bernice then added, "Rocket was Mother's horse, and one of his eyes was bad." Ray replied, "Well, he was a good runner. Quite a spirited deal. Dad was a natural handler of horses. He could have been a licensed vet."

Ray mentioned working twelve hours a day as a young man during the watermelon season back in the Midwest. Then he brought up his dear friend Allan Kelly, who was also no stranger to low-paying manual work. Allan was one of two sons related to the three well-known Kelly Ranches in North San Diego County in Southern California. "He was working as a service-station attendant at the Union Oil station when we first met in Oceanside fifty-seven years ago," Ray said. "He was making two dollars a week. He was quite a nice guy. He's wealthy now." Bernice mentioned that her friend Carol Kelly, Allan's granddaughter, had since moved to Colorado and had once joked with her, "I am never coming back to that place because my children are there." We laughed together.

Then the conversation took an unexpected turn and became

uncomfortable. Bernice brought up the events related to the family moving from Woodward, Oklahoma, to Wichita, Kansas. (My best estimate is around 1918.) "We lost the house in Woodward," she said matter-of-factly. Ray bristled. "No," he said. "I was there. It was a rough deal. But they didn't foreclose. We sold it before we went to Wichita. It sold for several thousand dollars. We didn't lose money." Bernice raised her voice this time. "NOW, RAY!" she insisted. "You can't possibly forget that. I was there, too."

Ray paused briefly, then tried to shift the conversation to more pleasant childhood recollections about their late brothers, Orville and Harry, and their surviving brother, Homer. Bernice twisted in her chair. "Oh, Ray! Please!" she persisted. "We moved to the fairgrounds and lived in the exposition building for two or three years. I was in the sixth and seventh grade." She hesitated, then finally said, "I never felt poor." Ray got quiet. He hadn't forgotten.

•••

By 1925, Ray's parents and what remained of the family were still struggling. The family had at one time included his parents, William Homer (WH) and Dessie; his sister, Bernice; and his brothers Harry, Orville, and Homer. (There had also been another sibling, who died as an infant and is buried in Woodward.) Work was hard to find in Oklahoma and Kansas, and farming was often uncertain. During the previous ten years, life had been full of hardships for the Wilcox family. Harry died from an illness in 1918, at age twenty-two, while serving in the military. And then Orville also died from an illness in 1922, at age twenty-three. The move from Woodward to Wichita hadn't really panned out for them, and Ray's parents began exploring options to move to yet another city or even another state. By July 14, 1925, Ray, then age twenty-two, had made a critical decision. He hardly had enough time to say goodbye to his friends and Dora in Wichita before quickly boarding a train to the East Coast. He was determined to make a success of himself—and his first goal was to find work in Florida.

It was on this long trip southeast that Ray began his first correspondence with Dora, who was living with her parents back in Wichita. The earliest dated item found in the hatbox was a brief postcard from the journey. Ray wrote just five sentences while on his way to the Sunshine State. It was the farthest he had ever been from his home and family. Little did he know it would only be the beginning of the greatest geographic and romantic odyssey of his life.

July 20, 1925
(Albany, GA to Wichita, KS via postcard)

Dear Dora,

I have reached Albany, Georgia and 1,300 miles from home. Two days more and I will be in Miami. Please excuse my penmanship on this postcard. I'm standing on the train while writing this note to you. Please write to me 'Care Of General Delivery' in Miami.

Ray

[Dora wrote a lengthier, affectionate letter almost immediately.]

July 23, 1925
(Wichita, KS to Miami, FL)

Dear Ray,

I received your card this morning, and I certainly was glad to hear from you—that you were safe and near your destination. I hardly knew whether to expect to hear from you or not, for I thought that you might try to forget Wichita all together.
    Did you have any trouble on the road? Didn't you get tired of riding all day?
    Friday evening ten of us girls had a picnic. Monday evening our Christian Endeavor church group had a picnic, or rather a steak fry in Sims Park. As soon as we got there it started to rain and it rained all night but we stayed until nine o'clock. We were

all soaked—surely had a good time and a wet time, alright. I had to hold the umbrella over the fire to keep it from going out. The Christian Endeavor misses you, too.

I went to Church Sunday, but Mr. Hamilton preached and you know how that is. Sigh . . .

Well, Ray, the impossible is happening . . . Last night in Towanda my sister-in-law taught me how to drive a Ford. I may know how to drive good soon—didn't kill anyone but I surely hit every rock that I saw.

I hope that you get a good position in Miami. I am quite sure that you will. Be sure to write me all about your trip, and position, n' everything.

I have just been raving on, so I expect I had better stop.

Write to me soon.

Lovingly,
Dora

July 25, 1925
(Miami, FL to Wichita, KS via postcard)

Dear Friend Dora,

Been in Miami two and a half days and swimming in the Atlantic Ocean twice. This is a wonderful city and very pretty. Business everywhere along the Coast is fine. I looked the West & East Coasts of Florida over before coming on down to the tip. Everybody seems to be in the real estate business here. Over 7,000 people engaged in that line of work.

Millions of dollars being spent on buildings and improvements. People from all over the world are here and the town is packed and jammed. More come every day. Plenty of jobs at 50 & 60 cents an hour. The climate is fine. Not as hot as Kansas. Temperature stays around 80 all the time.

Sorry your friend Dick cannot be here but it seems it was impossible for him to come.

Take good care of him, but don't forget to write to; Yours truly,

Ray

August 10, 1925
(Wichita, KS to Miami, FL)

Dear Ray,

I am so glad to hear that you have a good job, and I am hoping you get a raise soon. Don't get discouraged, but just keep on plodding and you will get there some day. But remember, Ray, it isn't the money that you make, but the money that you save that counts.
It really isn't any of my business I guess, but I am betting on you making good, and I certainly would hate to be disappointed—I am sure I won't be.

In the movies last week, I noticed some pictures of Miami. They were perfectly beautiful. I wouldn't mind seeing the real thing.

The weather has been wonderful here last week. One wouldn't want it any cooler.

Have you heard about our earthquake? Kansas is getting rather freaky. It was just a small one—the folks said that they never felt it, but most of the people on the hill felt it quite plainly. I didn't notice it because I was in Towanda. You never know what is going to happen here next.

School starts in a month from now. The vacation this summer has seemed so short to me.

My brother, Carl, leaves for Kansas University on the first of September.

My brother, Harry bought the Kelly Springfield wholesale tire place on South Market Street, so he moved his family down here. They live in the first block on North Grove. I have to go & see them every once in a while.

You needn't worry about Dick and me. I hadn't seen him for two weeks and I thought that he had gone to Florida, but last night he came out for a little while. He changed his mind about leaving town, isn't that the limit?

Well, I must tell you all the church news. Pastor Anderson has been away fishing for several weeks and just got back about a week and a half ago. I wonder if he will share some casting tips and demonstrate them for the congregation?

I did get through [leading] that Christian Endeavor meeting last Sunday, but it was funny. I had a backward meeting—you know, doing the things first that we usually do last. Everyone got so tickled when we said the benediction first. It certainly was a crazy meeting, contests 'n everything. Pastor Anderson was with us most of the time. I felt rather foolish, but everyone seemed to have a good time. Ryan said that I could lead all the time, but I declined—gently but firmly.

Miss Bailey has gone on her vacation, so I have the exciting and demanding job of playing the chimes during services in August.

Your Sunday School class is still wandering around without a teacher—and so is our class.

Mrs. Hill has gone to Columbia, MO., on her vacation. She asked about you. Also, I met Helen Doth on the street and she inquired about you. Everyone seems to think that I am the information bureau—why is it? Isn't it nice to be missed?

It seems so funny not to see you once in a while. I can't get used to it. Please don't get homesick and give up. I will do anything to help you. I answer your letters as soon as I get them, so the oftener you write the oftener I write. Let me know all about your work. Work hard, but have a good time, too.

With lots of love,
Dora

August 16, 1925
(Miami, FL To Wichita, KS)

Dearest Dora,

You are surely fine about answering and you write such letters of encouragement. It surely "peps" me up to get letters like those from somebody who cares. I have something to work for and surely do not want to disappoint my friends and myself.

So, you take Miss Bailey's place playing the chimes thru August? In the morning, that is noon, ring them loud so I can hear them down here. Gee, but don't I wish I could hear those chimes today especially when you play them.

Listen, Dora, did you ever change your mind about sending me one of your pictures? If I just had one of them on my dresser to look at when I'm home, don't you know how much better it would be? If you will, I'll send one of "yours truly." Can't see what it would hurt, do you? If you can't come yourself, send your likeness. Could you take a vacation and come down before school? I know you need one, and if you could I could show you a good time. Maybe I wouldn't let you come back. Wire when you start and I'll meet the train.

Now you know that I know that that would be an impossibility, but I do get a "big kick" out of just thinking about it coming true. "No Kidding," I would like to hold you in my arms tonight.

Yesterday, the fifteenth of Aug. was one month since I started out from Wichita. It doesn't seem over two years since I left Oklahoma, but now I am getting used to it and don't mind it so much.

Dora, if you still feel that you don't want me to have your picture will you do me a favor? I left those pictures I had enlarged of you and I, at Lauterbach's store, and if you will ask for them there I think they will find them for you. Will you send them to me? Is there anything here I could do for you in any way?

I should have sent you a questionnaire instead of a letter this time as I have asked so many questions.

With love and best wishes,
Ray.

August 20, 1925
(Wichita, KS to Miami FL)

Dear Ray,

When I came home from Towanda this evening, I was so tired that I didn't want to do anything, but your letter came and revived me, and here I am in bed writing to you. I knew that if I didn't do it this evening it would be several days before I would get to do it, so I decided to do it now.

There is just something going on all the time. I must give a couple of music lessons in the morning, go swimming with a girlfriend in the afternoon, and go picnicking in the evening with two other couples and a boyfriend. That is the way it is day after day—so I guess that I never lack fun. I must have been born under a lucky star.

Last night in Towanda my brother, his wife, and myself were invited by a young couple to a dance. They held the dance in a large room in the basement of their home—a beautiful room. It had tile floors, lovely furniture and a dandy fireplace (although that really wasn't needed last night). It was so cool, for they had four large fans going. I just wanted to sit and enjoy it all, but instead I danced from 9 o'clock until midnight continuously. We just had a dandy time. But, this morning . . . . Gee! I hated to get up early and teach Sunday School.

Do you have to work on Sundays, too? Just what kind of work do you do?

I am so glad that you are getting acquainted and that you are having a good time, for then you won't get lonesome and blue. Pretty soon you will forget Wichita entirely. Tell me all about your friends—gals and boys both. Hope that you and your "date" had a dandy time Sunday.

Gee! I wish that I could take a trip to Florida and see you, but as you say I guess we will both have to imagine it. There seems to be no other way.

About those pictures, I haven't a single picture left and I don't want to get anymore made, so I guess you will just have to stand it!!

Use your imagination instead. I am going to get rash someday and have some snapshots taken, and if they are any good, I may send you some. You do the same, won't you?

I hope that nothing happens so you will have to come back so soon, because you are doing nicely, and you had better stick and do better. There isn't anything here to do. Although we would all like to see you, I hope you get to stay and have success.

Lovingly,
Dora

August 25, 1925
(Miami, FL to Wichita, KS)

Dear Dora,

By now you know that this is going to be a letter instead of the inevitable postcard. But at that you can hardly blame me for having some post cards handy. I fill them up, or usually do. But cards are not quite the proper thing to carry on correspondence with a girl back home. Tonight is the first time that I have written a letter to anyone, even the folks at home.

You don't wish you were here any worse than I do. Kansas is all right and a dandy place to live. . . . but Dora this country is wonderful. Coconuts, bananas, oranges and everything else in the index grows and flourishes here. The Bahama Islands are a short distance away, also Cuba.

Rich people, nationally known celebrities, multi-millionaires, famous manufacturers have their winter homes along the East Coast. I took a trip the other day out where they are spending one hundred million dollars on a tract of beautiful land and are turning it into the most wonderful suburban city in this country. It is called Coral Gables. You will read of it soon in all the magazines and newspapers. They are contracting for three hundred million dollars' worth of fine homes there. That's quite a sum of money if I say it myself. It's the same all over.

You ask whether I had a job yet. You bet I have and you can tell the world it's a lot better than the one I left at home. I work for the American Express Company. They are rushed all the time. This city is literally packed and jammed with people from the whole world. They say next to New York City Miami is made up of more representatives of all nationalities than any other city. People from everywhere I don't care which place you might mention. I get 25.00 a week straight for an 8-hour day and then 75¢ an hour for overtime. We put in overtime everyday so far and will for some time. They have electric trucks and two men to a truck. When I know the city a little better I will have charge of a truck and that won't be long. I expect September, and then I get an increase in wages of $4.50 a week. Miami lives up to its name of being the "Magic City."

But the Real Estate business is the one line that is really making money and that's my ambition, to get into that as soon as possible. It's been pretty hard "sledding" for me here alone but you will know that I am not a "quitter" no matter how hard it comes. I came down here for a change and I got it (now laugh) but my real purpose was to make a "stake" and that's what I am going to do. They want me to stay and I am going to stick.

No, Dora I have never been up in a plane but I am going someday. Seaplanes are common as flies here and they are always flying over the Bay. Also, many steamships and yachts.

I see that you are still dreaming of me and that this time I am sunburned. That's no mistake and your dream hit it about right. I am about the color of the early American Indian and about as healthy. Still going over to Towanda are you? Doesn't seem to be any let down for you is there? (now smile)

I am so glad that you have mastered the art of swimming. It makes life something different anyway. Wish you were here to go into the ocean with me at Miami Beach. The ocean is salty, but otherwise very fine.

Well, old girl I know that you have been patient in reading this stuff but listen here. I want you to know that I think of you and miss you terribly. I shall never forget those wonderful nights I have spent with you, those dances, gosh they make me homesick, but dearest, this is hard to stand but I guess I can make the grade if you write real often.

Tell me all the news and gossip. Tell all the Christian Endeavorers "hello" for me and tell them not to be afraid to write. My address is 126 N.E. Third St.

Lovingly,
Ray

August 28, 1925
(Miami, FL to Wichita, KS)

Dear Dora,

Your last letter received and I was glad that you had time to answer mine. I know that you are as busy as you can be and glad that you are having such a fine time.

Well Dora, I was disappointed about the photograph but if that's what you think, you have the right to your own opinion. You are surely steadfast when you make up your mind. I shall not ask you again.

Had a letter from my father saying that he had made a deal and made a new Flint car as a commission. Hope it is better than the old car he had when I was home. I also received a nice long letter from Pastor Anderson. He urged me to keep on and go to college. It was as fine a letter as I ever received. He is one fine man. He said that I never would be satisfied until I had an education. It gives you an appreciation of life that you rarely have without it. Well, Dora this is short and snappy. I work hard every day and am saving my money for school.

Sincerely,
Ray

[Author's note: We now find a thirty-day gap in correspondence between Ray and Dora. There is no written documentation or mention of what prompted Ray to suddenly leave Florida and journey back to Wichita and then on to California. It seems practical to assume that his parents may have reached out and asked him to support the family in their own transition from Wichita to Southern California, a 1,420-mile and (back then) multiday journey by train. The Wilcox family at that time included his parents, WH and Dessie; his older brother, Homer; and his younger sister, Bernice. Ray notes that while working in Miami he had lost weight and suffered from an infected foot, so that may have influenced his move as well. He also wrote that he was in California for his parents' health and to make some money. So perhaps he wanted to reconnect with his family too, as they headed west.]

September 28, 1925
(Oceanside, CA to Wichita, KS)

Dearest Dora,

Now that we are settled in California, I hope it will be for some time. I will take my old quill in hand and write to a really nice girl back in the old home town. We have a really nice house that overlooks the sea and from where I sit now I can hear the Pacific Ocean roar and boom. It is some water and sister Bernice and I are going in real soon. Have you ever heard the ocean? It makes a real noticeable roar all the time and the tidal waves bump against the sandy beach and splashes the foam all over. The Atlantic is not quite as rough notwithstanding the name "Pacific" was given to this quiet water.

    Well Dora how are you by now? Is the old school work getting the little girl down? I know it never did heretofore but now that "yours truly" is not now there, maybe you are not getting the proper attention. (Don't hit me)

    We have a dandy little house and some awfully nice flowers of all kinds. Homer and I are putting out some garden (Real work) and will have some radishes, etc. in two or three weeks. This is a fine country in many respects and not so very fine in others. The Mountains and the Ocean are wonderful and scenic and the paved roads thru the Mountains and along the Coast can't be surpassed in natural beauty and thrills. But it may be that we are too full of the plains and level country to ever get used to this country and make new friends. It is strange to step out on the street and never meet anybody you really know, only speaking acquaintances, etc.

Dora, you know that when I came back I was in bad shape. I was underweight about 13 pounds and had an infected foot. Well, yesterday or the day before, I put my regular shoe on again and I gained back my normal weight. So, you can see that Florida did not agree with me and that perhaps California is. We are really out here for the folk's health and incidentally to make some money.

How is your steady boyfriend now? Does Dick make his regular calls, or maybe Randolph M. has usurped the high place in the fair lady's heart? Are you dancing much, any more or yet?

Wish I was there so that we could have that long car ride or Sunday night on the front porch and make my arm twitch again. I did get a giant kick out of that and hope that you enjoyed yourself a little. Or that car ride before I went South. I had better quit or I will get up and start back home. Well, "bye bye" and write me all the local gossip and news.

With Love,
Ray

October 16, 1925
(Oceanside, CA to Wichita, KS)

Dearest Dora,

Your keen letter was received here by the folks and held here several days. Then when I came home from Long Beach where I had been working, I found that they had forwarded my mail and I had to wait till it came back. That made me feel not so well but your letter was certainly worth waiting for.

Say, Dora I can't write more than this page as it's the last one. Bernice has used up all the good stationary. But next time I will write one of those long newspapers that I have sent you from time to time.

I can't make up my mind which part of the country I do like best but I know it is not Florida. This country is fine for climate and scenery but as for making money I have yet to find out.

We are just a little ways from Mexico, about as far as Hutchison from Wichita. I've been to San Diego—the border town—about 4 times and am going across to Tijuana real soon. Tijuana is the saloon town of Mexico and the "toughest town in the far west" so I am going to watch my step.

Yes, Dora you have about the finest Dad I know of and if you don't appreciate him now you will when you get older. I wish every girl had as good a Dad as yours, then there would be less tears and more smiling Maybe that's what makes you so good natured.

I am sorry that the ankle-popping and arm-twitching titles are resting on other brows more noble. Maybe I can regain them when I get back to Wichita.

I've been to Los Angeles and Hollywood and have seen some snappy looking women and men but they are not natives. I still insist that the Middle West has the best and keen looking women.

Dora, get your spy glass out and read this. [print is small] Next time I will break the long-distance record and when you get through with it you will know that you have scanned an eyeful. But that don't mean for you to wait to write. Please "do your duty" and then I'll have a nice box of stationery.

With love,
Sincerely Ray

October 21, 1925
(Wichita, KS to Oceanside, CA)

Dear Ray,

I was quite surprised to get a letter after such a long time, for I didn't know whether you were still in California, or whether I should look for you to "pop" up here someday. One can never tell about you—here one day, and there the next day. Also, I had another dream about you—I dreamed that I was sitting in our regular place in church and someone came and sat down beside me and whom do you think it was? . . . You!! It must have been in the winter for you had on your overcoat. Such dreams as I have—but they come true once in a while.

So much has happened since I wrote you last—a week ago Friday Jo (Josephine) and I drove up to Salinas in her Ford Coupe to see our basketball team get beat by the Kansas Wesleyans of Salina, but it was a dandy game anyway, and then we went on to Abilene and stayed the rest of the week and at a girl friend's house there, and we came home Sunday evening. Friday evening this girl had a little party for us, and I danced until the music ran out—we used the radio. They surely have some fine dancers there. Saturday we started the day right by getting up and playing tennis at six o'clock—(I nearly froze to death doing it) then fooling around, going out for lunch going to Junction City and spending the afternoon, and having another little party in the evening. Sunday was also another full day. Gee! We had a good time, but we only had about three and four hours of sleep each night, so I could hardly keep awake in school Monday.

This week I had such a cold that I did nothing at all, and Mother and my Aunt left Saturday for St. Louis, so I am trying to keep house too for Dad and me. It seems just terrible to come home every day to an empty house—of course, Dad is home in the evenings we get along just fine—he eats what I cook—and that is more than some people would do.

Tomorrow night Dad and I have a "date" together—we are going to see "Abie's Irish Rose."

I am so anxious to hear how your inventory at the store came out. Let me know as soon as you find out.

Today has been one hot sultry day—regular Kansas summer day.

Please write real soon, dear, for your letters mean so much to me since we can't be together at this time. I love you and will love you always.

Yours,
Dora

October 30, 1925
(Oceanside, CA to Wichita, KS)

Dear Dora,

It has been sometime since I received your last letter and I am sorry that I have not answered it sooner. I have been awfully busy, the usual excuse, but that every day that I would answer it that night. Somehow I did not have a pen or stationery handy and could not if I would. But, today I made up my mind that I would, so I bought this paper and a new fountain pen. Maybe I will be more prompt after this. I hope that you will not wait as long as I have. Please don't.

How is every little thing now? Do you have any trouble keeping warm? When you get this, Halloween will be over and the cold month of November will be ushered in. Gosh, how I dreaded to see November come in Oklahoma. It was the windiest and coldest & worst of all the months it seemed to me. Out here now you can notice a slight difference in the temperature but that is very slight. The breezes blow warm against your cheeks and flowers continue to bloom. Gee, but this is truly a wonderland. I certainly wish you were here to enjoy it with me. Maybe you can come for vacation in summer. That is if I am still here. But whether I am here or not, Dora, you should see Southern California. I have been with you on a great many enjoyable nights and know what you think is fine, or think I do. Here, everything is just like you would have it if you had your heart's desire. You can find wonderful fertile valleys and orchards and fields and gardens. The ocean is always near and the mountains all around. The sunshine is just like an April day in Kansas. And there is no end to the places of interest you may go to see. I may change my mind sometime but right now I think that here is the place for me to make a home.

Dora, I don't suppose you care about all this, so will ring off. No, I won't either for a minute. There are some simply immense mountain roads close hereby which are dandy for auto parties and picnics. Some are steep and wooded and almost impassable. Others smooth and nearly level and some of the deepest ravines and canyons and oh boy, the sunset over the mountains is great. Makes the rocks and trees all look golden and purple.

If you like keen hiking you can surely find it here. Last Sunday afternoon a bunch of Christian Endeavors (six) went out to the Palomar Mountains and took some pictures and did some other stunts. We had such a good time we are going again, this time all day. We will have four couples and two cars. Did you ever read the book of Peter B. Keynes, "The Pride of Palomar?" Well, here in these mountains is where he had the setting for the story. It is one grand pretty place, so darned picturesque and all.

Listen, what did I tell you about that long letter I said I would write? You didn't expect one about the country did you?

Sister Bernice and I are getting acquainted [here in town] some now. Been to one dance and a party myself. Down on the beach last night to a Halloween party about 50 feet from the old salt water. Had a pretty keen date, red haired, snappy tempered too. We danced in a thatched pavilion and later went out and roasted weenies and marshmallows, drank cider and ate apples. Lucky to be able to get around today. There were about 12 couples and although I knew about 5 couples I had a pretty fair time.

How is Carl [Dora's brother] making it at law school? Did he make the Kansas University football team? I surely wish he has and sincerely hope the old boy makes good. Has he another crush on any college girl?

You wrote that you saw some bimbo in a drug store who resembled me very much. I wish him the best of good luck but he has an awful handicap to start with. Did he act like yours truly? Maybe it was him. I saw a big 3-page advertisement in the Saturday Evening Post 3 weeks ago that had 3 full page pictures drawn by Ray Wilcox, just like that. When I saw that, my heart jumped over a couple of times. I would like to know that bird. He even prints his name like I do—to some extent. The advertisement was for Fashion. Parl Clothes for men. Ain't the world small after all, (now laugh).

The races start at Tijuana on Thanksgiving Day and the biggest mob in the world usually comes through here on the way down to get a drink and gamble on the ponies. The pavement is always full up on holidays here as everybody has a car and maybe two.

Are you keeping up with your music? I do miss those keen nights at your home. And the "arm twitching" contests. Gosh, I work so hard now my arm can't hardly do it anymore. I got a good job with a chain store Company. They have about 325 stores in Southern California. They are called Safeway Stores.

How is Dick Van Dolah getting along by now? He caused me some worry if you will remember. He had full right to as I cut in on him. Do you see Randolph M.? Tell that big louse to write and give me the dope on everything.

Do you see and talk to Mildred [Van Dolah]? Are you still planning to major in music out at Friends University or will it be somewhere else? There are so many questions in this letter that you may start at the first and say yes, no, yes, no, no, hardly don't know, and then mail it back. But how am I to know if everything is O.K. without asking what I want to know?

Another question you see.

Does Pastor Anderson still preach such good sermons?

You will have to get yourself a wheelchair and a pair of crutches when you finally finish this. Don't let it get you down but write real soon and then I'll know you are out of danger.

Now I am going to (pen drawing of a bed) and not wake up till (pen drawing of a sunrise)

With love,
Sincerely Yours,
Ray A. Wilcox

Nov 5, 1925
(Wichita, KS to Oceanside, CA)

Dear Ray,

Well, you did just about use the whole box of stationary—Three cheers for you! I certainly do enjoy your letters—though few and far between—but with your wonderful description of California, you make me want to come out there. I see no hope of doing so now, but if I ever get the least little excuse to go, I expect to pack and go. I wish that I could make Kansas sound as attractive and interesting, "but you know how it is." I do love to hike and explore, but what fun is it here to do it? What could one explore? I know that you are having a lot of fun and I am glad of it. If I don't stop talking about it, I will be packing my bag and coming out—anyway I want a vacation so badly.

I don't know what to do. Housekeeping is a fine occupation if one doesn't have to do a dozen other things besides. There is something all the time. If Mother doesn't come back soon, I may go insane. Dad and I get along famously, but it seems that I never have a minute to myself.

We are having perfectly lovely weather—snow 'n everything. It is raining tonight, but it has snowed several times and it has been cold as "Heck" lately. Unusually cold for October & November.

This Halloween was certainly different from last year. I didn't go to any parties,—although I was supposed to go Friday and Saturday. nights. Friday night I went to the Crawford and heard Percy Grainger, pianist and composer—it was wonderful. Saturday night. I had a date and we just fooled around—rotten time.

I will try to answer all your questions so this letter may be a little disconnected.

I am not taking music at all at Friends University—but take from Mr. Fischer. I hope to major in music at some large university some day—Chicago maybe. I also gave up my class of pupils in Towanda—great relief, but I have four pupils here. It is enough for the time I have.

I haven't seen Mildred [Van Dolah] for months and Dick is still going to college, works from 6 to 12 at night, and has a job on the Beacon newspaper writing for it or something.—If I remember correctly you never cut in on him, but he did on you, and it caused him some worry too, after he found it out.

The fellow that did look like you is quite a little different from you. He is a little taller and not nearly as fast as you are—I mean he moves around slowly. That isn't you, is it?

You may be some relation to Ray Wilcox, the artist, for you showed some of your talent in your last letter—One can never tell.

Brother Carl is getting along fine and he made the football team, but there are 40 on it and he hasn't played in a game yet. Kansas University is having a hard time—lost nearly every game. He doesn't tell us any more about his crushes. We make too much fun [of him], I guess.

I will tell Randolph to write to you, but I think it is your place to write to him first—write to him at school for I don't know his address.

In Christian Endeavor, we are having a contest to get more members, and the side that loses has to treat the other side to a turkey dinner around Thanksgiving. I can picture myself going out and hunting a turkey—we are behind. Wish that you could be here for it. Friday night a whole bunch of us C.E. are going to Newton to a C.E. conference.

I can't tell you about Pastor Anderson's sermons for I haven't been to church for a couple months—I study all day Sunday from 11 o'clock until evening, and then I have a good time.

Which church do you go to? I wish that you would send me some of those pictures you took of your bunch and Yourself and the Scenery.

Let me give you some advice Ray, you must be careful of these red-haired girls (over) (ran out of stationary—please excuse this) [remainder of letter written on the backside of a page]—You never know what they will do next. You had better try a blonde—pass out some more suggestions please.

So, you have decided to make a home in California? Please let me know when you start it—so I can send you something for it as a souvenir. I didn't know that you had a "case" out there as bad as all that. Sounds interesting.

If I haven't answered all your questions, just ask them over again. And I will try to answer them all the next time. (I try to please) This is certainly an information letter all right.

How long do you work a day? You mustn't work too hard, you know. Wichita is about the same as ever. How large is Oceanside?

Let me know all the news and answer P.D.Q. [Pretty Darn Quick]

Love from Dora

P.S. If this letter sounds blue, excuse if please but it is the way I feel, and I have to take it out on someone and as you are the farthest away—you are my victim.

November 9, 1925
(Oceanside, CA to Wichita, KS)

Dear Dora,

You are getting prompt results from your last letter. You're surely up to your neck with work and I know how you feel. I have been in the same boat myself and now I work six days a week and ten hours a day at that. But maybe I should be glad I have the chance and the health to work. Could be a dozen times worse and I want to tell you tonight that you have a whole lot to be proud of and if there are times when you feel like "blowing" up and quitting, then don't, because there are a million girls who would gladly exchange places with you.

 I have seen some of them and talked to them and I know what real trials and troubles they have and maybe if you would only think of the people you have seen whom you wouldn't think of exchanging places with, you would feel better. Maybe you do by now anyway. So perhaps this is all useless. I will not try to reform you by any of these poorly written letters, besides I need some of my own medicine. But Dora don't get blue enough to do anything "rash" and I won't.

 You said in your letter that it was raining that night and had been snowing too. Although there has been no snow here, it has been kind of "snappy" in the mornings here. We get up and "shiver" around about an hour and then the sun warms us back to normal. This may be a "way down south" but we do get chilly too.

 Dora, old girl I do wish you could take a vacation and come out and see us and the country. There is no end to what we might see and do. Yesterday we all went over to see the Motorcycle Hill Climb at San Diego, in the mountains. Gosh, maybe you have seen them in pictures but to see the real thing is some thriller. The grade was about 70%, which is some grade even to climb on foot. Not one of the riders made the top of the hill, but many of them took spills and some went over backwards. One amateur rider went higher than the professionals. We went over with the Flint [the family car]. Bernice and a friend and another keen girl and myself in the back seat and Papa and Mama in the front, driving. It was about 45 miles over there but we had a dandy time. Then in the evening I went over and took "her" to Christian Endeavor and after that for a ride.

Altogether a very fine day. She is not the one with the red hair. But maybe this won't sound interesting to you. But I have nothing serious "on and any case" that I may have won't be on such short acquaintances. No. I have not fully decided on a home in California. We never fully decide, because we may change our minds. But from the standpoint of climate and good people, Southern California can't be beaten anywhere I have been.

I want to get in some good hard years of money making and experience before I take up the duties of a husband. Every day, in every way I get foolisher and foolisher.

We have a good bunch of Christian Endeavor here and that makes a decided difference in living here and not meeting anybody. We have a boys' basketball team and we played the strongest church team in San Diego and beat them. Next Saturday another team from San Diego comes over and then after the game the girls are going to "throw" a supper. Hot Dawg, that's where the money goes, but I like it.

Oceanside is very small and town-like. It has about 3,500 in population and is coming to the front. It is the metropolis for the northside of San Diego County. It has a pleasure pier and ocean drive and palm trees n' everything. Wonderful fishing, but I don't have time yet for that. The ocean view is so great it makes you gasp for breath and now and then you get a glimpse of some seals going by. This town is the headquarters of the famous Rosicrucian Fellowship that has members in all parts of the world and is said to date back as far as the Masonic order. The big San Luis Rey Mission is about three or four miles from here and is the finest mission in California. You no doubt have heard of the old Franciscan Missions?

Well, Dora, you see I can't get down and say what I mean. I ramble along and say a lot but don't get anything over. But really I miss you Dora, regardless of what has ever happened and I hope you miss me. Someday I hope to know you better and I know you are a fine girl. And I am sincere. Don't think that I am writing this because of anything else. If I go back to Wichita and you are still there, I want to see you and if you can come out here on the least possible excuse, do so, and we will have a lot to talk over. Maybe you could have a "nervous breakdown" and come out to recuperate. These mountains and the sea will do wonders for anybody who is the least bit under the weather.

Did you hear of the death of our Grandmother in Cimarron, Kansas? She was 85 and had a stroke of paralysis. She lived about two weeks. She was Mama's Mother. We will miss her dreadfully. But after you reach the age of 85 years, there isn't much in life left, I guess. And then we can but believe that, "God's will be done" is our only comfort because she probably is happier by far, now.

Write soon Dora and keep the old ball rolling'. Tell me all the news. With lots of love.

Sincerely,
Ray

November 14, 1925
(Wichita, KS to Oceanside, CA)

Dear Ray,

I have been getting so many shocks this week, but when I looked in the mail box and pulled out your letter, I was so shocked that I should have been equipped with "Shock absorbers" for safety first.

Your letter cheered me up and it made me feel foolish for writing that last letter, but if it brings such prompt replies, I may do it again (just for spite) I got over my blue spell and I am just as happy as usual you are right—I have always had things so good that I can't appreciate them, I guess. So, you get blue, too? Do you want me to write you a letter and scold you for getting blue?

Do you like your new job? Is labor plentiful and are things cheap? You know Dad has been trying to buy some oranges—most of the stores don't have any and those that do are charging $.90 a dozen for real small green ones. It is terrible—there must be a scarcity of them.

The last time I wrote it was snowing, but the last few days it has been just like spring—so warm. It was so beautiful today that Dick and I walked home from school. This is the first time that I have talked to him for a long time—I found out a lot of things.

You know Ray, I have just about decided to make another "rash" move. Hold your breath and listen—I get so darned mad at boys sometimes (not meaning you) that I have a notion not to have any more "dates". I go out with them several times, and they get so darned (excuse my swearing) serious. It makes me mad. Isn't it the limit? I can't understand boys and all. Oh well, I should worry. I have started on that resolution already, for I was supposed to have one ("date") tonight, but I turned him down. I don't suppose my good resolution will last long—(you know me). That is enough on that subject.

Last week the teacher's convention was held here—the town was packed. I met a lot of old friends.

My brother Carl has been in "paradise" lately for he played in the last two games with the first team—one game in Kansas University and one in Oklahoma, and he gets to play this week in Iowa. He plays guard instead of center.

I must stop writing for I have to make some plans this evening for a party, or rather a dance, that the Junior Musical Club is giving Friday evening in the Twentieth Century Club House you know where it is right across the street south of us. We meet there all the time. I am glad for I don't have far to go.

I wish I could have a nervous breakdown but Good Night, I am in perfect health, so I see no chance to get to come to California.

Maybe someday you will get homesick, and come back here, but I expect that you are having such a good time, that that will never happen. Anyway, you are getting your education by seeing different parts of the country, which sometimes does more good than college.

Our Christian Endeavor group is getting livelier—last Sunday we had 40 people there—me included.

I was kidding you about your "case". Don't take it seriously, for you have a right to have any kind of a "case" that you wish.

As I said before I must stop and hang my close (clothes) on this line

With lots of love,
Dora

P.S. When you write, just ramble along like you want to—I like it. Give my love and best wishes to your folks.

November 24, 1925
(Wichita, KS to Oceanside, CA)

Dearest Ray,

What is the matter with you? You have been answering so promptly lately, that I am afraid that you are not feeling quite well, or there is something wrong—at least I would like to know the reason. I hope that you keep in the same mood for a while for it suits me fine.

Well to get this "serious" business off of your mind. I don't know whether I should tell you or not, but I won't tell the folks about it for it would worry them, and as I had better tell someone, I guess that you are a good person to pick on—you won't worry will you?

A couple kids have gotten a little serious, but some boy had the "nerve" to propose—I call it "nerve" for I had never seen him more than six times and had only four dates with him. He calls it "love at first sight"—I don't. Anyway, as far as I am concerned, he has gotten the "last sight" of me. You don't know him—I'm sure. I don't give "two snaps" for him, and we quarreled most of the time that we were together anyway—you can imagine how long I would live with him; can't you? If he were a millionaire, it would make no difference. Dad just can't understand why I won't take any more dates with him, but I don't want to tell him the real reason as all I can say is that "I hate him" on which I do.—If the "right person" ever asks me, I may marry someday, but heavens! I am not ready to settle down yet.

So, you have just about quit having dates?—I seem to be setting a good example. I have quit having dates with Dick, so since I won't go with him, he has sworn off of having dates too. I didn't know that I could affect anyone that much. I have only broken my good resolution twice in ten days—pretty good, isn't it?

Do you remember Josephine? She spent the weekend in Abilene, and to-day she came back wearing a diamond on her third finger, left hand. I guess that I will have to spend the weekend out of town.—That's enough on that deep subject.

Mother isn't back yet, and she hasn't said when she would come back—I wish that she would come soon. Dad and I are still surviving I am waiting now for him to come home for supper. He is serving on the jury again—it just about gets him down.

You needn't talk about your wonderful weather, for we, too, have some grand and glorious weather here—just like spring. It may be the weather that affects some people—I'm not sure.

I hope that it stays lovely like this for Thanksgiving so we can beat Fairmount. Kansas U. beat Missouri U. Saturday, the team that has been winning all year. I hope that we can do the same.

Tomorrow is Tacky Day at school and everyone must dress tacky. I am going to wear the worst looking apron—I am afraid that someone in a street car might take up a collection to help this "poor little girl."

One of my girlfriends is going to go to California with her parents as soon as school is out to visit some relatives in San Diego, as far as they know now, and they want me to go with them, but it is so far off, I cannot tell what I will do for they may change their mind about going. We have a lot of fun planning it anyway, and you should see us save our money—we surely think hard before we spend any.

Maybe Santa Claus will be good and send you a ticket to Wichita, if you ask him very sweetly. Let's hope anyway that he brings you "oodles and gobs" of things. I haven't thought much about Christmas yet.

Oh Ray, you always thought that I was so good natured, but I surely ruined that reputation this weekend. You know when I was elected president of the Junior Musical Club, I understood that I was to run it for the year, but one of the sponsors seems to think that she is the only one that has anything to say. She won't let me do the way I want to, and I don't like her method, so we had one grand fight this weekend, which is ending in my resigning from the club—also several others are handing in their resignations. I don't know when I have ever been so mad. She wants to build up the club, but she doesn't want us to have any social functions, and one must have social life in a club or it will die. Dad said that if I went to another meeting of the club, he would spank me. He is so mad at her, so I am resigning and she can run it to suit herself. It's a great life if you don't weaken—but I am weakening.

Oh yes, I just about forgot one of your questions. It is just a little bit too cold in the evenings to sit on the porch and listen to foot popping and arm twitching contests, and anyway remember my resolution.

How often do you take that wonderful drive that you spoke of? Don't take it too often or soon it will get monotonous and you won't get any thrill out of it.

I don't know whether you are hard to satisfy or not, for look whom you went with in Wichita, I am not the person to judge.

Everyone at school had to have their picture taken, so of course, I did, but no one liked mine, so I have to have them taken over. I hate to, though. Have you had your picture taken lately?

George Dean I believe that is his name—the boy that you went to Sunday School and church with a great deal keeps asking me about you—so does Randolph M? Why don't you write to them? This is some sisterly advice—take it seriously. You see some people still remember you.

Did Bernice find out who owned the railroads? You know you

should always help your sister when you can, or someone else's brother will.

Do you have good shows there—the latest I suppose? I don't go to the show very often—I haven't time. Must close now or write on imagination. Write soon or (on edge of stationary) sooner.

With most of my love,
Dora.

December 4, 1925
(Oceanside, CA to Wichita, KS)

Dear Dora,

This one has been delayed awhile as you know but maybe the next one won't be so long between times. I have been terribly busy, here and now, and am not out of the rush yet. In the first place the store has been invoiced and checked in and of course that meant extra work. Then the Thanksgiving rush and long hours. But Thanksgiving Day we got away and went to Tijuana Mexico for the inaugural of the horse racing season.

All of us went and had a "keen" time. We saw some fast races and the big crowd and the cabarets & saloons and bars. The bars were crowded with all classes of humanity and the singing and dancing was dreadful. The music was sort of dreamy and funny. Bernice and I went into one of the best and stood up to the bar and ordered two beers. The bartender fixed 'em up and of course Bernice couldn't drink her glass so I "killed" it. They charge "two bits" for a glass about as big as a thimble but that don't keep people from drinking what they want.

The race track is across the river from the part called "old town" and we parked the car and footed it over the bridge. It was a long trip through the crowd. Saw a lot of drunks but none of them were harmful. I was not scared for myself, but was worried about Mama and Bernice. Surely wouldn't want them there, unprotected.

I want to thank you for sending the papers out and can say that I surely enjoyed reading them. Seems like home to read the old *Beacon* & *Eagle* newspapers. Another package came today. The Sunday papers were fine and of course I was sorry to learn that 'Friends' basketball team? was beaten again. Someday that school's luck will change and they will give Fairmount the beating of their lives.

I am sorry that you are quitting the presidency of the Junior Musical Club but if that is necessary to preserve your peace of mind, I say do so at all hazards. I have run up against people like the lady you mentioned. You feel like fighting, I know but resigning will maybe "ease your pain." Let them have it and go to ------ and stay put. Excuse me ladies.

I have been reading about the rain and wind storms in Florida. Gosh! Fourteen inches of rain in twelve hours. And in that country. I can scarcely believe it. I saw it rain about five inches there and Flagler street was shoe top high with water. And the wettest rain in the world. That old damp sloshy kind. And the lightning was purple and scarlet not white or sparkling like Kansas lightning. I'll bet the natives down there thought the old Atlantic Ocean had spread out and flooded everything. They have an average of 55 inches each year there. The average here is about 11 inches.

That's enough about the weather!!

Now that Josephine has become engaged, how soon do you look for the actual "scrimmage" to begin. When will she start telling somebody when to get off and on? Does she appear any happier than before? Don't you think girls are happier when they are going to become brides?

Some time ago Bernice and her date and my girlfriend and myself went out to Lake Hodges Dam and "threw" a picnic dinner and exploring party. We hired a boat and rowed over to an island, or almost an island, and went up into the mountains and found the finest place to eat. The grass was green and the trees covered the whole hillside. Only thing bad was that it was so steep that we had to "dig in" to hold on and we had to almost bury the easements to keep them from sliding down.

We took 4 rolls of pictures, real snapshots and climbed to the top. Had a bushel of fun and the girls rowed back. Had tuna sandwiches, olives, fruit salad, cakes etc. Never enjoyed eating like that for a long time. I will send you a picture or two if you want them in the next letter. The girl I took is a senior in high school—a Catholic girl, so there can be nothing serious ever with us. Wouldn't want to be married to her [even] if she was protestant. So that's that.

I have a chance to work out of an office over at a little inland town 9 or ten miles from here. On commission basis 50-50. An Oceanside man maintains an office there. Real Estate-Loans-Insurance and he has offered to let me have the office. Vista is a really nice little town and is the heart of a new irrigation district that will have water in 60 days. Now I don't like to quit a job of the kind with wages like I have now, but it may be that if I don't try something else, I won't know what else I can do. So, I think that I will take the place. I can drive over in the morning in 20 minutes and back at night. The country will fill up with farmers and they will build and improve.

If I can sell them insurance on buildings and then any other insurance such as life, accident and windstorm etc. I can make a decent living and more. If I take it I won't expect to make much the first two months and yet I might make 3 or 4 hundred dollars on the sale of real estate. I won't be out much expense but my time so I think the logical thing to do would be to do it now. You can't imagine how wonderful it is to live here in California near San Diego—along the coast the back country as yet underdeveloped except by pioneers less than two hours' drive to snow and ice. Think I will go over to the Palomar Mountains and get some snow down my back so I can feel natural like the other twenty one years.

You see Dora, I just wander off and go telling a lot of stuff and the first thing I know is that I have spilled enough "gab" for one time. Maybe I will see a doctor about it. Maybe you are a doctor. Can you tell me what to do when I have so much to say that I can't write fast enough to keep my mind on it?

Give my best regards to your Dad and Mother. Keep one long kiss and a Sunday night hug for yourself

Sincerely,
Ray

December 12, 1925
(Wichita, KS to Oceanside, CA)

Dear Ray,

I started to write three or four times to you, but every time something happened, so here goes again. I am in the dining room trying to do this, but Mother and Daddy are laughing and "kidding" each other, so of course I have to join in once in a while and give my opinion, so I am getting along rather slowly.

Mother came back last Friday, and glad! I don't know when I ever was so glad to see anyone. Daddy was as glad as I, for he said that it seemed like at least six months since he had seen her. She got in at 9:00A.M. and at 10:00 o'clock she was cleaning the house, so you can imagine what she thought of my housekeeping. (now laugh)

I had the "blues" for about four weeks (I don't know what about, and I always thought of what you said, but I couldn't get over them) but now I am feeling just dandy. I guess all I needed was Mother to tell my troubles and joys to.

I am glad that you are having such a good time, and you like it so well out there, but I don't suppose that you will ever come back to Wichita, for there aren't any attractions here like in California.

By this time, you may have your other job. If you think it is any good, I hope that you take it for I know you could handle it all right, and there doesn't seem to be much advancement in the grocery business, do you think?

So, you had your wild trip to Tia Juana? Is the "beer" the hot stuff and full of "kick"? I expect Tia Juana is always full with visitors. I had a dandy time Thanksgiving also; In the morning I baked a cake for Carl, then several of us girls had dinner out at Josephine's then we went to the football game. Although we lost, it was the best game I have ever seen and exciting—the score was

7 to 3 in our favor until the last two minutes of the game. As usual "Arny" was one of our stars, and he is the Captain of next year's team. We girls fooled around until about 7:30, and then couple of the boys called and took another girl and me to the show. It was just about a perfect day. I broke my resolution then, but it was accidental, but I haven't broken it since, although some one is always calling up for a date. I am having lots of fun, anyway, and I don't want a date, so why should I have one? It certainly is a funny feeling—the kids think that I am silly—but I should worry.

I had a talk with Dick the other afternoon, and we had it "out" no fuss, but we just came to an understanding, so we still speak to each other and we are friendly, but that is all. You should have heard what he said he thought of me, and of himself—forever running after me like he did. It was all very plain at least.

Jo's ring was all a disappointment. When she came back, she never told us she was engaged, but we all just thought she was, for she has gone with this fellow for four years. We thought that he had "popped" the question. I wanted to give her a "shower", but she said I couldn't until she was engaged. Finally, she said that the ring did not mean anything, but I still don't know where she got the ring. It is all a mystery and some of it sounds "fishy". I believe girls are happier when they are engaged, for you should see some of the bright & smiling faces at school. So many kids at school are either engaged or on the verge of getting married—Christmas day is the set time.

What do you want for Christmas? I wish that I knew.

I want a floor lamp for the living room and Santa Claus (in the form of Daddy) said that he would get me one, so I am satisfied.

Mother and I are going shopping tomorrow.

Our Christian Endeavor group had their turkey dinner last Friday evening. The side I was on gave it to them—just my luck—there were about 40 there and we had a wonderful time—all that was lacking was—you.

The church is also trying to start up an orchestra, but I don't know whether it will be a success or not. I am still the president of the Junior Musical Club. I had a talk with these "old ladies" and they won't let me resign—they are just as nice and sweet as "honey" to me now. My advisor at school heard about the affair and she won't let me give it up, so I guess I have to stick, but I told them a few things anyway—just for good measure.

We had a dandy meeting Wed. evening too. Mr. Miltner of the Innes Cosgrove Music Company brought up a new Orthophonic Victrola and entertained us the whole evening. I just love these new Victrolas—I wish Santa would bring me one, but there is no hope of this. Have you ever heard one?

Please, Ray, do send me some of your—"snapshots"—I would like to see them.

You see I need a doctor worse than you, for I have written all this and said nothing—except about myself, but I will try to send you the papers oftener so you will know what is going on here. You remember the new building that is going up at Lawrence and Douglas—it is going up quite fast—they have twelve floors already. Just one more week of school and then two week's vacation. Hot Dawg! Don't forget to address the next letter at home, instead of school, for I won't be over there.

How are your folks? Do they like it out there better than here? Please tell them I said "hello."

The ending of your letter was lovely, and I accepted it, but of course the real thing is always better than the imaginary.

Well, I must close now before I ruin my reputation—

With lots of "you know what."
Dora

December 30, 1925
(Wichita, KS to Oceanside, CA)

Dear Ray,

I just had to write and tell you that I received your picture this morning, and I surely do like it. Thanks so much. You couldn't have sent anything that I would have liked better than this.

Do you want to know a secret? Shhhhh . . . you are getting better looking every day. Sunny California surely must agree with you. Several girls came to see me today, and they thought your picture was so good that they just about ran off with it, so I will have to watch it closely or someone might go off with it. Right now, I have it on my dressing table—looking me square in the eye, so I guess I will have to be good.

I just received so many nice gifts for Christmas. The folks gave me a floor lamp, and Carl gave me the most beautiful silver compact with his fraternity crest on it. Then I got stationary, perfume, three other pictures (all girls), flowers, and the other usual gifts.

What did you get? The usual ties and socks? Dad has always gotten enough socks at Christmas to last him a year, so about two weeks ago mother told him to get some, but he said it wasn't any use for he would get a lot at Christmas, but this year he didn't get a single pair. A real surprise to him!

I didn't want to send your present so early, but I wanted you to get it just about Christmas day, but this year we sent all of our packages about a week earlier than usual. Last year we waited about two days before Christmas, and Dad got into such a crowd at the post office, and had to wait so long, so we resolved to do differently this year. Many others must have made the same resolution, for he had to wait in line nearly an hour then.

Did it seem like Christmas to you without snow and cold weather? Didn't you miss seeing all the Christmas trees that line the streets downtown? I can't imagine Christmas in California. I suppose you went picnicking Christmas day, or something else that would be perfectly absurd to do here?

Nothing exciting happened here. We had our whole family here for dinner, and had a real good time—then I went to the show in the evening Something nice did happen though—your telegram came Friday morning—it certainly was unexpected, but I liked it all the better because of that—I like surprises.

Brother Carl came home a week from last Friday—and he is bigger than ever—195 lbs. I can't hit him and get away with it at all.

He likes one of the girls that lives here now—"another

wonderful girl"—quite well. He is taking her to the Crawford theater tomorrow evening. Hot Dawg! He will get over it soon, the way he usually does.

I was so surprised Monday—met two girls I haven't seen for four years—used to go to school with them. They live in California, and they are just spending a week here visiting. They were nearly frozen to death, for this climate is a little bit colder than California's.

What are you doing New Year's Eve?

I don't know what I will do. I think a bunch of us will get together and watch the New Year come in. Well anyway I hope that you have an unusually happy New Year. Expecting to hear from you soon, I still remain just the same old "kid" with the same old love.

1926: LONGING, LAND, AND LEVERAGE

The beginning of the new year in 1926 launched Ray and Dora past the initial "friendly" letters of their courtship to a new phase: a longing to be together. It had been almost half a year since they'd seen each other in person or even heard each other's voices. The options for long-distance communication and the speed of message delivery are of course radically different today from those in the 1920s. We now have affordable phone services, texting, instant messaging, email, social-media channels, and high-quality video conferencing with virtually no lag time. During Ray and Dora's time, though, the only practical option was letter writing. But these messages took time to compose by hand on paper—and days to send and receive. Sending a telegraph was a faster option, but that required quite a bit of additional money, so it was only used if a matter was urgent or worthy of the expense. Letters and packages were their only method of communication; although those were frequent and heartfelt, the young sweethearts couldn't bridge the large gap they both felt, and the distance and heartache resulted in a new depth of loneliness—for both of them.

Twenty-three-year-old Ray realized that twenty-year-old Dora was the only woman in his life who inspired and fulfilled him. On January 7, 1926, he wrote to her, "I know that I can hardly wait until I see you 'face to face' again. It has been five months already and it might have been five years according to the worry and yearning that I have in my heart... All that I ask is that you wait, Dora and I shall make good."

◆ ◆ ◆

Ray was ambitious and farsighted. He knew and saw things that others didn't, and he looked for opportunities that would make him more successful. Dreaming and planning were two important themes running through his young life. And what made his dreams come true was the incremental change he created by taking action. We can see in his letters to Dora that even though he enjoyed all the exciting and unfamiliar things that new places like Florida or California had to offer, Ray also consistently put in the time and work to improve himself and his standing in life.

These steady achievements meant all the difference in the arc of his life. They helped him to not only reach a level of success that satisfied him personally but also support Dora and his future family. And from my seat in the front row of life's classroom, even decades later, I can see that it created a meaningful and gratifying life.

By early 1926, Ray also knew that he wanted California to be his home for good. He realized that he never wanted to leave this new and enchanting land near the Pacific. So he began putting down roots there and casting about for options to earn a satisfying and secure living. The idea of selling and investing in local real estate appealed to him, and he formed a plan to leverage the money he saved from his full-time work with the local Safeway grocery store. He earned $200 to $250 per month and estimated that he could make $300 a month in the spring and summer. (In 2022-adjusted dollars Ray would have been earning roughly $3,100 to $4,300 per month.)

For her part, Dora was emerging as a leader in her own right. She was (still!) president of her Junior Musical Club and active as a leader in her Christian Endeavor church group. She was also fiercely independent and gaining more confidence in all the arenas of her life. She demanded that her father let her mow the lawn, and even began going to the gym two nights a week—at the Elks Lodge! Dora's sense of humor was on display again, in the form of her running joke, as readers may have noticed, of a boycott on dating men.

Dora's work at the Mentholatum Company and business courses in school seem to run counter to her sense of adventure and playful personality. But she balanced the practical needs of steady work and useful study by participating in fun things like tennis and social and sporting events. A deeper look into her letters indicates that Dora was raised in a fairly liberated household, at least for the Midwest during that time period. This home environment also allowed her strong, sometimes sassy personality and her sense of humor to emerge.

At this stage in her relationship with Ray, she appeared to share a little less about her personal thoughts and feelings than he provided, but it's clear that she cared a great deal for him. She'd begun her relationship with Ray as a friend, and by early 1926 that friendship remained intact, though it was also now tinged with romance and a deep and growing love. She continued to root for his success and happiness and remained empathetic to the challenges and hard times that he and his family endured. For example, when Ray was promoted to a managerial role with Safeway, she wrote, "Nothing makes me happier . . . Now, please make good at your new job, for you can do it. If one just has confidence in himself, he can do nearly anything . . . so, go to it. I am behind you."

Throughout this period, Ray wrote about his dreams for his new hometown—and he shared them with Dora, giving them immediate energy. This was significant, because as I look back on their lives together, and on his as a civic leader, much of what he envisioned came true in a way that contributed to making a section of North San Diego County what it is today. That we see the first seeds in these letters written a century ago seems important from a historical standpoint.

Throughout their twenty-three total months of correspondence, they had only one significant argument that I could find, which we see play out in this chapter. The backstory is that Dora believed Ray had written a letter to another woman in Wichita named Mildred, in which he suggested he would return in the spring to visit *her rather than Dora*. (Readers may remember Dora hinting to Ray several times in her letters thus far that she might enjoy his returning for a visit, but up to this point he never had.) In the ensuing dialogue, Dora blasted Ray—or, in 1920s language, "She really let him have it!"

Ray referred to Dora's high-octane letter as a "little sarcastic note and I was surprised by the nature of it and hardly thought that you would do that . . . That was a stinger for sure, Dora. I don't think I deserved that." Dora later asked Ray to burn her hurtful letter. He honored her request, so there is no remaining physical record of it.

During their months of longing, personal photographs of each other were like sacred objects. As Dora noted in one letter, "I see you every night now—so, no matter what time I get in, you are here (on my dresser)." Likewise, Ray would find happiness in the evening hours by looking at Dora's photo on the mantel of his family's fireplace. Sometimes he would take it down and hold it and talk to her about his plans and dreams for their future.

It's easy to imagine Ray in the small Wilcox home on South Horne Street: The air smells of the ashes of burnt wood resting in the fireplace. He is alone in a modest, dim room. A mirror reflects the yellow light of a small lamp. He stands and gazes at the photo of his sweetheart, looking deeply into her dark-brown eyes, feeling and thinking about what a life with her might be like. And then, sitting down, he finds a pen and paper and writes his next letter.

January 3, 1926
(Oceanside, CA to Wichita, KS)

My Darling, Dora,

Your jolly letter, written in installments came on the 1st of the new year and I got off to a good start when I read it. You certainly can write encouraging letters, Dora. I walked into the little post office and wished with all my might that there would be a letter waiting. Sure enough—there it was. The folks were outside waiting in the Hupmobile for me but I had to keep them waiting a little longer while I opened my mail. Sometimes I wonder if I am not just dreaming after all.

Can it be true that someday you will come and be with me forever? I can think of nothing more pleasant. Just thinking of it thrills me and makes me feel a peculiar sensation that inspires me to be a better man. There's something about your personality Dora that would make, or does make a man live a better, cleaner life, because of having met you. But to know you is to love you. Anyway, I think so! And I shall always think the same.

You certainly did get a position in a short time. "Lucky," I calls it. But did you think you should go to work so soon? Do you ever get tired of working? Please "don't" work too hard now when you are so young. It means so much to both of us to conserve our health when we have so many years yet before us. I am trying to take care of my health to the best of my ability and with the advice and care of my folks, think that I will live a long time, barring accident. That is a gruesome thing to consider when you are young and feeling fine; but Dora these things are worthy of consideration now before it's too late. I have a policy of twenty-five hundred dollars with the New York Life Insurance Company and a thousand-dollar policy kept up by the Company as long as I am in their employ. Besides these I have an Automobile Accident policy that pays compensation for many things that may happen while around an auto. If I should meet death by accident while riding in an auto or struck by an auto my beneficiary would receive by double indemnity $11,000.00. Perhaps I am worth more dead than alive, what say? When I was examined for life insurance about a month ago I passed a perfect examination so the doctor said. I just naturally feel good and am sincerely glad of it. More than anything else I am glad that you are happy and healthy, too. When you come to California next summer you can understand why most of the girls live out of doors here.

I can hardly wait until I see you and can tell you something of what I love for you to listen to and enjoy. We have so much to talk about and to see out here that we never shall catch up. It seems that the little petty things of life slip into the background and are rarely brought forward out here. There are so many more delightful things to occupy one's attention than just work and worry. By this I mean that you hardly even hear two people discuss over a few minutes the different crop situations the farmers have to face. If market conditions are bad, well it's all right, etc. Back home you always hear the farmers bemoaning their fate and cussing Congress, etc. But hardly ever have I heard anyone say anything radical regarding the government. Here they wink at the Washington scandals and pass them up. California absolutely satisfies them and they are in a world by themselves. Southern California is a little world unto itself. Across the Mountains and Desert in the East lies the rest of the Country but to Californians there is no other "Country beyond."

I do not know of any place that I have been where people are so doggone sure of their knowledge of having found the place that suits them. Oceanside has just started construction of a $100,000 pier and many other things. San Diego is going along in great shape. I forgot the clipping last week but I am sending under separate cover literature about San Diego.

Dora, I am just a "wearying" for you. I am yearning until my heart will break. I know that you are the girl of my choice. Many have come and gone. But you represent more to me than all the others. I know that you love me enough to wait for me. By the grace of God some day we shall make up in love what we are missing now and with a love that can never die. We will enjoy the rich fruits of a happy married life. I love you, as ever . . .

Ray

P.S. Miss Kullman—I would give a farm in Texas just to hear you play the piano and dance with you—see!!!

January 7, 1926
(Oceanside, CA to Wichita, KS)

Dearest Dora,

Your New Year's letter came on the fifth and I will say that you could not start the new year off better than to write to yours truly. I need your letters so much now, Dora. They are a part of you at least they seem like that to me. Everyone seems just a little bit better because they are like you. I know that you shall grow better as the years go on. Now you are as near perfect as any man could ask and I am lucky to have you as my sweetheart. How much longer we shall have to wait before I can be with you is the big question. You are putting it mildly when you say that we must see each other soon. I know that I can hardly wait until I see you 'face to face' again. It has been five months now and it might have been five years according to the worry and yearning that I have in my heart.

All that I ask is that you wait, Dora and I shall make good—I know it. And then only can we become man and wife. I am 23 now and you are 20 or is it 21. That's about the age to get married I think. Don't you? I hope that we can make it before I am a year older. Can you imagine us married? I can and I see a future happiness that will be unparalleled in our lives. I want you to be brave and have courage, because I know that I can make you happy. During the time that we have been separated, I have come to realize how much I love you. When we meet again I will tell you and prove to you most emphatically my regard and love.

It seems that you are surely lucky Dora Working in such a nice office. You have so many friends & no wonder. But Dora, dear, wouldn't it be fine if we could work in the same town so that we could see each other after working hours? Out here I can dream of you by the fireside after the family has retired. Some nights Bernice and I go out and I have to go to San Diego every Tuesday night for a while, so the evenings pass and another day rolls around. The biggest kick I get now is to come in late at night when nobody is awake and take your picture down then stir up the fireplace and just look at you. Maybe talk to you if I am in that kind of a mood. Honestly, Dora the picture has been a life-saver.

I have been working at real estate on the side, a little, lately and I like it. Last Sunday I looked at a lot up on the hill here in Oceanside. The owner wants to sell and I think I can handle the deal. It's well located and I can make some money on it. I will write to you as soon as I know how the deal goes. If this one does not materialize, another one will so I am keeping my eyes open.

Since the first of the year we have a new system in force in the Safeway stores. My store is switching over nicely and I hope that we can make the change without much trouble. By the new arrangement I should make $200.00 or $250.00 per month after the first

30 days. The District Manager gave me every encouragement and is going to buy-out the fruit stand and let me share in the profits of the vegetable and fruit business. I think that I can make $300.00 per month in the Spring and Summer. Of course, it will take work and energy, etc. and I will have to be here on the job for three months anyway.

But dearest of all girls, another summer shall not pass without seeing and being with you. I must not keep you up in the air about our plans. So, Dora when the spring and summer comes, if you don't come out to California, I will come to you. I promise this even if I have to quit my job to do it.

I sent you some pictures of San Diego which I hope you will enjoy. The city is approximately 35 miles South of Oceanside. It is very pretty down there and opportunity seems everywhere if one has any money.

We have had company all evening and if this letter seems disconnected you may know how it happened. A man in Long Beach is singing "Always" over the Radio. He makes me rather sad the way he sings it. "Not for just a year, not for just a day, not for just an hour—but always."

Please write me everything, Dora. I love you.
Best regards to all the family. O.K. about the ring. You know best, as Ever
Ray. (Love and Kisses) (many of them)

January 14, 1926
(Oceanside, CA to Wichita, KS)

Dear Dora,

I have thought many, many times that I would write to you and tell you how much I appreciated your last letter thanking me for the picture and telling me lots of news about the old home town. But tonight, I thought that I have waited so long now that this letter won't be welcome, but I am taking a chance. I hope you won't wait so long to answer, but write real soon.

Well how is Miss Dora Irene by now? Still kickin' and doing your stuff? I hope that you have recovered fully from the effects of the holidays. You know those late hours and heavy dates will make a good-looking girl use rouge. But I believe in having a good time while the sun shines and then get an overcoat when the evening grows colder. We're only kids but once and maybe never men and women. New Year's comes only once a year at that.

Bernice and I and the rest of the family spent a very happy Christmas. Although it was warm and sunny on Christmas day we had seen them [like that] in Kansas so it was no novelty to us.

We motored about 40 or so miles back into the mountains on that day. We enjoyed a turkey that was given to me by the Safeway company. Altogether, in a strange land we had a keen time. New Year's Eve Bernice and I were out again till morning. She at a party and yours truly at another dance. You might get the impression that I dance a lot but really I have only been to about 5 or 6 dances since we came here. You know how much I need the practice. Your shoes that I ruined are a constant reminder to you of those keen nights in your front room when I did my best to imitate a tractor and you graciously said that it didn't hurt your toes.

About that picture: it was a token of affection, and while I cannot be there in person, I want it to keep you company, safe and in good health. Really, Dora I would like to see you face to face again and go places with you and take you home. But now that I am away and can't be with you for a while, I can but hope and wish you the best things that the world has to offer.

May 1926 be one grand chapter in your life and one to be long remembered. If all girls were as good and kind this would be a very different world. May God be with you and keep you. I like to think that there is lots of joy and happiness for you yet to come.

I went swimming about two weeks before Christmas. Another fellow and I got up our nerve and did that very thing. Gosh! Gee! Oh Boy! That water was cold. Cold. Whee! Reminded me of the salt water that runs out of the drain hole in an ice cream freezer, just that cold and salty. But by running up and down on the sandy beach we warmed up and really felt exhilarated. But I don't think I will try that again for a while.

So far in this letter I have spoken of personalities and said a lot about myself but from now on I'll not mention myself quite so much. Isn't it funny how much of a letter is filled with "I this" and "I that"? I guess you want to know what I have been doing with my time so I naturally write it to you. The picture that I selected was one that Mama didn't like. She said it looked like a prize fighter or something. There was one proof that she liked better. It was sort of stern and dignified, but I wanted this one that wasn't quite so hard looking. A mother wants a picture of her boy to be quite dignified, you know, so maybe I will have one made for her. She cried when she saw the picture.

Well Dora are you getting by in college? Is the work pretty hard? Wish you would write me what you are taking and how you like it. Brother Carl must be a good looking fellow to have so many different girls. He is lucky in many different ways.

How is your mother now? Does she mind the cold weather? I wish your folks would come out for a winter in Southern California. It would be a fine place for them. And, say Dora, I wonder if you can plan a trip out here next summer? Just think you can come here in two days and a night. And then the many, many places to go and beautiful things to see. It's a winter wonderland. Do you think that you can come out in the spring or summer? What do you say? I would like so much to see you again.

We drove to Pasadena on New Year's Day and saw the Rose Tournament. And such a crowd—about 400,000 people. What I saw of the parade floats was wonderful. Such an array of flowers. And the cars were thick as hops.

Anyway, Dora, please write to me and let me know the lowdown on Wichita and the vicinity. I surely do appreciate the papers. I know that they are tokens of your love and remembrance of me and in appreciation I offer to do anything in my power here in this Country for you. Maybe you would like the San Diego papers. Tell me if you would and I will send them.

We think San Diego is the best place to go to. Just as soon as

Bernice graduates we will move there. There are lots of things that I don't like here. Business isn't so good and the people are just different a great deal. But I want to make a home by the Western Sea. Even if I have to stay here in the winters and go East in the warm months.

With lots of love and xxx
Ray

February 26, 1926
(Oceanside, CA to Wichita, KS)

Dear Dora,

Your letter and picture came early this week and I have been so awful busy that I have not acknowledged the receipt of either. But tonight, I feel I must, by all that's decent, let you know how much I appreciate them. Dora K. you are surely getting to be a fine-looking young lady. In fact, you always were good looking since I knew you. But I feel that I am especially privileged to have you as a friend. Certainly, to me, you have been one good girl. There may be at times a little streak of, shh!! (the devil) Pardon! in you but if there was not, you wouldn't be human hardly.
    Dora, I want you to know that I am more than willing to let bygones be bygones and forget everything that is not what it was meant for. I am afraid that I am too quick to feel—pride I guess. But it comes naturally to me and is not in the least false—if I think that I am being taken lightly or at the point of a jest I just fly off and say things that later I am ashamed of. But in the case between you and I—you had some grounds to say what you did—but it's all over, let's forget it and each resolve to do better. What do you think about this idea?
    About the picture.—I like to see you in the picture—I've seen you so many times that way, But I would like to see you face to face again. Do you think that you could induce your father and mother to let you come to California for a vacation? Do you? I know that

after you are here we can have the most wonderful times—and you will be safe and secure.

Dora, I want you to ask them and reason with them that you are old enough to take care of yourself. Don't you think so? Wouldn't you like to come to San Diego and Oceanside?

There are so many wonders and delights to be seen here. After all, it's just a few hours on the train. Mrs. Thurman who stayed with us in Wichita is visiting us here now as you know. She is going back soon after she goes up to Long Beach and Pasadena.

She left Wichita one Friday night after dark and got into San Diego at 3:30 the following Sunday afternoon. We met her there and brought her up the coast in our car. You can do the same if you are willing and you know that you are more than invited to come and stay as long as you like. I can't tell you all that you can see but I know that it would be a wonderful trip and adventure. Although we do not have the finest house to be had it is all right for Californians who do not need much shelter. Write to me and let me know whether you would like to come or not.

Today sister Bernice and about six other girls went swimming. She said the water was fine. Tonight, she went to senior play practice. She is always on the move it seems. Today the weather was really warm and I knew swimming would be good. I have been in once about Christmas time. That Wichita swimming suit has been wet with the salt water of two oceans. But it likes the western sea the best—you bet. I am going in again real soon. It is so zestful. It makes you feel the joy of living.

Last Sunday we motored down the coast to a suburb of San Diego called La Jolla (pronounced La Hoy Uh). They had a big real estate development and opening. Had some movie stars here—we saw Jackie Coogan and others. We saw a Hawaiian surfboard rider do his stuff.

We also saw some members of the San Diego Rowing Club competing in two canoes in the rough Pacific waters. One of the boats got caught broadside with a breaker coming in and it filled up with water—some water? Do you know the joy of riding the waves buoyed up with a rubber shark? Boy—but when one of those man size wavelets comes rolling in and you try to out jump it and don't.

It carries you back and if you are not a good swimmer you are apt to get water logged and strangled. The best way is to keep down and let 'em pass over the top of you.

Well, Dora, I could rave on and on but I don't dare. But do you want to know how I feel about coming back or going home? I think now that I never want to go back. California has cast its spell upon me sunshine and all. Never more, I hope will I have to stand one of those Kansas blizzards and spring dust storms. It's no wonder that people are nervous and strained back in the middle West. The air is charged with high tension (static) if you please. I have spent 21 years there and if I don't know I should anyway. Here it is different, Dora. The people lose that drawn look; they are more universally happy—it's the climate and sunshine—you feel free and want to really live and do something. I know that you won't understand all this unless you have been here. You have to experience it to really know what I mean. There are times when the air blows from the East from the mountains when the air is rather chilly and cold. But it is enough to exhilarate you. Then it begins to warm up and such perfect warmth it is. Not that lazy, springtime kind of atmosphere, but peppy healthful sunshine. Pardon all this please but . . . . .

We were down on the highway that parallels the beach, the other night there was just about half a moon showing—and the waves that are forever coming in, were rolling calmly and when they would break, the moons radiance filled them with the most perfect silver shine and glow it was wonderful beyond description—and the air—so clear—oh, I wish you were here to enjoy all this. It's a fairyland—the time might come when I wouldn't like it here and go back but I hope not and I do not think so.

Living is better here and it has been proved—Statistics show that people who are born in California live 12 years longer on the average. The person who comes here in middle age has his expectancy in life increased by 5–6 or 7 years.

While expenses here are slightly higher than at Wichita the difference is overbalanced by not having any coal or ice bills. Nights are cool and all summer long, the natives tell me you need blankets to keep warm. What a joy that will be here when I recall the hot sweltering nights I have spent back there. Do you blame me for liking it here, Dora? I know that it has not the steady firm agricultural basis of Wichita but in their line the California farmers are just as dependable.

I'm going to quit right here and give you some rest. Please excuse it all and chalk it up to a "fevered" Californian, but you know I have no earthly object in telling you this except that I am full and running over with it.

How is the young woman by now? Is she "dating" now or has she continued her "boycott" against young men? Would I have the privilege of escorting her to a dance should I ask her? Tonight? I am going to ask her to a moving picture show and see what the answer is. It said to come at 7:30. Ha!

Please excuse this penmanship? Will you?

I am glad to know that your mother has your father at work. A little work doesn't hurt anybody—He needs it don't he?

The papers are appreciated—I know that you go out of your way and are at considerable expense to send them and you send them for me don't you? That's one of the many reasons why I care for you, Dora. You are so thoughtful.

I got a raise at the store where I work. Needed it too. Ha! Don't laugh. With lots of love.

Sincerely,
Ray

March 4, 1926
(Wichita, KS to Oceanside, CA)

Dear "Californian,"

Your fine letter was received, and from the way you wrote you surely do have the California fever. Is it contagious? I am afraid that it is, and that you sent some of the germs in your letter, because I already show some signs of getting it. I am just "crazy" to come to California, but I doubt if I can talk the folks into letting me go. it will be hard to convince them that I am old enough to take care of myself, for you know how much more parents worry about a girl than a boy. I know that I would be safe and secure there—with you around, but you know how t'is. Thanks for the invitation, and I will do my best.

Maybe you can come out here and stay a while. Wouldn't you really like to come back to Wichita? Just for a visit? You know that you are always welcome here. And really Kansas isn't so bad. I can't describe the beautiful spring days and moonlit nights that we have been having lately—but of course there isn't much to see—no ocean or anything—I admit that. If everything is as lovely as you describe it, it must be a fairyland.

I certainly am glad that you got a raise—you are showing them what you are worth, eh?—Keep on doing so, and make them keep on giving you raises.

I am glad that you liked the picture. It is "me" all right. Yes, it was nice of you to escort me to that dance the other night—I enjoyed it. 7:30—Yes. That does sound rather familiar, doesn't it? Do you remember the "last street car" one night after a dance? I see you every night now—nso matter what time I get in, you are here (on my dresser).

I have lifted my "boycott" against boys, and have been dating some—you know there are some places that a girl can't go to without a boyfriend, parties for instance. I have been gone nearly every night for the last month, and have been having the best time (not "dates" every night, you understand). With all the wonderful things to see and such wonderful nights, you must be gone every night, too????

Of course, I send the papers for you, and it is no trouble to do so. Is there anything else you would like me to send?

Yes, Lewis Lauterbach still works at the store, and they are doing all right, so far as I know. I very seldom go to the store. I haven't the time.—It keeps me quite busy going to school, studying, going out at night and practicing (I am taking 2 lessons a week now in piano).

I must stop, for you will get so tired of hearing about "I" but nothing exciting has happened lately. Write me some more of these "fevered Californian letters." Bushels of love (give some to your folks from me)

From your "Kansasn"
Dora.

March 5, 1926
(Oceanside, CA to Wichita, KS)

Dearest of all,

This is the first chance I have had to write a note to you, darling. Sunday was inventory day and we inventoried my store and one down the coast at Encinitas. It was a long hard day but I think it will all come back to me when the results are known. Monday is always busy and Monday night was play practice. I am glad that the play will be the day after tomorrow, because it's always a strain on nerves and keeps one up so late practicing. I wish that you could be here to see it, it's a good one "Kempy" is the name.

This note is written at the store and we are rather busy but I knew that you would be waiting to hear from Papa.

Dearest, every hour draws us closer together and then we can have that loving companionship that means the most in life. To have you by my side and hold you ever near and in fact to love you means the world to me.

To have something to live for and to work for is enough. Then to have a love that will endure through the ages will be wonderful. There is more to life than just strife and gainful pursuit. More than work and worry and petty and trivial matters. There is love and happiness and joy.

We will find them side by side in California. I know that you will love California and the coast. I know that I will love you always—

As ever,
Your Ray

P.S. another letter following

March 22, 1926
(Oceanside, CA to Wichita, KS)

Dear Dora,

I have neglected writing to you lately but I have been so very busy. You know how it is. Now when I should have answered your last letter, I felt that I didn't have a thing to tell you that would interest you in the least and what is the use of just writing because it's scheduled. I like to feel that when I do write I will have something to say except rave about this climate.

How have you been lately? What has happened around Wichita that is exciting? Do you still get good reports on your work at school? That's enough questions for a while.

Our family is as well as usual and I am feeling tip-top. The winter here has done me a lot of good. My folks think that they feel better here than back there. I don't know. But we have been hearing fine reports of the conditions there, especially the coming wheat crop. My father thinks sometimes that he will drive back perhaps in May if the wheat crop continues to come along in good shape. He says that a person can tell in the last of May whether or not the wheat will make good.

We have sold the Flint Car, and have just bought a brand new Hupmobile Six Sedan. It is a very pretty car and runs fine—we are just breaking it in. You know a motor car is tight when it's new and has to be driven slow at first. We haven't driven over two hundred and fifty miles yet so the motor is still tight.

I don't suppose that your dad has ever changed his mind about owning a car, has he? Of course, every man is entitled to his own opinion but I know that you would enjoy a car to the utmost. He thinks or did think a car is very dangerous. He is right and wrong because it all depends upon who is at the wheel and what kind of car he is in.

All of us drove over to San Diego yesterday (Sunday). Had a swell trip 'n everything. The weather was just perfect and the beautiful scenery along the Coast was certainly inspiring. We visited the Museum of Natural History—drove out to Point Loma—and Loma portal past the Army and Navy Academy—hospitals and barracks. Saw the famous San Diego Bay from a great height. Drove thru and around Balboa Park, which is in the city limits of San Diego. The park contains 1,800 acres. It is the largest park in any city in the U.S. This was where the Panama Pacific Exposition was held in 1915. Many of the grand old buildings still stand and are used by the city. We were glad to get back to our little town of Oceanside, where we feel at home. The city is so strange but you have to get used to that.

I haven't written to Pastor Anderson but once when I first came here. I suppose that he is just as successful as ever. I know that he keeps busy. Do you still go over and hear him on Sunday Mornings? I used to enjoy sitting with you and listening to him preach. If I ever come back I want to do the same thing if it is possible. I hope that you and I will still have the same kinds of ideas and that you haven't changed much from the delightful girl that you were last summer.

Doesn't it seem funny what has happened in the last 9 or 10 months? So much has taken place. But for all of it I hope that it's all for the best.

Bernice and I were swimming again the other day. We enjoyed ourselves to the limit. We can hardly wait for the summer season to open so that we can have a dip every day. Gosh, but I never get enough to satisfy me of salt water.

How does Carl stack up? Is he engaged to be married yet? I know that some girl will capture him some day. He's a dog-gone good fellow even if he is big. And the girl who gets him will find a first-class citizen on her hands. That is if he is still the same as when I knew him. And his sister is not so bad?? She is a good scout and gives a fellow a square deal if he deserves it.

Well, Dora I have told you a lot of what was on my mind and I still have a lot that I can't say now. You and I have been good friends and of course there have been some misunderstandings. Who has not had them? And I think you care just what becomes of me and I am sure that I am more than interested in what happens to you. Who could not be who has known you?

When I asked you for that picture and you would never let me have one or send me one it made me feel that you did not care. But now that I have your smiling likeness here with me, there is somehow a stronger link than ever between us. It makes me feel good to have you for a friend and the fact that we may perhaps meet again makes my heart pound just a little harder and faster. Possibly I cannot come this summer. Maybe you can come here. But to see you and talk to you again would be wonderful.

To renew an old friendship—that's it—the "kick" that comes to those who wait—

I will write longer and better next time—also sooner. Can you beat that combination?

Answer soon,
Sincerely
Ray

Care of . . .
Box "S" in Oceanside.

April 18, 1926
(Oceanside, CA to Wichita, KS)

Dear Dora,

This letter comes to you quite late but several things have come up lately that made me put off writing for a time. But I have thought of you every day and I hope that you think of me too. We have been unusually busy at the store again. Several changes have been made and then we invoiced again. The manager that I have worked under has been let out of the organization, for many reasons. Also, one of the clerks, too, has been dropped from the payroll. The district manager is here for two weeks—trying to straighten out some "kinks" in the local store. He also is here to try to break yours truly in as a manager, but what success he has will soon be shown. This store is one of the best in the district. If the company decides to make me the manager it will be another step up the ladder for me. But if they don't I am not going to lose any sleep or quit because I have been with them about six months. And it is a great responsibility, managing somebody else's business. But I believe that I can make good. (That's enough about business.)

Dora, you may be sure that I am glad to hear that your Dad has again engaged in business. Perhaps he will not only succeed but will find happiness in work. And, if he does, it is a wonderful blessing because really happy people are scarce. Don't you think so? In fact, I have met but very few people who seem to be supremely happy. There should be more than there is and I hardly see why there isn't. Now your father has made a good home, raised a good family and now has sufficient money to keep him until the end. While he might never be satisfied, he has many reasons to be content. But what does he lack? Only something to occupy his time and now that he has that, I am glad.

I would like to work for your dad but I don't know how he would take to me. I might need a job if I came back to Wichita.

I see that you answered my questionnaire thanks—so much. Now the information I so desired has been given to me. And I am glad to hear that you are the president of the Christian Endeavor. Don't forget to attend the Convention and Senate when it convenes this summer. Randolph and I had some time last year and if you had come along we could have had a better time—I know.

I am awfully sorry that this letter has been delayed. But don't you forget to write. I hope that you don't.

How about that trip out here this summer? Write me all about what you plan to do when vacation comes. I would so love to have you here. Can't you come and enjoy these wonderful days and nights—I get so lonesome in this little town, for a girl who knows me. So far I have not met any girls that I care a darn for. Maybe it's just me—hard to satisfy.

So, you and Marion McNabb gave Independence the once over? Glad you had a swell time and sorry you "scuffed" up a pair of "pumps." They have brick factories there too like Coffeyville, Kansas—one on every vacant lot.

When you finished the last installment of your last letter you mentioned the fact that it was snowing in Wichita and Vicinity. I saw in the papers that the entire Southwest had a return of Old Man Winter (Some country—Spring one day—hot like summer the next and on the third day snow a foot deep. It's a good Country—to be from But Dora I will quit this "ragging" as I know that you are a loyal Kansan and I have a big spot in my heart for my old states; Oklahoma & Kansas.

It is still our plan to go into San Diego this summer—that is if we find that we can do better there. I never want to move away from the sea if I can help it. I have come to love it—it's so big and rollicking and wonderful. Here at Oceanside the beach is wonderful, sandy and smooth, etc. And the hills and valleys and mountains around here are rough and pretty—the country is not squared off in section lines—just a winding road here and there.

Dora, every time I hear the song or sing it myself "The West, the Nest and you" my heart throbs just a little faster because I have come to know about what that would mean.—"Beside the Western Sea." Sometimes I take a walk by myself down on the long pier that juts out into the ocean and out there I sit and dream—and think—after a hard day at work—how restful that gentle roar and surge of big water is Dora, I don't think that you can feature this unless you have lived by the sea for a while.

Do come and see for yourself. Talk it up at home. Save your pennies; I will look after you. You know I can.

Keep up the old pep and answer soon, with lots of love

Sincerely,
Ray

April 27, 1926
(Wichita, KS to Oceanside, CA)

Dear Ray,

I was certainly glad to get your letter, and hear that they are trying to make a manager out of you. It will be a step up the ladder for you, and I hope that you succeed. A few responsibilities help to make a man out of a person, and if one learns how to bear them now, it will be much easier to do so in years to come, so go to it, and succeed. Please let me know how this all comes out, for I am interested, and I think about you often. So many things remind me of you, and often I wish that you were back.

You should have been here last Monday. The Christian Endeavor had a "kid" party, and we had the most fun. It just felt wonderful to be just a kid again. You should try it.

I cannot tell you what I will do this summer. I feel as if I should go to work, so if I can find a job I will do so, but jobs are terribly scarce here, and everyone wants one. It is terrible but I am so undecided about everything. I rather think that I will stay out of school next year, for I can't decide what to specialize in, or what I want to be, so if I stay out a year, by that time I may have made up my mind. I hope so. Anyway, I don't want to go here any longer. I am tired of Wichita, and I would like to get away from it for a while, but I doubt if I do. I hope that something happens soon to make me decide one way or another, for this way I am so dissatisfied.

Mother and I went to Towanda [Kansas] yesterday to the dedication of the new Christian Church. Mr. & Mrs. M. Orban of Whittier, California (they used to live in Towanda) built this $100,000 church for the Christians. It is a beautiful church, but really too large and nice for Towanda. I was "bored to tears" all the time I was there, for I didn't know any of the girls and boys my age except one boy. Had a good time after I got home though.

Ray, what is the matter with you? With that wonderful climate, those moonlight nights, and everything so wonderful, and you aren't in love? We don't have such attractions here, only spring weather, but everyone is in love, except myself. Every girl I run around with is madly in love with the only boy in the world, of course, and that is all I hear about. It is a good thing that I am still sane to keep them from doing any more silly things than they do. I have a good time with the boys, but like you, I don't give a darn for any of them that are here, so something must be wrong with me, too.

Do you still have your terrible looking knife, Ray, that you used to carry around with you for protection? I have one now too that I carry for protection. You should see it—Jo gave it to me. Here is a picture of it.

This is the actual size of it—[a sketch is included, approximately one and a half inches long] Isn't it huge? It is a darn good knife for it will open letters.

Don't worry about why I did not send my picture before—you have it now, and that's enough. Write me real soon or sooner, and let me know how you are getting along—it only takes a minute to write.

With lots of love from
Dora

May 2, 1926
(Oceanside, CA to Wichita, KS)

Dear Dora,

Your "illustrated news" came to me two days ago and it was certainly welcome. I was indeed glad to hear that you now have a dependable weapon for defense and my wish is that I could be there to look after you more carefully. My knife was with me until a few days ago when my father lost it or hasn't found it yet which of course means that I am open to all manner of attack from the hidden foes of upright and honorable manhood. Don't I love myself? But really Dora, old girl, it is best that the knife is gone because now that I can't depend on the darn thing, I have to depend upon myself. The only thing that I used a knife for was to open up sugar sacks at the store and if I ever get out of the grocery business I won't need it for that! That's enough right now about knives.

 Dora, I think that we have both reached the age of restlessness, and dissatisfaction. You say that you are undecided as to what you are going to do with yourself next year and I might add that you are not alone in that feeling. I do want to settle down and not be a "rolling stone" all my life. But where and how to do it is a puzzle, and how best to do it is the next step. Dora, please don't quit school to go to work. It's really a shame and a tragedy because you have a real opportunity to make good in your line—music—and the business world doesn't need you, Dora! And I believe if you really knew what was best you would go on and finish; it means so much to you.

 The store has changed quite a lot now and things are beginning to pick up some. Although I did not get the manager's job here at present I am in line for that job and they brought their best man here to work at our store. He has been with the company 5 or 6 years and surely "knows his stuff."

 I had a talk with the superintendent of this district and he said that it was his sincere wish that I might have a store to manage and that with a little more experience he would see that I got one, that is, if I wanted the responsibility. So, you see Dora, I have reason to expect something better in the coming months. But even that is now what I would like to be doing. That's not all, but being handicapped in a financial way, I have to start slow. Maybe in the years to come the way will be easier, but right now it is slow. "Beginning at the bottom," that's what they call it.

 You have been a good friend to me and I hope to always keep you my friend. If only we were closer together where I could see you often—I remember and I hope you remember those nights when we were together. Shows, parties, dancing, church and home. How I held you in my arms and thrilled when driving, or at home in the porch swing. Oh! but that was good, too good because now I can't do it and it hurts. But, maybe someday, you will come here or I will come there and I will ask for the privilege of seeing you and if you say yes, then watch out. I can dance some now and I realize that before I was merely shuffling along on your toes. I owe you $20.00 for two pairs of "pumps" that were literally sacrificed on the altar of bad form. But try and get it Dora this far away—1,800 miles—But still I do hope to pay you someday.

Does Wichita bore you? What do you do with your spare time besides practicing? Golly, girl but I would give a lot to hear you play once more, say, "Moonlight and Roses" or some other keen piece. No Dora. I am not in love, just feel like I would like to have somebody who is agreeable and sporty and who will take a dare and who is full of life and pep. Do you ever feel like that?

My folks have been feeling about as well as usual and we are enjoying the car to the utmost. Last Sunday we motored up to a place in the back country where a pageant was put on called "Ramona" and then back by way of Lake Elsinore where they had a pageant on the water. Lake Elsinore is about 1 $1/2$ miles wide and 3 or 4 miles long. There are lots of folks there for their health—because of the hot mineral baths. The hills are beautiful now and we could see snow on the higher mountains. It was so hot down where we were that we nearly passed out, but up there on those mountains was real honest to goodness snow and ice. Then we came back home to the coast and nearly froze to death in the sea breeze. That's California—all in a day, every climate in the world.

Today, Sunday, we drove down to a flower show at a small town called South Coast Park. The floral display was gorgeous and the music was good, after that we went inland through the hills and mountains to the wonderful valleys of Northern San Diego County. Out here the wheat crop is getting ready to harvest; the wild oats, of which there are a lot, are being harvested now. The barley is brown and alfalfa has been cut many times since we came. The gardens of cucumbers and beans and peas and potatoes are past their zenith. Today we saw a machine digging a crop of great big new potatoes as fast as a crew of men could follow and pick them up. Many other things I have seen that you wouldn't care to read about so I'll quit.

This personage was elected President of the Epworth League

to succeed himself for the next term. We are just beginning to put some life into the service here. It's hard to have any really enjoyable meetings when so many people are disinterested or so self-seeking as to be boresome.

Last week I went to another beach party down on the sandy stretch fronting on the ocean and had a good clean time; had baked beans, "hot dawgs," coffee, marshmallows etc. Oh! I forgot potato salad too. We played some old-fashioned games and then went into an old deserted dancing pavilion and danced to the music from an old battered timeless piano which we unceremoniously confiscated for a few minutes. Again on Thursday of the same week I was invited to go "grunion" hunting with a party; grunions are a small silvery fish called smelts in some localities. They "run," that is, come up on the beach with the big waves when the tide is running high. Science can tell by the moon and the time of the tide when they are due to "run," so that when we hear that they will start coming in on such and such a date at a certain time of night we get up a party and go down with our bags and buckets and get a mess of them if we can. There is great sport in it. They are quick and elusive and when a beachcomber or big wave comes in with them they flip and flop on the sand and are quickly out of sight in a very few seconds. They come in to lay their eggs, it is said. The idea is to get them while the waves are not running full. They are about 3 inches long and resemble a sardine in looks but not in flavor. They are easily cleaned and fried crisp. They are a delicious sea food. I was talking tonight with the boy who is president of the Christian Endeavor and we are going to have a "grunion hunt" for the young people's society of the B.Y.P.U., the C.E. and the Epworth League all together.

Won't we have fun? It's wet work and everybody must be dressed to get wet. Every time you scramble after one of the little fellows you get caught with a big wave which soaks you to the last dry thread. We have to have something to get some excitement around here wish you were here to go with me, I would love to have you—write soon

With love,
Sincerely, Ray

Saturday Evening/undated
(Wichita, KS to Oceanside, CA)

Dear Ray:

I was "knocked speechless" when I came home and found your letter here Thursday. An answer so soon. It came nearly as quick as a "special." I am always glad to get your letters for they cheer me up, and also they help to vary the monotony. I like to hear about what you are doing too.

    You should have seen me work this evening. Daddy started to mow the lawn this evening and I was feeling so "peppy" that I made him let me do it. Daddy was afraid that I would disgrace the family and the whole neighborhood, but what do I care what people think? It costs nothing to think. The exercise I got was as good as an hour at gym.

    I have been taking gym two nights a week at the Elks Club. The director can certainly work one, but we have lots of fun too. Mother took it one night, but it nearly got her down so she says, "nevermore."

    You write as if I have been practicing a lot—I have, but I will have to work harder than ever now, for I must give a recital all by "me self" around the first of June, then I get my diploma. Mr. Fischer leaves the 19th of June for Europe for three months. Wish that it was I going. Daddy said something this evening about how it would be rather nice if I could go to California this summer. Maybe by the time school is out, he will be in the notion of sending me—at least, I hope so.

    What do I do all the time? The same things that I used to do. You know, the usual things. Tuesday was May Day at school, and they had a very pretty affair. Afterwards, we had dinner. A bunch of us kids were together and we went to Jo's afterward, but we all got so sarcastic to each other that we decided to go to the 2nd show at the Miller, before we really did say something "mean," but we did have a good time.

Only four more weeks of school but you should see the work we have to do.

I congratulate you, Ray, on your presidency. You must work fast??

If you get any good ideas for meetings, please pass them on to me. We have been having pretty good meetings all winter but now spring is coming., (I mean, here) it is hard to lure the kids in. What church do you go to?

Instead of a "grunion" hunt, we might have a "mouse catching" contest—exciting??? That reminds me, the other day I was sitting in the library at school at one of the tables with a girlfriend and Dick, when two boys came in and sat down by us, and they were laughing so, so I asked them what was wrong. I soon found out. One boy pulled from his pocket a small mouse and put it on the table. I broke a "record" in getting out of the library. It was a regular entertainment for the rest of the library.

Gee, Ray, I am going to get really jealous pretty soon. I have heard more nice things said about you these last two weeks, and most of them from girls, although several were from boys If I told you what they were, you would puff up so much that if anyone stuck you with a pin, "blooey," you would go, so I won't tell you what was said. A sweet girl said something lovely about you this evening. Don't get too excited, please!

Miss Bailey was operated on for appendicitis last Saturday at the Wichita hospital, and she is getting along fine.

I wish that we did live closer together—a few miles closer at least. I miss you, for you always were so lovely to me, and have been such a good friend. Maybe someday, somewhere, & somehow we will meet. One never knows for life is so funny. Anyway, I keep wishing for all this to happen.

Well I must stop, and please surprise me again.

"A little love A little kiss

And that's the end of this"

Lovingly
Dora

May 13, 1926
(Oceanside, CA to Wichita, KS)

Dear Dora,

Better dodge, here it comes another one; I'm doing this so that I will soon have another one of those fine letters coming my way. That is if you keep up the good work like you have in the past.

Dora, old girl, I can't tell you how much I really appreciate your letters. They are so like you and seem like I am talking with you face to face. Not quite, but just a whole lot like you. When I came down to the store yesterday after lunch I found your letter waiting for me—laying on the cash register—I opened it and had a talk with you for a while and found out that you were getting along all okay and that you had mowed the lawn 'n everything.

The interesting thing was that you might get to come out to California. Now if you can manage it, then I'll be happy! Dora, if you come I can promise you that you will be taken care of in every possible way known to people of moderate means. We don't have a lot of money but we can take care of our friends. We will probably be in San Diego in July. That is where we want to be. Then we can have some real times—many, many places to go and see. But I want to show you this hill and mountain country of San Diego County. It's truly a wonderland. But my words here cannot mean much to one who has never seen it.

I think that you really deserve to come and spend some of your vacation here. Don't you? And I would love to see you and greet you again. So many things have come up since I first met you and I have not forgotten the good times and happy moments that you and I had together. I hope that you enjoyed them quite as much as I.

Dora, about those papers that you send me—I am going to relieve you of some responsibility. You know that Mrs. Thurman has been staying with us and now Mr. Thurman has subscribed to the "Eagle" and is having it sent to us. How much I appreciate it, Dora of your thinking of me and going to the trouble to do that thing for me. So, Dora, your kindness has been deeply felt and I want to do something to partly repay you. Will you tell me when your next birthday will be? For no reason at all. In your next letter please.

    I took my class of small boys (Sunday School boys) out for a dinner and hike Sunday and we had the time of our young lives. We went out, way out into the keenest mountains and then on a one-way road into a deep valley between higher mountains where the nicest kind of a mountain stream ran along the rocks. I made the coffee out of sparkling water and it was good if I do say it. But Dora this is just a short letter and I will send it to you wishing you the very best of everything—

    Answer soon and I will have a long letter the next time . . . .

With lots of love,
Sincerely Ray

June 8, 1926
(Oceanside, CA to Wichita, KS)

Dear Dora,

This time it is a trifle late! But maybe better late than never. This letter will find you in good hopes and spirits I hope.

    We all have been terribly busy these last few days. Yesterday and today we moved and it's a job I hate worse than any other. To be all torn up and out of place in new surroundings is the bunk. Then the lifting and tugging and sweating—gosh it's awful. But the new house is lots better and that's something. This moving and strain, etc. is enough to make a confirmed bachelor out of what was once a fairly decent citizen. To see all the trials and tribulations of married life, all but makes me think that never will I have the iron nerve to ask a girl to be my wife. There are times when the joys of a married couple seem to overshadow the cares and worries but I am inclined to think the great majority of people seem to take marriage as it comes along. Sort of something to be bored with through life. Then again, many people get married because it is the seemingly logical thing to do. But it's for the individual to figure out for himself. Hold on tight now I'm going to switch over to a different ink. I don't like this one that I am using.

Your last letter was very interesting indeed. Dora, and I was surely glad that you write in that frame of mind. It is so cheerful. And I know that you mean it when you say that you wished that I were there. So, do I and some day when I have something of my own I am coming back and then if you are not averse to having a good time, be prepared.

School is out, here in Oceanside and sister Bernice is the proud possessor of a diploma. She is getting to be quite a girl and wants to go to college. But the next few months will bring the answer to that question. For that matter, I too would like to spend the next four years at USC or Stanford but that is almost too much to expect. My plans are now to go to a good business college in San Diego and get some training in my system. I feel that I can make good with the practical education that I have, plus some business details that can be acquired only through study and work. I would like to know how to sell myself and merchandise and to handle a set of books from start to finish. Also, to learn to write legibly would be very good too, don't you think??!!

We took a trip up to the top of Palomar Mountain a week ago Sunday during the two-day vacation. It was wonderful. It is over a mile high and the vegetation and beauty of the big trees is beyond description. The big mountain is inland from the sea about 65 miles and while the surrounding peaks are mostly dry—this mountain is very luxuriant with ferns and plants of all kinds. The rainfall—mostly in the form of snow—is over 60 inches a year—which beats the average for Southern Florida. The lodge on the mountain has a keen maple floored dance hall and altogether is a very nifty place to spend your vacation. Many mountain streams flow up there and iron springs furnish ice cold water the year round. Oh, Dora, this country is the one ideal spot to live. With the mountains and the ocean and pretty homes and sunshiny days.

There is nothing like it anywhere to my knowledge. My ambition is to own a pretty home, a car and a good business and live in

San Diego County along the Western Sea. If you were only here to see as I do the wonderful possibilities. But excuse me Dora for Raving and answer soon.

Loving
Ray

June 15, 1926
(Wichita, KS to Oceanside, CA)

Dearest Ray,

I was talking to Mother this morning, and I said since I haven't heard from you for so long, I guess that you had gone and gotten married and ended it all, when here comes the postman with six letters for me, (I nearly fell over -6-) and among them your "missile" on the wonders of married life. Like you, I can't understand marriages. One day I think there is nothing more wonderful, and the next day (as you say) "I don't think I will ever have enough nerve to ask any man to be my husband"?????!!X.

But Ray, really I can't imagine you as a bachelor. Someday when the right girl comes along, you will slip and fall just as hard as any of the rest of them. Then instead of helping your folks move, you will be pulling, tugging and tearing around for her. Aren't I right? (Women always are.)

Well, it is all over. I gave my recital last night, and I got my diploma tonight. I didn't get a bit excited or thrilled last night, except when I received four huge bouquets of roses and carnations, and a corsage. About all I did all day was sit and look at them. Nothing thrills me more than flowers.

The last time that I told you good-bye, I hardly thought that it would be so long before I would get to see you again. Now I am afraid that it will be an awfully long time. Since for several reasons I can't come to California (and I am sorry as can be) I am going to St. Louis in a couple weeks to visit, and if I can find some kind of a position there, I am going to stay and go to Washington University there all next year. Won't it be grand? Gee, I wish that I could see you before I leave. I suppose that is impossible. Ain't life funny?

I hope that you get to go to business college, for it would help a great deal, but if you don't get to go, why don't you get some good books and study some at nights? Really you can learn so much that way. Try it anyway.

The Emporia Conference was this last week, so of course I didn't get to go, but four of the boys and four of us girls, and Mrs. Witt drove up to the State C.E. Convention at Hutchinson, and stayed last Saturday and Sunday. It was a wonderful convention, and we enjoyed it very much, and we had one grand time. I don't know what Mrs. Witt thinks of us now, for we did some things she didn't approve of. Two of the girls and two of the boys sat out in the car and talked one evening for about ten minutes, and she just raved. Saturday evening after the meeting two of the boys took me to a show—she doesn't go to shows. She said that we could go, but I don't think she liked it, I should worry.

Are you going to move to San Diego?

In Hutchinson we visited the Reformatory—never again for me. It depressed me so—it was a pitiful sight. Nearly 900 boys between 16 and 25 yrs. old there. I never realized that there were so many bad fellows in the world. If I don't stop raving on, I will be sent to the insane asylum. Harriet Jones, the girl that Randolph goes with, left for San Diego Saturday. You might run across her someday. I don't know her address now, but will tell you later. I don't know how Randolph will stand it all summer.

Just write to me here, and the day that I leave, I will write to you my St. Louis address.

Keep on working toward your ambition, and be as good as ever.

Much love and many kisses

Prescription: Take one when you feel you need it (arrow pointing to kisses)

Lovingly,
Dora

June 21, 1926

(St. Louis, MO to Oceanside, CA)

Dear Ray,

Well, here I am—isn't that a surprise? I was going to write you before I left Wichita, but I decided on Wednesday to leave Saturday, so I was rushed until the last minute. I left on the Sunflower Saturday evening at 5 O'clock, and got here at 7:30. The trip wasn't so bad, but I was rather lonesome, for I didn't know anyone on the train, and everyone was so unfriendly—and wouldn't even say "boo." It was every man for himself. So, I went to bed at 10, and got up at 6, but I can't sleep on a train, so I think that I got one hour of sleep altogether.

It feels so good to be back in St. Louis again—I am staying with my cousin and her husband—just a young couple—and full of fun.

Yesterday afternoon we went to a big-league baseball game between Washington and St. Louis. Gee, it was thrilling. In the evening we went to a movie. I wonder what Mrs. Witt and the Christian Endeavorers would think of that.

You can't imagine what we had to eat yesterday—watermelon. Gee, it was good—it is the first one that I have tasted this year. Have you had any yet?

I don't know how long that I will stay here, but write to me here, and often,—I might get lonesome.
My address is
4110 Margaretta Ave. St. Louis
Missouri C/) W.E. Kloepfer

"Gob" and "gobs" of love from your St. Louisian now.
Dora.

June 29, 1926
(Oceanside, CA to St. Louis, MO)

Dearest Dora,

Dear St. Louisan: Gee! you're getting good away out there, away from home an' everything. But I am glad to see you get away from Wichita, even for a while. Maybe you won't ever go back, but I am betting that you will go back to Mama and Papa.

Oh! Dora, after all there is no place like home and I have come to appreciate it more than ever. But really you must see everything you can and meet everybody who might possibly interest you. It's a great world and we can't expect to see it all but I want to see a lot of it if possible.

How do you like to live in St. Louis? Do you find it more thrilling in Downtown St. Louis than in Wichita? I mean more night life and excitement and crowds, etc. I expect that you have already taken some boat rides on the Mississippi River. Isn't it the biggest thing? I crossed it at Vicksburg Mississippi in 1925. One year ago, this July. Whew! How time flies. One year older and wiser—tee-hee.

We are still in Oceanside as you see and I am still working. The sun shines very brightly here in the daytime but the nights are cool. I am reminded of this time last summer when in Wichita and the stifling hot nights! These nights out here, gosh, they are wonderful. I sleep under a sheet and two comforters every night. Boy it's great—No more sweltering or dreading to go to bed. But the hard part of it out here is to really want to go to bed. There is so much that one wants to do. And while the weather is dependable at all times it is so much more pleasurable than to be put out by unexpected weather.

Do you want to hear about what I have been doing? Besides working I find time to go on beach parties, dances, hot dawg roasts and horseback riding, swimming and surfboard riding. The real kick of life is after the working hours. This country is a motoring paradise as you will find when and if you ever come here. Mountains, trees, creeks, Oceans, lakes, hills and valleys and canyons—Desert and waste land. Oh, yes, there are some rivers here, too!

Last Saturday night a bunch of us went out to a ranch out in the foothills, and staged a riding party on horses. There were seven of us and we traveled over and through hills and valleys and woods down into canyons that looked really bad to me from above. I got enough kick out of it to last me for a while and the after effects are the worst. I walk around like an old man with rheumatism. I don't want to stand up or sit down. Do you get what I mean?

But it will wear off soon, I hope. In the meantime, I am planning to go again if I recover entirely.

The young people were three young Christian Endeavors home for vacation from college, Bernice and I and a young man who lives on the ranch and his cousin, a boy. We met at the ranch house and left a watermelon I brought out in my car. We saddled the horses and took the wieners, buns and dill pickles on the horses and started out. The moon was full and you could read a newspaper out there. It was so bright, we traveled many miles and over some of the prettiest scenery, through the fine trees. One time we were traversing along the edge of a cliff in a canyon which was straight down on one side and perpendicular on the other with only room for the horses to walk. They were experienced mountain horses and they picked the trail carefully. But that didn't keep me from shifting the gum I was chewing to the right side to balance the load. Gosh it was a kick. If one of those horses should have stumbled, they would have had to pick the remains up in a basket.

We made camp and a fire and soon had our "Airedales" barking. Gee! But I wished for you so that you, too, might have enjoyed the perfect time that we had. We raced some on the way back and then at 1 o'clock we ate the watermelon, out in the yard 'neath the tall trees. We got in at 2 O'clock and got up and went to Sunday School. Went swimming with a few boys Sunday afternoon way up the beach. Rode a surf-board, in with the waves and cavorted around in general. Great Scott! But the sea is great. I want you to see it and to feel the surge of a mighty wave rolling along and bumping you. Nothing quite like it.

Dora, I have just picked up a box of photographs and in it I have found those two pictures of us taken over in the yard when I lived on Pearce Avenue. Do you remember the ones by the big tree? The pictures I had enlarged. Well they were taken when I was very happy, when I was with you. I can remember very distinctly the Sunday they were taken. Can you? So much has happened since. So much has taken place. We have had some little spats and there were times when I felt that you didn't care. But tonight, Dora after all I think that you are the girl that has meant more to me than any other. I hold dear to me those memories of those wonderful nights that I spent with you. No others can take their place and if I had known then what I know now, there might have been a better understanding between us. I get desperately lonesome for you now and sincerely wish that you were here to help cheer me, but again I know that unless I made some money you could not hold me very dear for long. Not that money is everything but because it means a lot to be able to spend and earn money honestly.

Someday I will have made some real money and then—well—Dora I just don't care for the girls I have met.

Prospects of nice business in real estate are picking up and by fall I think that there will be a stampede out here.

Will you please pardon this letter? It has been so "variable." Keep me informed about all the "dope" and gossip—

Write me what you like, it will get no farther than the heart of
. . . . .

Yours Sincerely,
Ray.

July 9, 1926
(St. Louis, MO to Oceanside, CA)

Dearest Ray,

Are you in a good mood? If you are not, just postpone reading this letter, for I know that you are just going to rave when you hear what I am doing and what I am going to do. I am going to be a St. Louisian for a while until I have a chance to go to someplace else.

A week ago, Monday I started in business college, and I am going to try to finish this course in three months, and then work for a year or two—and after that some more college. You are saying right now that I should finish my college course. First I suppose I should, but I don't know what I want to take in college, or where to go (no more friends for me), so I feel that in a couple years I will know what I want to specialize in, and also I will appreciate it much more, and get more good out of it. I am not too old to do this. Please don't scold. Everyone here thinks that I am doing a wise thing, but the kids back home think that I am silly. Of course, they want me to come back to 'Friends' (University). I won't do it. I could have stayed in Wichita and have done the same thing, but I was entirely too dissatisfied there. I feel much better already since I have been here. I would be much happier if my folks, my friends and you were here, but this might be the making of me.

School is just fine. It lasts from 8 a.m. to 2 p.m.. I am taking Spelling, Shorthand, and Typewriting. I can write things now that I can't read (in shorthand). Five of us started in school last Monday, and we have been so brilliant in shorthand that today we caught up with a class that has gone two weeks longer than we have. It certainly takes study though—2 & 3 hours every day at home. I wish that you could go—you would like it.

I walk to school—We have a park across the street from our house, and I just have to go through it, and about three blocks more. Yes, it only takes 15–20 minutes to go across the park if you walk real fast. That's not bad.

You certainly have been having one grand time—I wish I were there. I have been having quite a lovely time too—for just the sight of a bed gives me a thrill. Every night we go someplace or have company, and it is usually midnight or after before we begin to slumber—and 6:45 A.M. comes mighty early in the morning. It is after 12 O'clock now, and we have company, but I sneaked to my room. There are three salesmen and one saleslady here, and everyone is as funny as he can be. We have laughed all evening. One plays the cello and zither beautifully, and one plays on the piano on just the black keys (he has never had a lesson) and another one jigs. The lady is from the south.

I am supposed to go swimming and to dinner tomorrow night, but I have refused, for I must have some sleep.

No, I haven't been on a boat excursion yet, but we are planning to go soon. St. Louis is certainly more thrilling than Wichita—any place is, I think.

You are one year older, aren't you? Do you look older or younger or just indifferent? I will soon be one year older too, but I don't feel like it. Several people here have asked me if I was 15 or 16. Imagine that—should I be insulted or complimented for keeping my youth?

Your horseback ride must have been thrilling. I wouldn't have just shifted my gum from one side to the other, but I would have swallowed it, after giving one look at the trail.

I was looking through my purse the other day, and I found those two pictures of us. I remember the day very well. In fact, I remember most of the times that we were together. I don't think that I will ever forget them. Those times have been some of my most happy ones. You don't know how often I wish you were here; every time I go out, I wish that it was you instead of someone else taking me, for really I don't care for any of the boys that I have met. Usually after the second or third time, I can't stand them, so you know I must have liked you to go with you as long a time as we did, and don't you call this real love to sit up at this time of night to write to you?

I wouldn't do it for anyone else. I think it is terrible that we live so far apart, and getting farther away from each other as the years go by. Let's hope that it will reverse soon.

I must stop this raving now, and maybe the next time I can talk about something but myself. I am glad that you are having such a good time. Have one for me too. Write sooner and oftener. Lots of love and kisses from

Just "Me"

July 19, 1926
(Oceanside, CA to St. Louis, MO)

MISS DORA IRENE KULLMAN!

Dearest Dora,

I must have been in a good mood when I received your letter

because I am surely in favor of what you are doing. While I know that you are planning a career and have the highest ambitions, I believe that you will never regret having spent these few months in business college. It really is, in my way of thinking, the one thing that will get your mind off of the scholastic course that you have been following. Dora, old girl I truly believe that you are a sensible girl and you know how many girls I have ever told that to—none—other than you. Believe me, they are scarce. I love to see you do something for yourself and know that you will accomplish a great deal more that way.

You may get homesick for the old 'Friends' (University) bunch but Dora, stick it out and finish because it means so much to you. Of course, the bunch back home possibly think that you have a silly idea, but they are not thinking of your personal good. They like you and want you with them for that reason. But Dora, please don't give in and go back there to the same old gang. I know you realize the good that it will do to have the fundamentals of a business education. I am going to start in September. I don't know when I will finish but I have made up my mind to go. There is a real first-class Commercial College in San Diego that is going to be burdened with another "straggler" pretty quick. I realize more every day that I will have to equip myself for the better job and the bigger money. I have fine health and am still young (but not handsome) and I do like to work and the world pays respect to the fellow who knows how to work effectively. Don't you think so?

Really Dora there's a challenge in the air for the fellow who has to wrest his living from the world because of being born poor. I am glad that I have had to struggle for what I have now and for what I do know of the world. But, Dora I am not poor in many ways because I come from an honorable family and good father and mother. I have an honorable name and that's not to be laughed at when you see so many these days that don't have a shred of reputation left. (I've said too much on this subject for this time. We will now have ten minutes intermission.)

My sister Bernice is 19-years-old tomorrow the 20th and she surely is a big girl. She is nice looking I think and enjoys life a great deal. She probably will go to college this fall. I hope she can.

By this time, you probably are getting pretty well acquainted with St. Louis. I know it must be quite metropolitan to you after living in Wichita. I always did like Wichita but it is not a city as large cities are thought of. I hope that you are careful and don't get "accidented" while you are there. I wish I was there to see after you and enjoy your company. I can imagine what a fine time you and I could have in St. Louis or anywhere else for that matter. My heart beats just a little faster when memory brings back to me some of those beautiful evenings spent in your presence. It seems a shame that we are apart now when I know that I could make you happy and enjoy myself doing it.

Just one year and four days ago I left Wichita for Miami. It isn't so long but it seems ages. So many things have happened since that day I kissed you good-bye. Do you recall that night? We took a trip on the paved road to Valley Center. The car would not stay on the road.

Dora, this is going to be long—catch another breath and hold on.

I hated to leave, yet knew that I had to break off working for the store. But the many sights and experiences were wonderful and to see that great development (in the best of it) which has caused millions of people to think it was worth the trip and time. Now isn't it a coincidence that I should come to the very place on the Western Coast that is to experience about the same kind of conditions that existed in Miami. (San Diego is the most talked of city in the west at this time and the developers and real estate men are beginning to boom this country which is so much better in every way than Florida will ever be.)

Oh! Dora you cannot imagine how much you would love this wonderful place, once you come here. I am sitting here with the door open and looking out at the great Pacific that rolls and surges on the beach. The moon is bright and casts a silvery blue color on everything. Our house is about 3 or 4 blocks away from the sea and I can see and hear the majestic king of waters that reaches away for five or six thousand miles, to the other side of the world. I never want to leave the coast if I can help it.

Last night after church a few of us fellows were sitting on our front steps talking and I suggested a swim. One of the fellows has a little car and we all piled in and on and went down to the beach and drove down the coast a ways and we all stripped off our clothes and went in "a la natural," of course. We had a good time and will again. Excuse the "ands." The night was moonlit and the waves were breaking heavy. One of them caught me with my back to it and gave me a good jousting and rolling, but gosh! how I liked it.

One week ago, Saturday another fellow and I drove out to a dance at a place called "Live Oaks." It's about 20 miles from Oceanside on the pavement up the valley of the San Luis Rey River. We danced with girls from many towns in this part of Southern California. It's a real smooth "slick" cement floor well-polished, out under some spreading oak trees. Pretty lights an' everything. Peppy music, "Zowie!" Some time ago I was at a party at the Mission Beach Ballroom in San Diego. It's wonderful and some class to the floor there.

I don't dance so very often but I have a good time when I do go. I would like to have the pleasure of dancing with you again/promising not to spoil your shoes any more.

We are enjoying the new Hupmobile car so much now. It's quite different from the old Hupp. that we had in Wichita.

Yesterday, Sunday—Papa & I were showing some contractors from Long Beach the city and they were here to do some building if things can be hooked up right. They are real builders and business men and I want to get into the business of selling real estate and handling deals on new houses. There is lots of money to be made here in San Diego County if things go right and "who knows maybe someday my dreams will all come true" and I will make a neat sum of money and get to own a home out here. With the Mountains in back of us and the Sea in front, there is nowhere else with this ideal climate.

Dora, you spoke of a bed giving you a thrill. Would you get a kick out of sleeping here every night of this summer with a sheet and two heavy blankets to keep you warm in July? (Am I boring you about this climate talk? Write to me if I do.)

Keep up the old pep, Dear and so will I and I think that I will be able to see you in a few months, maybe sooner or later, but I hope sooner. That is if you still care to see me. I have reasons to think that you really care for me and I want you to know how near I carry you to my heart. Write me soon and everything that you wish because these letters are yours and mine only.

With many kisses and worlds of love.

Sincerely,
Ray

August 13, 1926
(Oceanside, CA to St. Louis, MO)

Dearest Dora,

I know that you will pardon me for not writing sooner when you know all that has happened. We have been all torn up in the store and I have been working nights and have been so busy that I can hardly find time to write or sleep or anything else. The store has been completely remodeled throughout. It now has a new meat market, vegetable stand and open front, etc. But the main thing is that I am to be a manager soon. So, I have been doing night work and will continue to work nights for some time. I am learning the system and the "red tape" of managing.

I feel that I have neglected to write to you, and ask that I might be forgiven. But I think of you almost constantly. I am so sorry that you are having eye trouble and hope and pray that all will be well soon with you.

I have been talking with the District Manager and I know that they want to give me a store. I want this store in Oceanside. It's a good one. The manager here is taking his vacation soon and I am to have charge of the store and if I "make good" I will soon be the manager in charge. It's a real step ahead and I think that you will be glad to hear of this because you said that you did.

I can't forget you Dora and I don't want you to forget me. I know that you have a birthday this month but the date I have forgotten. It has probably passed by now but I know that you will hear about it before the month has gone.

This note is written late at night after I came home from the store. I couldn't bear to have you wait any longer so this is to let you know that I am still here and that I care for you and am homesick to see you.

Please write soon and don't wait and then I have a big fat letter in my system that I need to get off my chest. Don't get discouraged, Dora, and give up your course. I am proud of you and want to see you go ahead and live your own life.

Pardon this haste and scribbling answer soon with all the "dope" 'n everything.

With a goodnight hug and a lingering Kiss that means something and only waiting till the time comes to fulfill that statement and more,

I am, affectionately and sincerely,
Ray

August 23, 1926
(St. Louis, MO to Oceanside, CA)

Dearest Ray,

I have just come in from a 50-mile drive on one of the roads around St. Louis. Every time we go out riding, we take a different road, and we still have many more roads to go over—All the way home we ate peaches so I feel just like a peach now.

I am crazy about riding and also driving now. My cousin, Bill, has a Dodge Sedan, and he has taught me how to drive it, so I go out quite a bit in the St. Louis traffic. The other evening my "sweetheart" came, and insisted on me taking him for a drive—He has a wonderful Buick Sedan. I have never driven a Buick, but that didn't matter, I drove it anyway.

I suppose that you are wondering who my sweetheart is—he is

an old pal of Bills! About 65 years-old but looks about 40—married with a half dozen kids, and more grandchildren. He is a dandy musician, a fine old man, and lately he has been calling me his "sweetheart" so that's how it is. He has names for all of us. I have never told the folks that I drive, for they would worry themselves sick.

Gee, Ray, I am glad to hear the news of your advancement. Nothing makes me happier. I knew that you would get there soon. Now, please make good at your new job, for you can do it. If one just has confidence in himself, he can do nearly anything, so go to it. I am behind you.

I am not discouraged about my course, and I would not give it up for anything—I am working hard and enjoying it. I believe that this is the course that I should have taken all along, for I am more satisfied doing this kind of work than I have ever been before.

My music comes in handy also. Last week I was asked to play for them during a recreation hour that we had. Also, I am not sorry that I had as much college education as I did. It has broadened my viewpoint in many things.

My eyes are all right now. I very seldom ever wear glasses. I think of you all the time, Ray, and I will never forget you, for you have meant more to me than any other boy. I am waiting here for you to fulfill your statement—and may it be soon when we will meet.

Lovingly as ever,
Dora

P.S. I will take you "buggy riding" sometime too—we went riding through some of the parks here the other night, and we nearly got lost in it. Imagine that!

RINGS AND PLANS FOR A HOME BY THE SEA

Their words moved.

Their words began as countless thoughts and questions in their heads, then changed from this fluid form as they were shaped into sentences. After moving from mind to pen to paper, the paperbound words were then folded and sealed into envelopes. Two-cent United States postage stamps were applied to the top right corner of these envelopes, and mailing addresses were carefully added. Their words were then moved by mail carriers to Kansas and California post offices, where they were sorted and ink-stamped with a circular date and time seal, then prepped for cross-state motorized transport, moving toward their future delivery. Days later, their words were finally picked up by their recipients, our two friends, who tried to make sense of their deepening relationship by interpreting each other's words in these love-filled letters.

Later their words were put in a hatbox, where they rested for fifty-eight years. When the box was opened by their descendants, their words were read anew, then rebirthed as mechanically typed characters struck against a black ink ribbon and onto plain copy paper by a spinning metal ball within an IBM Selectric typewriter. Their words eventually found themselves laid out on a seafoam-green carpet in the great room of their house on the hill. They were then driven to a printing shop, where photocopies of them were made into cheaply bound "books" that were delivered to family members. And so, through the next thirty-six years, their words and my original book of their love letters moved with me as we traveled to different places that we called home. And now their words reside in digital format on Google Drive, and they can be accessed from anywhere.

Unfortunately, and all too often, handwritten papers eventually get discarded, because, really, what else are you going to do with these things? Their usefulness is like that of an uncle's relic of a fishing rod or your parents' fine china stuck in your garage when you have stopped fishing or entertaining. What are your choices? It seems best to give the rod or china to someone else who might use and appreciate it—or throw it out.

During this process, how much of the real love story was lost? How much of the love and dreams and planning faded as their words moved, and then vanished altogether when Dora and Ray left us? Those answers are difficult to determine, yet I do know their love story is still very much alive within me. The experience of reading their letters reminds me of a classic black-and-white film in which, during a key moment, the images transform into bright and vivid Technicolor. In my mind, Ray was like a filmmaker, and in his storyboard this visual effect would happen just as he described to Dora the panoramic views and stunning splendor of his beloved CALIFORNIA. Ray wrote the screenplay, and the landscapes he featured for Dora were at once evergreen and flowing, like an old-growth forest or a fast-moving river. Ray fully embraced this wonderful love affair with his new screen star named California. He wrapped his arms and heart and soul around her. And he basked, bathed, and rejoiced in her natural beauty.

•••

The letters near the end of summer 1926 revealed Dora's self-confident spirit rising and becoming more visible. She'd reached her full stride in life. She was adventurous and had moved to St. Louis, where she studied at a business college. She amused herself by taking long-distance drives alone, sometimes up to a hundred miles! She played tennis and danced, and her interest in sports was growing—she closely followed the St. Louis Cardinals baseball team as they competed for the 1926 National League pennant. And her pursuit of business classes and professional work demonstrated her own ambitions.

Dora kept things lively with her correspondence too. Her humor was witty and sometimes surprising. For example, in one passage she told Ray, "I am all alone this afternoon. We have company, so all the men went out hunting in the country, and the women have gone hunting too, house hunting, so I was elected chief cook. I can't cook, but they will all be so hungry that they won't care what they eat. The family around here says that I should learn to cook here, for they can stand it, but my poor husband may not be able to."

Dora was practical and sure of what she wanted—and also sure of the things she didn't want. "I don't like this kind of life where I live from one day to the next, and not having any definite plans," she wrote. "I am not satisfied here, but I wouldn't be in Wichita either, because I only want to be where you are. I bet that I will be there next summer, too."

Their relationship was growing stronger, and it was obvious they were committed to one another. Ray even noted that "something has happened to me." He knew he was in love and sent her a ring—a friendship ring. It was also clear that more planning was needed, as well as more money saved, before they could even begin considering a real path to forging a life together. Ray and Dora also needed to find out what Dora's parents thought of their deepening commitment and a possible life together in California. And there was the looming critical decision of whether Ray should stay in the grocery business, where he was doing well but was uninspired, or if he should shift gears and hitch his wagon to a power source where his true passion lay: the bustling land business in the growing place of wonder and plenty that was Oceanside.

Ray, however, was committed to giving his best effort to whatever project or business he was engaged in. He wrote, "I do not feel like I will follow the grocery business all my life but I know that while I am in it I am going to do my best and go as far as I can . . . Dora, I am not dreaming dreams, I mean it! I love you more than any other girl I have met. I want you. Tell me, can you see it that way? I have a good job now and am going to try to save some money. Write me everything you have in your heart for me—soon."

August 30, 1926
(St. Louis, MO to Oceanside, CA)

Dearest Ray,

I received the [friendship] ring, Saturday Morning, and I want to thank you so much for it. I have always wanted one of these rings—and to think that you were the one to give it to me. I was all excited Saturday, still am, and always will be over it. You are a dear to even remember my birthday, and then to send such a lovely present, you are dearer. I can't thank you enough.

—Maybe if I were there I could thank you better, but anyway, you know that I like it fine. I hope that someday I can repay you in some way for the fine way that you have always treated me.

I don't remember whether I told you in my last letter or not, but my birthday hasn't arrived yet—not until Sept. 17th, but that doesn't matter. I know that I will value your present more than any that I get.

I was wishing that you were here to go riding with me this afternoon. I went all by my lonesome. The rest of the family went to the ballgame. St. Louis is near the top in the National League—fighting for the pennant—50,000 at the game yesterday and about that many today. I got in that jam as they were leaving the ballpark, but here I am safe. Wouldn't Dad have a fit if he knew it?

I imagine the folks will be coming soon—I hope so. Dad writes as if he was homesick for me. I am homesick for the folks, but not for Wichita.

Saturday starts the greater St. Louis Exposition, to which people are coming from all over the world. It is a great deal like a World's Fair, only on a smaller scale.

Friday, I am leaving to spend the weekend, and Labor Day, at St. James, a small town over 100 miles from here, at a girl friend's home. I think that I will have a good time.

Do you remember Labor Day last year—when you arrived from Florida?

I suppose this evening you are nice and cool, but it is terribly hot here, so I have the electric fan going at full speed. I am crazy for cold weather to come, for I just got myself a new sport coat and everything to match which can be worn in the fall or winter. That's where my money goes, eh? I wish that it would get cooler anyway.

School is about the same as ever—tomorrow I go to the advanced class in shorthand. Today the vice-president was talking to me and reading some of my shorthand, and he said that I had written one word wrong. We had quite an argument about it, and finally he admitted that it could be written that way. I have lots of fun with him, for he is so jolly. I knew the word could be written the way he said it should, but I like to argue with him. He is very smart—knows four (4) systems of shorthand. Imagine! If I ever learn one, I will be doing well.

How are you getting along in your business? Fine, I hope. Write to me often, Ray.

Thanks again a million times for the present. The ring fits perfectly, and I wear it continually, so you know how I feel about it and you.

Lovingly,
Dora.

September 6, 1926 [?]
(Oceanside, CA to St. Louis, MO)

Dearest Dora,

Mighty glad to hear from you again and to know that you like the ring. While it isn't much of a present as value goes it does bear with it much of my love and admiration. I know that you will always think of me when you think of the ring and that is as much as anybody can ask. Just to know that there is somebody who cares and thinks of one is really a whole lot in life. Many times, when I am tired and feeling badly as everybody does at times, I think of you and the good times that we have had and I smile again and the tired feeling goes [away]—Gee! Isn't the world better because of memory?

We have all been so busy lately that we can hardly find time to live, but this is such a delightful place to live that it makes one have new pep and life every time the sun comes up—or goes down. I haven't been to a dance in a long time and possibly won't go for a while. I'm just burnt out and "fed up" with dances and particularly some people you meet at all dances.

I am very glad for you Dora that you can have the advantages of big city life and really enjoy yourself. But please be careful when you drive. It's so dog-gone dangerous that you never know when a drunken man or woman is going to smash into you. Out here on the Coast highway that parallels the ocean, the drivers returning from Tia Juana are either sleepy or drunk and there are so many accidents and arrests that the jails and courts are crowded.

Today is Sunday following a hard day at the store. We did a big business Saturday because of being closed on the following Monday—Labor Day. I have been managing the store for two weeks now and sincerely believe that I am going to make a success of it. We did a total of $533.00 in "cash business" yesterday—nothing but groceries—no meat or vegetables—they are separate. The former manager has been transferred to San Diego, just as I expected and I was given charge of the Oceanside store. Now, Dora, this may sound like a lot of business to you but I am telling you so you will know how I am getting along.

I do not feel like I will follow the grocery business all my life but I know that while I am in it I am going to do my best and go as far as I can. The store here is second highest in sales in the San Diego district of 31 stores. The company must think that I can do the work to put me in charge. You may rest assured that I am going to try to make my store top the list in sales and build up a reputation for the company.

Our company is the largest Chain Grocery System west of Cincinnati and that's pretty far east. We have stores as far east as Nebraska and who knows some day we will locate some in Kansas. Now 850 stores and more every week or two. You will hear of our company someday. It's the Safeway Stores, Inc.

The grocery business has never paid very high wages proportionately but I believe the time is coming when wages will be higher and the little fellows can't make the grade.

I could tell you a lot that I know about this kind of business which probably would not interest you in the least. But Dora, this is what I am interested in getting ahead—and making a success.

Dora, this separation has not caused me to think less of you, it has caused me to know that a girl can be faithful. Truly I know that you are a very, very fine girl and that I value your friendship more than any other girl in the world. If that time comes when I shall see you face to face and talk to you again I will be happy and perhaps make you happy too. Do you think that I can do it? Have you forgotten those happy summer nights when I took your "pulse?" I cannot forget them, nor do I want to. I would dance with you all alone in the front room, then you would play so wonderfully, till I was charmed to death and then to hold you in my arms and kiss you—oh! oh!—and then go home all exhilarated, on the last bus. Is it no wonder that this is so vivid in my memory?

Do you still dream of me as you once did?

One year ago, tomorrow—Labor Day—I came home from Florida. I wonder where it will be this time next year? I want, this time next year, to be near you. If you are not here then I want to be there. That is if you are willing.

Dora, I am not dreaming dreams, I mean it! I love you more than any other girl I have met. I want you. Tell me, can you see it that way?

I have a good job now and am going to try to save some money. This all may seem new to you but I have thought on it for many months. Write me everything you have in your heart for me—soon.

With a world of Love
Ray,

September 13,[?] 1926
(St. Louis, MO to Oceanside, CA)

Dearest Ray,

I am so glad that you are a manager now. Just think how much you have advanced in a year. I hope that you keep on advancing as rapidly. If one makes up his mind to do a thing, he can do it, so go to it.

Do you work for a salary or are you paid so much of the profits? I am glad that you are saving some money. One shouldn't be stingy, but one should save—there is a great difference, and a few dollars put away each week soon amounts up. I hope that you don't think that I am preaching, but you know things can't be done without money.

I hope to go to work in a month, and then I expect that I will see how hard it is to make a living and save too.

Last week, I nearly accepted a position in the office at school. They have been trying to get me to work there, but I am glad I turned it down. The people are lovely to work for, but I would have to agree to stay at least 3 years, and it is a 12-month job with only 2 week's vacation. Three years is a long time, and I don't know where I will be by then.

I am enjoying myself—I try to do that every place that I am, but I always feel as if there is something missing. I know what it is . . . . It is you.

Can you make me happy? Ray, the only time that I am really happy is when I am with you. That is the truth! Yes, your question was rather new to me, for I didn't know if you felt that way toward me. Ray, I can see it your way. You are the only one that I have ever loved and I feel in my heart that you are the only one that I ever will love.

Do I ever dream of you? Night and day, Ray.

Gee I am just waiting for the day we can be together, and I am hoping it is soon. We could be having such wonderful times together now, and it seems terrible that we have to be apart, but I guess it is for the best—I don't know.

You told me to write everything that I have in my heart for you, well—Ray—my whole heart is yours—do what you want with it, if you want it.

Let me hear from you soon.

Lots of love
From Your Dora

September 17, 1926
(Oceanside, CA to St. Louis, MO)

My Darling,

I have read and re-read your wonderful letter many times and each time I am made happier by reading it. Somehow I have always felt that you cared a lot for me and now I know it. Isn't it wonderful to know that there is one who understands and cares and loves you?

Dora, I am twenty-two years old now and will soon be twenty-three on the sixth of December and I am asking you this . . . .

Will you marry me and will you wait until I make the money?

If you are willing to take a chance with me I know that I will be positively the happiest person in California. And I believe that I can make you happier than you have ever been before. I mean it in its fullest sense.

You know me and what my chances are for making good, I do not know how your folks feel about me. My folks have nothing but the greatest respect and admiration for you. I cannot write all that I feel and think about you Dora, we will leave that till I see you again. I love you truly and miss you so much.

If you can still see it my way, send me your ring size and I will do the rest.

This letter has been full of "I's" and "You's" but what else can a man write about when he asks such an important question?

Dora I have old fashioned ideas about marriage, if that is old fashioned to be like our fathers and mothers. I want a girl to stick to me through "thick and thin" as the old expression goes. I want her to have all the beautiful things that we can afford and to have the best time possible. We are all human after all and we are all trying to do our best. Each of us have our faults and we must overlook them as we pass through life. It is my plan to have a home by the sea if possible. Homes are not so costly out here—more like cottages. But if my work takes me away from the coast—all right.

I do not intend to stay in the grocery business all my life—it's too slow and hardly any money at all. But until I have something sure and better I am going to stick. I get paid a straight salary and bonus on the amount of sales. Groceries have never paid big money and I suppose never will.

I want you to write to me soon and tell me just how you feel. I did not think that you would be going to work so soon!

Many, many young couples have started with less than we have and made good, but you write me what you think.

I wish that you were here tonight, I could tell you, oh so much more in a much more graceful way than this. And I believe that you would like it better.

Sincerely Yours,
Ray

September 23, 1926
(Wichita, KS to Oceanside, CA)

Dearest Ray,

You may think that you are the happiest person on earth, but I don't see how anyone could be any happier than I am now.

I have only one answer to your question and that is "yes," and of course I will wait until you make some money. We couldn't think of marrying for a couple years, for you must have time to save your money, and I must work some, and save some too. That may seem a long time, but time goes fast and we are still young.

I don't think that I would be taking a chance with you, for by the way that you have always treated me, I know that you will always be wonderfully good to me and make me happy. You may be taking a chance with me though, but I promise you that I will try to make you the best sweetheart and wife in the world.

I don't know what the folks will say about me even thinking of marrying. I know that they like you a lot, Ray, for they have told me so often, and they are always asking about you, and are interested in you. Dad, in his last letter, said that he was so glad to hear of your advancement.

You know most parents feel that they are losing a child, when he or she gets married, and it may take them a while to get used to the idea, but they will see our way soon. I wrote to them about it so I will hear soon. I am pretty sure everything will be alright.

Your ideas are no more old-fashioned than mine. I wouldn't think of marrying unless I intended to stick through "thick and thin." That isn't hard to do if one loves the person—and I certainly love you, Ray.

Ray, money isn't everything. It is nice to have it, but most people are happier if they don't have so much and work hard for it.

A cottage by the sea!! I couldn't dream of anything more wonderful. It hardly seems possible. This all seems like a dream anyway.

Dear, you won't mind waiting a while before you get the ring, will you? I had better wait for the folk's answer.

You know a ring is only a sign to others that we are engaged—but we can be engaged without a ring—we can have just as good an understanding. I will let you know later when you can get it.

I should write some other news, but I can think of nothing but this.

Write me right away, and I am closing with a big hug and kiss.
Big Kiss & Hug

from
Just Your's,
Dora

P.S. Ray, I love you—love you—love you,—and miss you more than that.

September 30, 1926
(Oceanside, CA to St. Louis, MO)

Dearest Dora,

Wired you today knowing that this letter would be late. I am one happy boy now that you have said the happy words. I only hope that your folks will take the shock as easy as possible. I know and realize that they do think that they would be losing you and of course they would want to be sure that you are not making a mistake. Your father and mother are like all parents, they want the best possible marriage for their children. I expect that your father will want me to prove to him that I am able to take care of you. As you say I think that we could not think of marrying for two years at least. I wish that it could be tomorrow. But when we do get married I want to have some kind of a home and a substantial savings in the bank. These people who marry on a shoestring are taking too big a risk. There is one sure way to cut down the chance of possible failure and that is to have enough to live on for some time after marriage. Money isn't everything but it is the "majority" in this case.

About the ring—I will wait till you say the word and then send it. I do not anticipate any "trouble" but I will wait until I hear from you.

Dora, I want you to come out here for the Holidays. I know that you will enjoy it a lot and my folks want you to come so much. You know how I feel, I want you to be here and to see you and to hold you in my arms—again. If you come, Dora—and I hope and pray that you can. We will have so many good times together.

We will have a chance then Dora, to really tell how much we care for each other. If you find that I am the same boy you knew in Wichita (hope I am better than that) then you will know to a certainty that we are all "set" to be married.

I believe that you could get permission to come especially if my Mother would write to you and to your folks. She wants you to come and visit with us and stay as long as you want. I know that I can entertain you. San Diego has so much to offer and just to be with you would be happiness for me. Let's plan to be together again this Christmas! New Years! Etc. Write me what you think of this.

We have been swamped with work since Monday and I surely have been working hard and long. I am going to let up on this work a little now that it is under way. I am the youngest man in this district and I want to make good but I am not going to kill myself off—so I will cut out the night work for a while. I went back to the store almost every night for a month after taking it over.

Dora, these warm Southern nights "get" one, they are so lovely moonlight and the scent of flowers everywhere. Just a year ago we came here and now I love it and never want to leave permanently. I know that you would love to live in this country. Mountains, sea beaches, woods and everything.

Tonight, when I should think of things more material perhaps I long to be with you knowing that it is impossible. But Dora, just to have you with me by my side, close and to hold you and to feel your quick breath as I kiss you one, two, three times and more (I never knew when to quit and go home) Gosh! Why can't it be now? I remember those cold nights after I had my overcoat on I would have to have one more farewell kiss—and run for the bus.

Don't forget to take it up with the folks about the trip out here. Come and be with us again. I don't seem to be able to leave so it will be up to you. Write soon and I will keep in close touch with you as ever (a good night kiss—you know one of those long ones!)

Sincerely
Ray.

October 7, 1926
(St. Louis, MO to Oceanside, CA)

My dearest Ray,

I received your letter yesterday afternoon—I thought that it would never come. It takes mail so long to get here from you. Thanks for the telegram, for it was a pleasant surprise. I was going to write last night, but we went out, and again tonight, but I am writing anyway, although it is midnight—all the time that I was out, I was wishing that I was home writing to you.

I have pleasant news—you know that I wrote to the folks about our terrible love affair, so Dad answered immediately. Get prepared for the shock. He said that it was no surprise to him (can you beat it—I can't even surprise him), and he had been expecting it for some time. He said if we had both thought it over seriously, and we still felt that we wanted each other, that it was perfectly all right with him and Mother. Aren't they wonderful parents? I hardly thought that they would take it so calmly. You can see that they think quite a lot of you. Don't you think that it would be nice if you wrote them a letter? They would like it so much.

You can't tell me that my dad wasn't excited though, for he put the wrong address on his letter to me. That is something he never does. It's a wonder I got it.

I want to thank you and your folks so much for the invitation to come on a visit—I will write the folks about it, but I am afraid that I can't come. Gee, I want to come and see you so much—but if I don't get there [for] Christmas, I think that I will get there next summer. Oh! That seems like an awfully long time. I don't see how I can wait that long.

Please write real often—I will write again this week.

I wish I were with you to get those sweet kisses (receiving them thru the mail isn't nearly so good), and to give you a few. Anyway, you know my kisses are all yours—and so is my love

Only yours,
Dora.

P.S. Give some of my love to your folks—I would like to see them.

October 11, 1926
(Oceanside, CA to St. Louis, MO)

Dearest of All:

I Love You!

Sunday your letter came and most certainly filled me with pep and hope and enthusiasm. You certainly write so much like you talk that I cannot believe that you are not here. Oh, how I miss you so much that I can hardly stand it any longer. Tonight, Monday I went back to the store alone to work on the books and forms and I thought how much I could be enjoying myself with you. But Dora, if everything goes well and we meet again I know that these days of waiting and hoping and praying will not be so bad. But if I could talk to you just for a few moments and look into those wonderful eyes again I might be satisfied for a while. To see you would be a delight.

Dora, this has not come about by chance or by accident. I know that I have cared for you ever since my first date. There have been some little spats and other things but underneath it all I knew that you cared and that I wanted you. Not for any accomplishments that you have or any particular way that you dress, but just for you and you alone. You have been so nice and so human and so understanding to me—Oh I can't express it. But, I know that with your love and help and cheer I have every confidence in the world that I can make the grade and a success that someday we can rightfully take pride in.

You may be assured that I was surprised that your parents affirmed the agreement. Isn't it nice to be respected and to be looked upon as good enough to marry an only daughter? You know how proud I am to be in that position. And I will try in every way in the world to always keep the confidence of your folks. I know that I am not good enough to be your husband Dora, but I am trying to make myself better as time goes on. I can realize what it means more and more to marry one of God's noblest creatures—the noblest I should say—a real, pure, winsome girl.

Something has happened to me—I don't get discouraged anymore! Hardly ever blue—except for you. I can take sharp disappointments without a flinch and a hard job without grumbling. I have a constant urge within myself to keep moving—it isn't nervousness because I sleep well and eat regularly, etc. and I can put two pinpoints together and hold them there. I feel that ultimately there will come success—with all that it means. I know what's the trouble—I'm in Love! Isn't it Grand? Yet, isn't it painful? My heart's out of place—it's there with you.

Now that you are working and getting some business experience you can see what kind of a struggle the working people have to keep the wolf from the door. But I am really glad Dora that you are "on your own" so to speak. It's commendable to say the least. I have never heard of any particular circumstance just like it but I have confidence in your judgment for what's best for you. The business world is pretty rough and uncouth and may disgust you sooner than you figured. Do you intend to stay in St. Louis all this winter? I would like to be in on some of your plans, young lady. You know I am the "legal counsel" for this organization and perhaps will be "district attorney" as soon as I am elected.

I was elated to know that "St Louey" won the series and I was here listening in on one of the finest radios in America at the home of a Doctor. We got it word for word, clear as a crystal and louder than actual personal announcements. It's a marvel—these radios—we must have one in our love nest—when we get the necessary "dinero" or wherewithal! They are such an attraction in a beautiful homey home.

I will write to your Dad and have been thinking of doing it for some time. I have lots of respect for your father and mother and any help or encouragement or word that I might give to them is more than forthcoming. You know me Dora.

If you think best about the ring I will wait until I can place it upon your finger—personally—with a kiss that means much. I wish that it might be tonight.

I just cannot write like I feel or like I can talk. What we do speaks so much louder that we cannot hear what we say. There is a lot of truth wrapped up in that old saying that "actions speak louder than words," don't you think?

It is now terribly late and I will stop for now and let you try and read what has gone before—just try and read it. If you are unable to decipher it I will send you the "code" next time. With love—real love and lots of it.

From your Ray

October 12, 1926
(St. Louis, MO to Oceanside, CA)

Dearest Ray,

I will try to write you a letter, but there is so much noise that I don't know how much success I will have. All one can hear is cow bells, tin horns, cannons, tin cans and pans, and the streets are filled with paper. Why all this noise? The St. Louis team won the World Series, so everyone is celebrating. Tonight is a big night for the team arrives home, but yesterday was terrible too. A cousin of mine came from Chicago yesterday to spend the day, and we took him to the station last night. The streets were so crowded that it took us an hour to get there, when other times it takes fifteen minutes. This place is truly a city gone mad.

I still like work real well, but I would rather be with you. Work would be a pleasure if I knew that I could see you after work. Maybe it won't be long until I can—I hope it isn't long.

I am keeping my position for a while, I guess. I am getting $15 a week and a raise real soon, and pay for overtime work. The hours are easy—from 8 to 4:30, and on Saturdays 7:30-12. It isn't so bad for my first position, and I am getting dandy experience.

I hope that your work is progressing nicely. I want you to show the people what the youngest manager can do. I already know. I hope that your luck continues.

You speak of those wonderful warm nights. I can hardly believe it. Here we are wearing fall & winter coats and dresses. The week before last we had so much rain, that during the whole week the sun shone only for 5 hours. It is enough to make anyone blue. It was nearly the same last week.

I haven't received the folk's answer yet about a trip to California at Christmas. Impatiently waiting. That's me. The folks celebrated their 40th wedding anniversary the 2nd of Oct. Not bad, is it?

Daddy sent me this church pape—doesn't it look familiar? I love to remember those nights in church and Christian Endeavor . . . . and maybe a walk or ride with you afterward. Gee! I am so lonesome for you, Ray dear. Must close now.

With Bushels of kisses and love.

From
"Me"
P.S. I don't believe my pulse is working right—do you (??)

October 16, 1926
(Oceanside, CA to St. Louis, MO) from Ray's sister; Bernice Wilcox

Dearest Dora,

We were all so happy when Ray gave us the news that you were our promised sister and daughter. I can hardly believe it is true because real good things are so seldom true. I'm so glad it is 'you' because "you" will make the most glorious little wife in the world. So please accept my congratulations which I send along with my very best wishes.

Dora, if you could possibly come out this Christmas I'm sure the Wilcox family would be as happy as could be—we want you as badly as Ray if that is possible—I suppose Ray has told you that I, too, am promised and will announce our engagement at Christmas time when Fred comes home from school. Don't you think it would be great if both of our engagements could be announced at the same time, of course that is for you and Ray to decide. Please try to come, Dora, and we will all be happy. Anyway, I want you to meet your future brother-in-law. In all my life I have never been so happy and Ray just simply walks in the clouds all the time.

Last night Ray was showing your picture to one of the boys and honestly he was so proud and happy that he had to let out a little grunt and said, "Gee, how I would like to see her," and then put his head on his arms and was very, very still for a long time. Dora, if circumstances were different Ray would come to you but it is impossible you understand, I'm sure.

With love and best wishes and anxiously waiting for an affirmative letter.

Sincerely,
Bernice Wilcox

October 18, 1926
(St. Louis, MO to Oceanside, CA)

My Dear Legal Adviser,

That doesn't sound so good, does it? It sounds like I am writing to someone really terrible—I will continue anyway.

You think that you should know of some of my plans for the winter. I wish I could tell you, but I don't know myself. I don't know where I will be from one week to the next. I suppose that I will stay here for a while and work. Often I feel that I should go home and stay with the folks until I get to go further west. (I know what I want to do—that is to go to California (wonder why?)

Now since you are my legal advisor, what say? Remember you are supposed to be an expert at giving advice. I don't like this kind of life where I live from one day to the next, and not having any definite plans. I am not satisfied here, but I wouldn't be in Wichita either, because I only want to be where you are. I bet that I will be there next summer too.

I am all alone this afternoon. We have company, so all the men went out hunting in the country, and the women have gone hunting too, house hunting, so I was elected chief cook. I can't cook, but they will all be so hungry that they won't care what they eat. The family around here says that I should learn to cook here, for they can stand it, but my poor husband may not be able to. I don't know whether he will or not.

Ray, I have always wondered if you cared from the beginning. I think that I fell in love with you at first sight and that was long before we dated together. I never knew that I cared so much until you went to Florida. I didn't think that I could stand those few months you were gone. Then you came back and I saw you for about an hour during that whole week, before you left again, so I didn't think you thought much of me. You didn't even call up till late that

Sunday Evening—aren't you ashamed? That is all right now, dear, for you were forgiven long ago for that, and now I care more than ever. Since you've been gone, I naturally have gone with other fellows, but it has always been you that I was thinking of and wishing for. Someday soon we may be able to make up for lost time—eh?

You work hard now, and then some day there will be less work and time for more play.

I am so glad that you don't get blue any more. I very seldom get blue either. Being blue is the worst feeling on earth, isn't it? Being in love is another funny feeling—but it makes me happy instead of blue.

Surely we are going to have a radio and all the necessary "what nots" in our home. Radios are getting cheaper every year, so by the time we want one—we will have the necessary "dinero." (where did you learn so much Spanish?)

We have had company several times lately from California. The different families used to live here, so when they lived in California a while, they liked it really well, but they wanted to come back to St. Louis, but as soon as they arrived here—they were wishing they were in California. That speaks well of your country, doesn't it?

Company is arriving now, so here's a big kiss to you before they enter—from yours—only and always "Dora"

October 21, 1926
(Oceanside, CA to St. Louis, MO)

Dearest Dora,

I have been thinking of you all the time and tonight I must write. I think of you so much that it is a wonder I hold my position. My mind is with you almost constantly and I feel sometimes like chucking up the whole thing and coming to you. I get so homesick sometimes for the good old times that we had back home. On cold winter nights with a warm front room and you! Really Dora you must come out here or I will have to come there because I need you and want you with me. No foolin'. One or the other must make a move.

Night before last I wrote to your folks and among other things mentioned that you should be allowed to come out here for Christmas vacation. I, and all the family, want you to come. You must come, Dora and see us and be with us for a while. Let's do that one thing if we don't do anything else!

I told your folks of our engagement and, you know how hard that kind of a letter is to write. But Dora, Darling, I told them simply that I loved you and that you loved me and that we both were willing to accept the responsibility of married life. I told them how proud I was to have the honor of winning the hand and heart of their only daughter (Not those words you know! but similar! WOW.)

Gee! Dora.

Can it be possible that one day we will be man and wife? My only regret is that it can't be sooner and that we are not quite ready for the momentous occasion. I am lonely without you, Dora, and almost lost without your presence. Now that I know that you care for me as you do it's almost unbearable to never see you or hear you talk. But I am hoping almost against hope that it won't be long now.

I am very glad that you have a good position (the first one is the one to make or break) and hope that good luck follows you around continually. Keep up the old fight, Dora, and you will surely come out on top. But don't be afraid to give it up if anything comes up that you can't stand and still give your best. Here is what I have come to believe and practice, "if anything is worth doing, it is worth doing well." The bird that said that was a wise one because it is a living fact. In my work around the store I find so many times when I have to remind myself of that saying and go ahead and do the job well.

Say! Don't I get off the track and run wild when I get started? The store work isn't quite as bad as it used to be. The company has sent me about 4 or five different clerks and each time they take them away and send someone else. Oceanside is 43 miles up the coast from San Diego and there are many men with families working in our store in San Diego, but who cannot live away permanently, so the company tries to find a single man who is capable.

In some ways I absolutely detest the business I am in and in other ways I like it. I want so much to get ahead and make something of myself and if I get the chance I am going to make a change—but it must be positively proven to be better before I make the change.

The folks are all well and kicking and best of all I think my father is recovering some of his old-time health. Bernice has worked since graduation in the office of a Wichita Doctor who is here. They are so nice to her and she enjoys the work very much. She is rather pretty and has such a nice disposition and everybody likes her. She is engaged to a boy who is attending the Oregon Aggie College. He is a fine sort of a fellow and will be here on his Christmas vacation. He is completely lost in Bernice and wants to marry her right now but she has good judgment enough to not permit it at this time. My Mother and Father think quite a lot of him and I believe he is a good fellow myself. So much for that.

Wouldn't it be fine Dora, girl, if you could come out "home" at the same time and all be together? Just to talk with you and hear you play the piano and maybe a dance or two and just to be with you in this wonderful place would be wonderful and truly the height of happiness. If, however, you cannot come—then I don't know what I will do—something desperate.

We have a nice place to live, just a few blocks from the "Big Drink" and plenty of room for you to stay. Bernice and you would get along so nicely and my father and mother welcome you with open arms.

Last night Bernice and I went on a horseback ride out in the moonlight. 2 boys and 2 girls. We went out to a ranch back in the foothills about 5 miles to a boy's home that I have been to. There we packed up and saddled and started up the road to a valley where at the end was the finest little waterfalls and big rocks and trees out in the brightest, whitest moonlight in the world. Read a newspaper, etc. any time. It was on this land and at this place that the old Spanish Fathers brought water out of a canyon back of this valley to irrigate their land over 150 years ago—talk about history—this country is full of it. Oceanside is just 4½ miles away from the old

San Luis Rey Mission which was founded in 1779—One of the prettiest drives out there in this state.

Well Dora if this one doesn't get you the next one must. With love and many kisses

Ray—

P.S.
I have reread this letter and I think it is the dumbest piece of literature in America. I've been up too many nights lately and it's beginning to tell on me! Please, please forgive me for using the word "I" so much. I do think and talk about something else. When?

Oh, sometimes.

Ray

October 29, 1926
(St. Louis. MO to Oceanside. CA)

Ray Dearest,

You write the most wonderful letters of anyone in the world. You call it dumb literature, but in that case, I just love "dumb literature" and I hope that I get lots more of it.

I received a letter from Mother yesterday, and one from Dad today, and they both mentioned the fact that they had received such a lovely letter from you—I know that it must have been, for you do not write any other kind.

Well, Ray, I have just about decided on one thing—I think that I will go home [for] Christmas, and stay there awhile and work—for once in my life I am getting quite homesick—(the older I get the more of a baby I am)—I don't suppose that I will be satisfied there long. If you were there, I would be, but just think that I will be several hundred miles closer to you.

I am quite sure that I can't go to California for Christmas. The folks think it rather foolish for me to spend so much money for just the holidays. It would take from $150 to $200 [by rail], and Dad says that I will be wishing that I had saved it for our home. I suppose that is true.

He says that I should go out when we want to get married, but I don't think that he realizes how long that is—a couple years. Dear, I can't wait that long to see you. If you can't come to me, I am coming out there next summer, if nothing serious happens before then.

I wish that you would do something desperate, and come to see me, but I hate to ask such a thing of you, because you would have to give up your business, and that is a whole lot.

But, darling, wouldn't it be wonderful if you could come to Wichita and spend Christmas with us—and maybe many days after that? We have a terrible time trying to get to each other, don't we? There is that old saying "true love never runs smooth." Ours has run pretty smooth (except for a bump or two), but this question seems to be a regular mountain.

It is a wonder that I hold my position too. While I sit and type I am always thinking of you instead of my work. But my fingers always manage to strike the right keys. My subconscious mind must tell my fingers what keys to strike, for I never think about what I am doing, but I always check my work, and it is always right—it is a wonder, really!

I have a very nice place to work in, and I like it a great deal.

Bernice wrote me the sweetest letter. I am so glad that she is so happy too. I know that she and I will get along fine, for I have always liked her and I think that she is really pretty too. I am so glad that I am going to have a sister-in-law about the same age that I am.

That is fine that your folks are feeling so well, and I hope that they keep on feeling that way. I like your folks so much—and I hope that they will like me, and not be disappointed in me.

The more I write, the lonelier I get for you. I could cry right now, for I want to see you so much.

If you could possibly come Christmas, please do and spend it with us at home. We all welcome you.

All my love and kisses to the "Only One."

from
Just "Me"
Dora

You told me to write everything that I have in my heart for you, well—Ray—my whole heart is yours—do what you want with it, if you want it.

    Let me hear from you soon.

Lots of love
from
Your Dora

REFLECTIONS ON MOMENTS IN TIME

So many important things happened during the time needed to complete this story—my own marriage, children, a career, community service, the loss of my parents, and the reality and life lessons that proved I was neither a historian nor a professional writer and that this book would never be "perfect." I was comfortable with those events and things. Yet, the digital clock on my bedstand taunted me. Every minute that it rolled forward reinforced the need for deadlines, because by July 2022, it would be a mere thirty-six days until our eldest daughter (aka Daughter #1) was scheduled to deliver a small human, our first grandchild. We needed to prepare a guest room; we needed to be ready for the next generation of our family (Ray and Dora's great-great grandchild).

Thinking about this future addition brought great joy to our family, especially to my wife. Pending grandparenthood also created some unusual reactions for me. They included reflections on my life so far and on things yet to be completed.

Writing this book created a fresh and exciting chapter for me. It was what Daughter #2 may have referred to as my "fake retirement" and "the exploration of alternative life endings." This period in my life is something that future historians might study for years and describe as "a reawakening when he reconnected with his soul through great acts of leisure and bodysurfing." Actually, it was a period of time where I pretended to look busy on a "very important project" when my wife came home after a day of hard work. I started to feel like an old stained couch that was visible each time you walked into your living room. The good days of living a casual, semiretired lifestyle working on a book full-time were clearly soon to be over.

Throughout this transitional period in my life there were several important themes, including gratitude and laughter. Gratitude is connected with many parts of my past and present. This sense of appreciation rises up and crests regularly for me, like the waves nearby in the ever-changing playground of the Pacific Ocean. Laughter comes from and with many wonderful people in my life and includes the joys of sharing unusual stories and random events with friends and family. A playful sense of humor seems to be embedded in our family.

I know Grandfather Ray Wilcox enjoyed a good story and especially a simple joke. He was playful and humble enough to tell jokes about his own tribe of people who migrated from Oklahoma. Many of these people were poor and lacked formal education. The term "Okie'" became widely used due to the stories of a Californian newspaper writer named Ben Reddick. He covered the 1930s migration of Dust Bowl refugees who journeyed to Arizona and California. His articles included photos of hundreds of Oklahoma license plates. The term "Okies" became part of our culture during that period, and it was not a kind description for these people.

Nevertheless, Ray told "Okie jokes" about himself and his people. His favorite joke was about two Okies standing on a street corner together, *neither of whom knew how to tell time.* Ray would say that one of these boys was wearing a new wristwatch and was quite proud of it. The first Okie (without a watch) asks, "Say, fella, what time ya got?" The second Okie (with the watch) hesitates for a long time and eventually points to his wristwatch and says, "Well, there she be!!" as he holds his wrist out for the other man to read the time. The first Okie, who is now on the spot, pauses and looks the man's watch over slowly and carefully, and finally says, "She shore am!!" Ray delighted in telling this story and sometimes snorted as he laughed loudly about the simplicity and truth it captured.

◆◆◆

Sometimes our heroes in life and in love stories suffer defeat or die early, and sometimes we are blessed to have them share their lessons and wisdom with us throughout a longer period of time. My heroes Ray Wilcox and Jack Thill stayed with us longer than most, and this created more moments of joy, love, and laughter.

When I was younger, my strong love for my father, Jack Thill, and a desire to get to know him in a deeper way drove me to take on his passions and hobbies. The strategy worked and resulted in many meaningful moments and conversations between us. These mostly occurred when he was trapped in a truck with me for long periods of time, driving on hunting or fishing trips across the western states or in Baja California. This was how I learned more about my *other* grandfather, Aloysious "Al" Cloud Thill. It's hard to imagine in California's present highly populated and overdeveloped era, but both my grandfathers, Al Thill and Ray Wilcox, once lived on the same street in Oceanside and were close friends.

As a teen, Jack wondered if Al, his tough and practical father, was trying to break his spirit by sending him off to the lonely streets of Carlsbad to attend the Army and Navy Academy prep school. Jack viewed this as unfair and a little like punishment, because all his friends went to high school back home or in the neighboring city of Vista.

Al, an Army veteran, owned a barbershop and trained boxers in downtown Oceanside. He was one of the first local professional boxers and was undefeated in nineteen professional bouts. Dad said Al quit boxing, however, because he didn't have a "knock-out" punch. This all made sense to me, but what was harder to understand was that Al gambled on Jack's athletic gifts and bet money on his son to win running events during track-and-field meets in high school. He also bought Jack shoes that were substandard and ill-fitting, which seemed unfair. However, when you have an extra-large heart your running shoes don't matter—and Jack proved to be an exceptional athlete.

After Jack's death, as I helped clean out my parents' house, it became evident that he hadn't been very interested in reading books about other people doing things. His small collection of magazines and books sat within the cabinet of his nightstand. The only thing I found of much interest was his personal Bible. I recently opened it and scanned through some sections. No one noticed this before, but inside the book were two tiny, sepia-toned, and faded newspaper clippings. The first was a story about Jack's success at a divisional track-and-field event in San Diego, where he represented the Army and Navy Academy. His results there qualified him to compete at the state level in California. And the second was a story related to a group of Catholic sisters (nuns) in postwar Germany and their fundraising efforts. It noted that they were desperately reaching out to people in California to provide clothing, especially shoes, for war-ravaged families and young children. I would bet Al Thill a hundred bucks that these are the only newspaper clippings Jack ever saved. Jesus Christ.

• • •

As I looked deeper into the endless boxes of Wilcox and Thill family keepsakes, photographs, news clippings, and love letters, it became clear that even though they were nearly two thousand miles apart, Ray and Dora started thinking of themselves as life and business partners. Ray began to move more quickly up the rungs of the ladder of success. His progress included his income with Safeway and the appreciation of land values for two lots of land he'd purchased in 1926. Ray was careful and consistent when sharing specific guidance about business and real-estate investments, yet when people expressed concern about the risks in buying land or property, he would say, "Land? Well, I am strong for it. It seems sound and of good value to me. I know one thing ... they aren't making any more of it."

The idea of them living in a cottage by the sea was first shared by Ray. Initially Dora viewed the concept as almost too good to be true and "like a dream," but then the thought grew into an exciting piece of their correspondence and even a real possibility. Soon it became a shared vision for them to accomplish. For two people who grew up in landlocked towns in Kansas and Oklahoma, it must have seemed fantastical. Yet, it clearly was there right in front of them and eventually became reachable and ready for their taking.

Dora's fun sense of humor and the theme of living by the water was on display in this passage: "Well, I got here all right—Having a dandy time—I just got in from a stroll along the beach of Lake Michigan. I like the water fine ... wouldn't mind living near it."

Ray and Dora were falling deeper in love. Their distance couldn't separate them. It seemed as if the cliché was true: that their absence from one another had made their hearts grow fonder. Their passionate discussions of marriage and being together were taking center stage and almost became distracting to their work and studies. Dora was a desirable young woman, and it got to the point where she directly asked Ray for a ring to help "brush the boys back" while she lived in St. Louis.

Dora was smart and bold, and often I wondered who was leading whom in the relationship. She wrote, "It would be grand if we could become married a year from Christmas. Why don't we set that as our goal and try to reach it? Let's do. What do you think about it?"

When it came to Ray's professional prospects, she also had strong opinions. "I don't blame you for leaving your company if they don't pay enough. Don't be afraid to make a 'break away,' for often that makes a success of a fellow. It will be easier to break away from them now while you are single, than when married. Why don't you try some other line of work?"

Dora gave Ray encouragement to go after the work that he liked best. She fully supported him and what he wanted to accomplish. Dora wrote, "I am glad that something definite in your business has been decided. I want you to do whatever you feel that you want to do. Life is so short that I think one should always work at the thing that he likes best: I am for you, no matter what happens."

Ray wrote, "Your suggestions about the real estate business are fine and I know that you want me to get ahead. I am finding out all I can about the business and keeping up on values here. It's wonderful of you to say those words 'that you will wait for me.'" He later added, "Many nights I lay awake, thinking, planning and scheming ways to get ahead so that I may have you all for my own . . . I was pleased more than ever when you answered my questions about the money that I ought to have when we start out. I am in love with you more every time I get a letter . . . when I see you Dora and know in my heart that you are the only girl for me, I do not hesitate to make it known."

Ray expressed his excitement by sharing his other love, the glorious California, with her. "You never can see everything that there is to see in this country if you lived here a lifetime," he wrote. "Some day when you are my wife, we will travel over this romantic country and spend days looking it over and enjoying it to the utmost. Maybe when you come next summer we can see a lot of it before we get married. It gets into your system—this romantic country."

Dessie Wilcox with her five children on a horse in Quinlan, Oklahoma, 1905.

Ray and Bernice Wilcox with Rocket the horse in Woodward, Oklahoma, in 1910.

A CALIFORNIA LOVE STORY 125

WH and Dessie Wilcox and family in front of house in Woodward, Oklahoma. circa 1910. Left to right: Homer, Orville, Ray, WH, Grandmother Mary Egbert, Dessie, Bernice, and Harry.

Bernice Wilcox in a carriage powered by a goat in Woodward, Oklahoma, circa 1915.

Dora Kullmann in Wichita, Kansas, circa 1924.

JC Kullmann store in Wichita, Kansas, in 1920s.

Ray Wilcox and Dora Kullmann in Wichita, Kansas, circa 1924.

Ray Wilcox in Wichita, Kansas, in 1922.

Ray Wilcox (third from right) and three co-workers in Safeway store #422 on Hill Street in Oceanside, California, in 1925.

Ray on a hillside in San Diego, California, in 1925.

Plumosa Heights in Oceanside, California. The city's first subdivision began in 1924. This image includes a view of the intersection of Ditmar and Leonard Streets, approximately when Ray Wilcox arrived in town. Note the unpaved streets and freshly planted Cocos plumosa *palm trees. Developer and banker Bert Beers called it the last remaining undivided property overlooking the ocean.*

Ray speaking at an Independence Day celebration on July 4, 1946, at the beach stadium in Oceanside, California. Future California governor Goodwin "Goodie" Knight, speakers, and community members present.

May 1954: Ray and Dora Wilcox seated in their home at Citadel Lane in Oceanside.

Sketch of the "Wilcox Home" by artist Eileen Roberts.

Eternal Hills Memorial Park in Oceanside, California, with a view toward San Bernardino county in 1949. Photo taken by park founder and president, Ray Wilcox.

Coyotes drinking from a guzzler at Marine Corps Base Camp Pendleton, California. Photo by Trail Camera 16 on October 3, 2018. The artificial water holes provide water to approximately fifteen hundred animals each day.

October 29, 1926
(Oceanside, CA to St. Louis, MO)

Dearest Dora,

It is now time for me to go to bed but I would rather write to you! I think of you so much Dora and wish that you and I were together. It seems as if we are not to be together soon as Bernice had a letter from you saying that you didn't think you could come Christmas. Oh, how I wish that you were to be here at that time and could stay as long as you wish. But don't give up and let it worry you because we will see each other by next summer if it takes everything. I must see you and be with you again and I don't mean to be headstrong or anything. How can I stand it and wait until summer rolls around? It's like being in jail in a way only I have someone to love me and who will wait for me.

I love you, Dora.

I have not heard from your folks yet but I know that they will write when they have time. It may be that they didn't like my letter, but I only stated facts as far as I know. I'm hoping for the best and don't know how they will take that letter which was so hard to write.

I know that you must get awfully tired of working for someone who has no interest whatsoever in your life. There are lots of hard jobs in the world that are drab and uninteresting. Maybe your work is different and I hope so. I take lots of pleasure and hard work out of my job—mostly hard work. But Dora, someday maybe I will change into something that is good and then watch my smoke.

I am enclosing a check on my weight and also my fortune which means about as much to me as the next guy who might step on the scales—or maybe it might apply to the weaker sex too, it doesn't say. But I was delighted to know that I will travel considerably at times—maybe a trip to you. Who knows.

But seriously Dora, there is a lot to plan and to do in the next few months, until that day when you will change your name and become the wife of this Californian. We have some real thinking to do and some work, real pleasant work in the near future. Did somebody say something about two years? Surely not, two times 365 days and every day of anticipation and expectation and yearning. We shall see if it will be two years. Not if you were ready and I had the money. Would it?

One year from next Christmas would be a logical and a beautiful time to commence the life that means so much to both of us. The months to come will help us decide.

I have been a manager for some time now and if the company doesn't come through with "mucho dinero" pretty soon I am leaving them "pronto."

[We] Can't live on promises and dreams, etc. It's the real money that counts now when I am beginning to save.

Speaking of traveling—makes me think of the time when we will want to go and see the strange and beautiful things on this earth. Don't you love to travel? When I make a big deal some time and we can get away, let's take some trip, just you and I. Tell me if you would like it.

The family has gone to bed and it's a dark and stormy night outside—the ocean makes so much noise and I feel like you and I were together here alone, in a cottage by the Western Sea, with a home with a big fireplace and lots of books and magazines. You are playing the piano—our piano ever so softly and I have a big pipe to smoke, after a day of work. Do you see it all as I do? Happiness—I love you and must have you—please write ever so soon to your Ray

November 3, 1926
(Wichita, KS to Oceanside, CA from Dora's father; JC Kullmann)

Dear Ray,

Your nice letter came some time ago and I want to thank you for the manly letter you wrote. I am sorry to disappoint you, but I don't think it wise for Dora to visit you on Christmas, for in two weeks' vacation, it would only leave her about a week in California. It would make it quite expensive so I believe it is best to save until she is ready to marry you or until you are married. As it will help towards making a home, as I want her to do her part. Hope you will not be too disappointed, for as you grow older you will know, Life is made up of Disappointments. I wish you the best of success, and hope you will go higher in your occupation. Thank you again, also your parents for the invitation to come and visit them, but you know Ray I don't like to travel. So I cannot accept. Maybe sometime in the years to come, who knows. We are all well and hope this will find you and your folks in the best of health,

Your Friend,
JC Kullmann

November 3, 1926
(St. Louis, MO to Oceanside, CA)

Ray Dearest,

All day I felt that I would get a letter from you today, and when I came home—here it was, and the package also. That was a very pleasant surprise. Thanks so much, Ray. I always enjoy anything you send me. The fruit is delicious—that is about all that I ate for dinner. I don't mean that I ate the whole basketful tonight—far from it, but they did taste awfully good.

 Honestly, Ray, I just wait & live from one day to the next waiting for your letters, because they always cheer me so much.

 Everything is so quiet here tonight—my aunt and cousin are busy sewing, and I just came back from the store—and it is dark out, too, but Bill is away on a three-week trip, so I have to be the "man" of the family. I don't like being a "man." I would rather have someone else be it.

 Last night I worked overtime until 6:30, because we have so much work now—there is the usual Christmas rush, and I expect to work overtime the rest of the week.

 You had better come back and look after me, or I may get lost some day. Sunday night Bill wanted me to take him to the station in the car, so I did. I thought that I knew how to get home, but coming back I got on some streets that I never heard of before, but I finally arrived home safely. Such is life when you aren't here to look after me.

Speaking of traveling, I wish you were here this weekend. There is an excursion going on for $5 a round trip to Chicago and back, and since I have a cousin up there insisting on me coming, I think that I will go. So, when you receive this letter, I will be busy riding the elevated, tubes, and boats, or sight-seeing in town, and trying to keep out of other people's way.

I just love traveling, and I hope that someday, we—just you and I, can do quite a bit of it. Wouldn't that be glorious?

Did someone say something about two years yet? I believe that I did, Mr. Ray. Heaven knows I don't want to wait that long—I would do it tomorrow if we had the necessary money for a married life—so it is all up to you, Ray. The sooner you get enough, the sooner the great occasion will arrive.

Often I wish there wasn't such a thing as money, for there are so many things that one can do if he only had the money, but all things turn out for the best.

It would be grand if we could become married a year from Christmas. Why don't we set that as our goal and try to reach it? Let's do. What do you think about it?

I don't blame you for leaving your company if they don't pay enough.

Don't be afraid to make a "break away," for often that makes a success of a fellow. It will be easier to break away from them now while you are single, then when married, why don't you try some other line of work?

Can I see your dream of happiness? I can! And that is just the way that I have pictured it often, and that is just the way that we will have it someday—won't we, dear?

Write me often, Ray, please!

I love you with my whole heart as ever.

Dora

November 8, 1926
(Chicago, IL to Oceanside, CA (via postcard)

> *Well, I got here all right—Having a dandy time—I just got in from a stroll along the beach of Lake Michigan—I like the water fine—Wouldn't mind living near it.*
> *D.I.K. (Dora Irene Kullmann)*

November 17, 1926
(Oceanside, CA to St. Louis, MO)

Dearest of all;

I must write you and let you know how much I enjoyed your last letter. It was fine and I am proud of you, Dora. You know, the more I think of you Dora, the more I think how lucky I am to have you as a sweetheart. I admire sensible girls and girls who do not think of themselves all the time.

Oh, Dora, I think of you so much and need you so much if you were only here, how much happier I would be. To know that you were at my side to cheer and make easier the way would be wonderful. Can't we ever make our wishes come true?

We have been very busy lately at the store and last week the "Big Fellows" from the main office came through Oceanside on their way to the San Diego Meeting of Managers. I was at the store alone at the time they walked in and the General Superintendent came in with the President and vice president following. He came over and introduced himself. (He didn't know that I had met him once before) He introduced the President, Mr. Skaggs, and then Mr. Dale the V.P. Maybe you don't think that old Ray A. Wilcox was pretty much excited. But I recovered and they asked me how business was, etc. They stayed about a quarter of an hour and looked things over pretty closely. Oceanside store 422 is a good link in the chain.

This man, Skaggs, was really excited when he was introduced and made a lot of funny grammatical errors, etc. But he was sincere and is a self-made man. He started eleven years ago and when he consolidated with the Safeway Stores he had about 350 Stores and never borrowed a dollar at any time. So, he is a man worth listening to when it comes to business. I am proud to be associated with this company and maybe someday, if I stick, I will have something more to be proud of.

I received your card written in Chicago and was glad that you took the trip. Doesn't it seem big and bustling after living in St. Louis? Please write to me about some more of the side trips you take. I enjoy having you tell me about them. You see I am way out here in this little town and I like to hear about the outside world, especially back East. Dora, I am just way out West, working and waiting and yearning for a girl that I love. You are the girl and the sooner the waiting and worrying comes to an end the happier I will be and perhaps, you too, will be the same. You will be happier if it is in my power to make it so.

Sunday morning, a friend and myself climbed into a new Ford sport Roadster with green wire wheels and took a wonderful trip into the mountains. We left about 10:30 and ate Dinner or Lunch out in a little town called Ramona. We were on our way to a lake called Cuyamaca, the largest resort lake in San Diego County. It is situated about 70 miles from Oceanside and about 70 miles from San Diego. The mileage is purely guessing to me as I don't know exactly how these mountain roads are measured. But the region about the lake is very pretty and enchanting. Big trees, pines and oaks and cedars and firs. We had the top down and the air was chilly and it felt like back home in the winter. We had big top coats on but we were very cold. We saw the sun go down over the imperial valley and of all the pretty sights in this world it is the mountain and desert sunset. We drove on into San Diego to Allan Kelly's folks' home and later went to the Pantages show. We drove home after the show to Oceanside and altogether had a wonderful trip. You may realize how far we went when you know that San Diego County is larger than the State of Connecticut. We have here both the (I'm gonna' Boost the climate and the country right here) Mountains and the Sea and the wonderful farm land that will produce winter fruits and vegetables. We passed by an old gold mine away out there in the mountains where they had taken out over 5 million dollars' worth of Gold in the Olden Days. You never can see everything that there is to see in this country if you lived here a lifetime. Some day when you are my wife, we will travel over this romantic country and spend days looking it over and enjoying it to the utmost. Maybe when you come next summer we can see a lot of it before we get married. It gets into your system—this romantic country.

Dora, my girl, let's don't get discouraged and let things worry us because it only makes it worse. When you go home this Christmas, remember that a year from now, if everything goes well we will be married; never again to part. I am so anxious to see you and talk to you about a whole lot of things that mean a lot to our future happiness. When you come out next summer and I can see you for a while I can talk ever so much better than I can write. That is, I think I can. I know that I don't write to any advantage so maybe I can talk.

I have a new dream to tell you now. It's about our home in California. I want an orange or lemon orchard and some kind of fruit crop to have our own. I think that we could be very happy along the Southern Coast.

I want to work in the land business and real estate. I love the soil and would have been a farmer if I had stayed in Oklahoma. All my ancestors have been either farmers or merchants so it's in me to make my living that way, only I want to sell the land and have a little left to call our home. But dreams mean nothing—not even much pleasure when they don't work out unless they can be fulfilled by hard work and effort. I am trying and feel that I can make good.

The radio just came on with a solo called "In the Garden of my heart" and the moon is shining ever so full and mellow here tonight. It makes me wonder about the days to come and what they will bring to my love—with many kisses and much love I send this to you.

Ray

November 28, 1926

(Oceanside, CA to St. Louis, MO)

Dear Dora,

I know that you have been expecting this before now and I am kicking myself for not writing sooner. But Dora I have been thinking of you almost constantly. You are on my mind practically all the time.

I love you so, I can't forget you. This Thanksgiving season has been so busy for me. It seems that I have been getting in so late these nights that it's disgraceful. But these nights we're not dating. Bernice and I date out all the time now and I hardly have eyes for any other girls. The only girl on my mind is you. There is none other in all the world. Like you, I always think how you would like this and that that I do and say.

It won't be long now until you will be going home to see your Dad and Mother. Oh, how I wish that I were going home with you to stay a long time. I will sometime, dear little girl.

This is Sunday Morning about eleven o'clock and I am missing Sunday School and Church. It is a beautiful sunshiny morning and the whole world is bright and new. There's something very inspiring and beautiful about a Sunday Morning out here. With the beautiful mountains in the East and the deep blue, white crested Pacific on the west, it could hardly be otherwise. I can hardly wait until you come out so you can enjoy it too.

You spoke of keeping the date of our marriage, to ourselves, and I believe that it will be a good thing to do. Especially if we don't happen to make the grade by Christmas next year. But I have lots of confidence in myself now even though I have had a lot of tough breaks. Your father wrote me, among other things, that life was full of disappointments and was not so good as young eyes pictured it. But he gave me every encouragement and wished me the best of luck. I can understand how he feels and I believe that I can profit from his advice to a great extent. The last thing that I want to do is have a lot of self-pity. I have no use for people who are forever pitying themselves in their plight. Why not take the good with the bad and keep on trying? It's the everlasting keeping at it that wins in the end. No use giving up, it only makes it harder to start again.

Dora, you asked if I would mind telling you how much money I am now getting and I will say that there is nothing that I wouldn't tell you and think too that it is a very proper question that you ask. My last bonus check paid me with my usual wages, little over $300 a week.

But the officers are trying to find a way to install the partnership payment plan in this district so that the store managers will be able to make more money. However, if that does not go through I have a raise coming soon. But even then, I can't go on at this wage. I ought to make at least $2,000 a month out here and then I could save some. Rent is not so high out here as you would imagine. Houses are not so costly because they don't have to be built to withstand the elements. About all we have here along the coast is fog and salt air that is hard on paint and outside metal fixtures.

I have a plan now in my head that I believe will work out to our benefit. I am going into the land business on the side and later work into it permanently. Also, I have a job of taking the temperature and condition of the ocean water every morning for the University of Southern California. This makes me $15.00 more a month and it's a lot of early morning exercise. I draw up three buckets of sea water to the top of the pier and pour it through a silk funnel and catch a sample. Then I take a thermometer reading and make a daily report. The Institute of Oceanography has several stations along the coast from Los Angeles and in this way determine the rainfall. As the ocean water controls the air temperature along the coast and the air controls the rainfall.

Dora, I have written this while we have been having a sermon over the radio and it may be unintelligible.

Your last two letters are down at the store and as I left about midnight last night, I forgot them. Keep on writing every chance you get. They mean so much to me. I am sending this one on to you and will write another one before you get this one. With all my love—and lots of it

    to my darling

—Ray

December 1, 1926
(Oceanside, CA to St. Louis, MO)

Dearest Dora,

I promised I would write again soon and here it is. How are you by now? You wrote of being rather blue and just a wee bit sick and it worried me to think that you were at all feeling bad. Isn't it terrible to be feeling bad just at this season of the year?

It was my pleasure to receive your letter today which told of, among other things, your love of traveling. Gee Dora, I am glad that you like to travel. It has been one of my ambitions to see this old world, someday. To go to the out-of-way places, places that are strange and beautiful. Do you not wonder why I would feel this way when I have always loved home so well? Home has always been wonderful to me ever since I can remember and my most cherished memories are those of home but there has been a longing in my heart that I must someday satisfy that is to go and see some of the wonders of the world. When we make the money, let's start out, just you and I, to visit countries and cities that we have read and heard about. What do you say?

I want to have Southern California as a home to always come back to and live in forever. Dora, you will love it I know. The desert is only a short way over the range of the mountains to the South East. There they have the most gorgeous sunsets and dawns, almost past description.

Dearest of all, it will soon be Christmas and then just a year— Hot Diggity Dog! Can you imagine that? It can't be possible can it? Be of good cheer and always remember that I will love you to the end whatever happens.

There is a fog outside that is some fog—almost a rain it's so wet almost a cloak, it's so thick. It reminds me of a Kansas snow storm. The ocean is pounding away like nothing ever happens out of the usual.

In one of your last letters you wrote of dreaming of me coming back to Wichita and being so cold. Aren't they the most peculiar things these dream-minds of ours? Nothing could possibly be further from a reality than that dream. I only wish that I could come back and see you at Christmas time. I have a lot to tell you and I know that you can let me in on a lot of "news" that would do me good to hear. If by any freak of fate, I should get a chance to come to you, I shall not wait a second. Just know I feel as though you and I must see each other. Please promise to come out next summer if I cannot come to you this winter.

Had a talk with a real estate man this evening and he made a proposition to me that sounded good and I may take him up. If I make a change I will be sure it's for the best. I am not afraid that I cannot make good in the real estate game. I know I can sell this country out here. I am going to send you some poetry that I like. Do you like poetry? If you do let me know. I do not know the author of this sketch but he expresses it pretty good it seems to me:

ALL To—Myself

All to myself I think of you

Think of the things we used to do, think of the things we used to say, think of each happy yesterday; Sometimes I sigh—and

Sometimes I smile,

But I keep each olden golden while All to myself.

Some of the happiest memories go back to the hours I spent with you, dear heart.

Many nights I lay awake, thinking, planning and scheming ways to get ahead so that I may have you all for my own.

Let me know how and when you are going back home. With all my love

As ever,
Ray

December 7, 1926
(Oceanside, CA to St. Louis, MO)

Dearest of all,

This is written at the store in a hurry. Please pardon the pencil and stationery!!

I want to tell you how much I appreciate the fine gift on my 23rd birthday. It came yesterday and also your dandy letter. Dora, I have reason to believe that we can be married one year from Christmas and I am overjoyed at the thought that then I will never lose you.

Things are beginning to shape themselves in my favor and I can see my way clear to talk to you in this way. If I did not think I could make it, I surely would not tell you.

Dear, please keep up your courage and spirits and we will be with each other next summer if I have to come there to be with you. Maybe sooner, who knows?

Will write more, tonight if possible; please keep those cheery loving letters coming out. I love them and you so much. I understand your last letter and will write about it soon,

With love and a world of it,
Ray

December 9, 1926
(Oceanside, CA to St. Louis, MO)

Dearest Dora,

As I promised I am going to write to you again, dearest of all.

I have always thought since I wrote you in pencil that it was not best but I am glad that I wrote anyway. Please do not think that I have become in any way careless of you Dora, but that I think of you so much and want you to be happy. So, I took that time and material at hand to let you know that my love just had to be expressed in that method.

At every mail I look for a letter and when one is in the box I can recognize the writing and my heart gives a funny little jump that makes me happy. And the letters are so good. I enjoy every word of them. You write just like you talk, which is natural and unaffected. I have had so many happy times with you and the letters mean so much, it's no wonder that I love you so!

We have had a lot of rains here in the last few days and the atmosphere has been gloomy and the skies are leaden. Not at all like the sunshiny days of which I am so proud to write of and which I enjoy so much.

(on backside of page, an ink drawing of Safeway store #422. The sketch is very rough and the words GOSH AWFUL are written under it)

This side was written on and I didn't know it. Ha. Ha! Notice the date line—too (Oceanside, Calif. Nave. 28-'26) See below for an idea of how my store looks—some picture.

It looks so bad that I obliterated it! I feel better now. (next page)

I am sure that the opposite side of this page is clear and unspotted so I will try again.

Dora you wrote of some friend of the family that asked you for some date and of course you refused him. I am glad that you are that kind of a girl. I respect you for it. But the nerve and the idea of some fellow who is married asking a single girl to accompany him is ridiculous and makes me want to fight. There is no other thing that would make me more angry than to see that sort of thing go on. The world is full of hypocrites who try to fool the world but are only fooling themselves. I cannot understand how any man could be so darn low as to do anything of that kind.

Even in this case the man happened to have a wife and family. I am glad that you wrote to me of this, Dora. I can understand how you would feel. You probably had an illusion shattered and felt "queer" all day. And probably your confidence and faith in humanity were shaken. But be of good cheer Dora, all men are not that way. Just the same as all women are not bad. There are lots of good men and women left in this old world. I have lots of respect for the great majority of decent people whom we both know.

There is to be some big changes in the operation and method of payment of wages in the organization where I work. I think that it will be for the best. I am working hard for advancement while I am with them. If anything happens I will let you know.

You will find a picture enclosed here of a fellow that I go around a lot with and myself taken on our lawn here in Oceanside. We look awfully small but it is the way the picture was taken. I forgot that the picture includes the kitten that Bernice has adopted. I want you to notice especially the rose that I am holding in my hand. It was one of the most beautiful roses that I ever saw. It grew on the opposite side of the house. All the time I had it I kept thinking of my rose back in St. Louis who was just as perfect and beautiful to me as the rose here.

I just got the pictures back today and they were taken two weeks ago Sunday or maybe three. The fellow who is here in the picture is the Allan Kelly who runs a ranch for himself and father out in the backcountry. I had Dinner at his home in San Diego Sunday.

I am going to send you some San Diego papers during the holidays with love and kisses

—Ray.

December 15, 1926
(St. Louis, MO to Oceanside, CA)

I was surprised yesterday—I expected a letter, but two of them was rather unusual. They both came in the same mail, but I was glad that you wrote both of them—it does make me happier to hear so often from you, Ray.

About all that I can think of now—besides you—is going home. I was never so homesick before, although I am glad that I came to St. Louis. If I had to do it all over again, I would do it the same way. I told the "boss" Saturday (when he was in a good humor) that I was leaving. He said that he was sorry and a lot of other "apple sauce." I didn't believe him, but I guess he meant it for he has talked to me several times since, and he is trying to get me to promise to come back after Christmas. He will give me another raise n' everything, but I don't want to come back. If I come back, I am afraid that it will be "ages" before we ever meet. It seems like ages already since we have seen each other.

I will leave for home Wednesday or Thursday evening—The girls in the office were going to have a Christmas party Tuesday evening, so they have begged me to come, for they want to make it a farewell party for me. I think that I shall go, for they are so nice to me, as far as that goes. Why? I really don't know.

I like the picture that you sent this time much better than the last one—when I saw it, I fell in love with you all over again; your friend looks like a fine fellow—I know that I will like him.

Bill is painting the kitchen furniture, and the odor is terrible. The fumes have nearly put us all to sleep. Someday you may be painting kitchen furniture—what say?

Do you really have such beautiful roses growing at the side of your home? I can hardly believe it. I love roses, and I think it would be wonderful to have them around all the time.

Ray, I wish that I were just half as sweet as you think I am. I try to be just as you would like me to be, but you know I am human and I have a good many faults like everyone else—sometimes I think I have more.

Give my regards to your folks and Bernice.

I will write later in the week. Write to me often, and I hope that there is a letter waiting for me at home when I arrive.

Lots of love and kisses From

Yours Forever,
Dora.

December 16, 1926
(Oceanside, CA to St. Louis, MO)

Dearest of all,

Your fine letter came yesterday and I could not answer it last night so now I can tell you how much I enjoyed it and how I look for more like it. I have a drawer in my desk at the store where I keep my last few letters and every now and then when I am feeling pretty blue, I go and get one of them out for some inspiration.

At last I have some definite good news. We managers were all called into San Diego the night before last to be told by the president of the company, Mr. Skaggs of the new plans and changes that are to go into effect on January the first. They certainly make me feel considerably better now that I know how much better our new jobs will be when we get going. By the new plan the managers will all be paid $300 a week and receive 30% of the net profits of his store. We are to be the partners of the corporation and if the company makes money through our efforts, then the managers get 30% of the said profits. In the Northwest where the Skaggs stores operate the managers make an average of $34,000 per year which can be duplicated in Southern California, so Mr. Skaggs told us. Beginning on the 1'st of January all the stores take an inventory and then can operate under the Skaggs plan of retailing at prices which the manager himself sees fit to put upon the merchandise. By this way each store can be the leader in the community and so increase the volume of business and eventually make much more money for everybody concerned. Mr. Skaggs is a man of few words and I believe he knows whereof he speaks.

But I would not be writing this to you unless I knew that you would understand how I came to be in this situation. I was about at the point of quitting when this came up and now if things don't go right I will anyway. But if I can make $25,000 or 30,000 in the next year with the company, it will be best to stay with them. That's enough about business now.

We have had a snap of cold nights and mornings out here that reminds me of home. I can stand on the ridge that surrounds Oceanside and see snow back in the mountains. Gee, but the wind off of the ice and snow is cold. I think that I will go out there next Sunday and see some snow again. I missed it last year. It is remarkable and beautiful that I can see the Pacific Ocean in one direction and snow-covered mountains in another direction. I am certainly glad that you can go home at Christmas time. I sent a small gift to you at "616" in Wichita. It isn't much but maybe you will like it.

I gather from your last letter that somebody has been talking to you in regard to marriage who has not made it so good herself. You can count on it when one person makes a failure of marriage, they try to make everyone else think that it is the "bunk." I do not know how it will be but for me I think it is the best thing that I can do. I know many happy people who are very much in favor of it if the right kind of girl is found. We both know that we can't have the same freedom that we have always had and that we will have to give up a lot of personal pleasures we have known. But there are always lots of little things that give enjoyment in married life. Just to have the one you love with you, at your side in the battle of life is enough.

Dora, I have talked to fellows who were so very pessimistic, and who looked upon the sacred vows of marriage as something to be taken lightly, but I have never thought that way and if I have you all through the years as my sweet-heart—oh how happy I will be! But Dora, we want to be sure and have enough money at first.

This letter should not have been written tonight. It is not up to standard. I know that you won't like it. I came home weary and tired this evening. And when I feel exhausted I can't write intelligently. But I am not unhappy or discouraged. All I need is sleep and rest. Going to get it, too.

Your suggestions about the real estate business are fine and I know that you want me to get ahead. I am finding out all I can about the business and keeping up on values here. It's wonderful of you to say those words "that you will wait for me."

When you come next summer out to this glorious California and we can be together again to swim, to play, to motor and see the wonderful sunsets over the Pacific, then and then only will we appreciate how much we mean to each other. I know that I will get the opportunity of having a true-blue girl who can be a sport and who can play the piano to perfection. Isn't that enough for any one?

Don't forget, Dora. I love you—
and want to kiss you goodnight Ray

December 20, 1926
(St. Louis, MO to Oceanside, CA)

Dearest Ray,

Madame Schumann Heinch is singing over the radio from New York this evening, so while listening to her, I will endeavor to write to you.

Tomorrow is my last day of work here, and Wednesday evening I will take the train for home—I wish that you were going with me, Ray.

The "boss" is still after me wanting me to come back after Christmas. He says that he will give me a raise, and he wants to put me into the advertising department. This summer they are building a new plant and making it three times as large as this old one. I would like the advertising work, but I feel that I should be at home with the folks.

Sometimes I don't know what to do. Here I have a good position offered to me, and at home I may not be able to get much—I would like to be nearer to the folks and I want to be with you. Often I wonder how it will all turn out.

Ray, I want to warn you that most likely your Christmas present will be late. For the last two weeks, I haven't had time to go to town after it,—I know what I want so I will get it tomorrow or Tuesday and send it, so you know that it will arrive sooner or later.

It has rained most of the day, so we have stayed home all day.—Emma gave me a cooking lesson (she does that nearly every Sunday), and the rest of the day we have been packing and laughing. No wonder I am so healthy, we are always laughing. We have a silly fortune telling book, so some nights we lay in bed and tell each other's fortunes just to have something to laugh about. I don't know what I would do if I had a gloomy disposition. Ray, this is just a note, but I will write you more when I get home.

Anyway, I wish you the Merriest of Christmases and the Happiest of New Year's

With lots and lots of love and kisses

From "Just Yours," Dora

December 21, 1926
(*Oceanside, CA to Wichita, KS)

*"Where life is worth living"

Dearest Dora,

Four days before Christmas, or is it only three? I can hardly realize that it is so near and no cold weather yet. The sun shines here almost continually and it doesn't seem a bit like Christmas. Tonight, the sky was cloudy and the wind was blowing rather hard and it looked like we might have a storm. I am getting so I like a little storm now and then to keep things interesting and to break the monotony.

    The folks are feeling lots better now and I believe that they are beginning to enjoy life much more than they did in the past few years. They have certainly been through a lot of hard experiences in life and it is my wish and prayer that they may be spared the suffering and disappointments that have been theirs in the years gone by. If I can be of comfort and help now that I am old enough to realize my responsibility I certainly will do what I can. You know Dora, life is a great tragedy for the most part and anything to cheer up life is worthwhile. Sometimes I smile to hide an inward tear and I think that most people do the same thing. Do you ever catch yourself doing that? Of all girls that I ever knew, you are the most consistently good humored and jolly. I can remember when you have made me feel so much better after being with you a while. Do you ever think of those fine nights when you and I learned to love each other and to care for each other? I do, and I never shall forget them—Gosh how I love you and feel that if I don't see you pretty soon I will go "plum nutty" and run amuck. Just to have you with me and in my arms to know that you will never leave me. I lay awake nights thinking of you and wondering how you are and what you are doing. Then I dream of you, Dora. You do mean a lot of good in my life and I hope that I can make you happy, more happy than you have ever been before. We are young and energetic and have both had a taste of the world's experience. We know that there will be the usual small discouragements and disappointments but we are both rather philosophical and good humored, and our marriage will be a success. I will love to work for you and a home of our own. We can have each other forever and forever, which is more than the world to me. Sweet little girl, I love you.

It is my plan to have our home out here on the Southern Coast. There is opportunity here for young men, more so than in the Middle West.

I am so sorry that you got so terribly homesick in St. Louis. Dora, there is nothing quite so bad as being homesick, unless it's being homesick and out of money I have had both at the same time and I know. Money isn't everything but it sometimes seems like it is. But now you are home and can enjoy being with your folks again. Do you think that you could live this far away for any length of time? After a while it won't be so bad. I know how it feels to be away from all your usual relatives and acquaintances. But you will soon have many friends here in California—here the handwriting changes color—(see I have changed ink) I have found many worthy people out here whom I am glad to call my friends. But of course, you and I will never quite lose contact with the folks back home. I never want to leave them entirely so why try?

I love that little verse you sent in one of your last letters. Write some more of that kind and say, little girl, why not send a snapshot of yourself now and then and give a fellow a chance to look at you as is?

Shortly after Christmas we will take inventory at the store and start out on the new system. I am all up in the air right now about everything but think everything will come out fine in a few days.

I sent you last Saturday a little remembrance which I hope you will like. My best wishes go with it and all my love. Darling girl, I love you more all the time.

Dora here is the first and last verse of a poem written by Ella Wheeler Wilcox. Entitled—"My Ships"

> If all the ships I have at sea would come a-sailing
>   home to me
> weighed down with gems and silk and gold ah,
>   well! the harbor could not hold
> so many sails as there would be if all my ships
>   came in from sea.

> Oh, skies be calm! Oh, winds, blow free. Blow all
> my ships safe home to me!
> But if thou sendest some a-wrack, to never more
> come back,
> Send any, all that skim the sea. But bring my love
> ship home to me!

I have been reading more than usual lately and run across a lot of interesting things that I never knew were written. Some day when we have books of our own, won't it be fine to just enjoy them and many more good things in life? I feel like they will come to us. Be good and write often to your lonesome "boyfriend." Here's hoping that you have the "bestest" Christmas ever—

From Ray.

December 24, 1926
(Wichita, KS to Oceanside, CA)

Dearest Ray,

You are a darling! Your gifts were here, so I opened them, and I certainly was surprised and pleased. The set is beautiful, and I am so thrilled about it. Every time I get a chance I look at it and think of you. The box of fruit looks delicious. I don't know how I will ever be able to thank you enough for all this. I know that I will receive nice Christmas presents, but yours means more to me than any other, for it is sent from one who loves me in a different way than others. I will repay you for it someday.

I sent your gift Tuesday morning. It was too small to send alone, so I put it in the center of some Christmas cookies.

Well, Ray, I am safe at home by the fire.

I left at 6:30 yesterday evening on the Sunflower Special. I anticipated a dull evening, for you know how it is when one travels alone, but I had just become seated, when a young fellow came up and started to talk. He was a boy that used to go to high school with me. He goes to Illinois University and he was on his way home. He entertained me until 9:30. By that time the porter had all the berths made up except the one we were sitting in, and had turned the lights and heat off—and that seemed a real hint for us to retire, we did. After all, the evening wasn't so dull, but I hadn't thought of meeting anyone that I knew.

I arrived in Wichita with my suitcases and bundles—looking like Santa Claus.

The folks are fine, brother Carl is home also. He already has found a lot of typing for me to do.

Wichita is the same old town, but it seems terribly dull and dead after being used to St. Louis. I expect that I will get lonelier than ever for you.

I am glad that something definite in your business has been decided. I want you to do whatever you feel that you want to do. Life is so short that I think one should always work at the thing that he likes best: I am for you, no matter what happens.

You think that someone has been talking to me, who is unhappily married herself. It happens to be just the opposite. She and her husband have been happily married for ten years, and to see them, one would think they had just been married. Each one is always doing something to please the other one. She believes in marriage, but she thinks that we have plenty of time yet to get married.

At the rate that I am sending letters, I will soon fill that desk drawer of yours. Don't forget to help fill my drawer.

Thanks again, Ray, for the presents, and with all my love and a good night kiss, I am

Just Yours.
Dora.

December 27, 1926
(Oceanside, CA to Wichita, KS)

Dear Dora,

Your letter came this morning written from Wichita and the box with the gifts this evening just before the mail was all distributed. I went over to the P.O. just in time to sign up for the registered or insured mail. You are a dear to make and send those fine cookies and the pen was just what I wanted and needed. I cannot thank you enough now but some day when we are together I may be able to express to you how much they have pleased me. I think that the pen is the best looking one I have ever had the opportunity of seeing. I hope that I may be able to keep it forever and have it as a remembrance of you. I am going to get a "gadget" that slips on the bottom of the pen when I wear it, to keep from losing it. I wouldn't have it lost for the world.

I know that you must have had the finest of all Christmases. (some language) At any rate, I hope you were happy and will be all through the holidays. When we start on a new year we want to be happy, truly happy if possible. Isn't it remarkable how much different the morale of the people is during the holidays when most of them are thinking of friends and home? Everyone is just a little more considerate and thoughtful and seems much happier than usual. It would surely be a fine world if the Christmas spirit would continue throughout the year. But when you are in love almost everything is fine and is for the best. Common difficulties are no longer in the way, they are easily passed and little things that usually are enough to make a person "peeved" never make any impression at all. It's a funny thing this being in love. I can truthfully say that I never was in love before I met you. Of course, I had the usual little affairs with pretty faced girls who later meant not a thing when I knew them better. You must have had the same thing happen to you when you were in school. But Dora, I love you. And I know that and that is enough for me. I have quit looking at other girls, and in fact I don't feel like I want to. You mean a lot to me, Dora, and as soon as I can make the "maguma" we surely shall both be together again. You are the one thing on my mind that makes life worth living.

I just came home from the store, where I had been writing an order for more merchandise. Gee, but it is cold out here now and the store feels like an ice box most of the time.. But San Diego County is wonderful because of the difference in climate that can be had in the winter. You can go into the "back country" up in the mountains and find "plenty" of snow and ice. And in just an hour of average driving you may be down where the orange and roses are blooming. Isn't that remarkable when you think of it? There is enclosed a clipping from the evening paper that sounds awfully bad but don't let it give you the impression that everything is snow bound out here because that is not the case. I have tried to describe and to picture to you the "romance" and the atmosphere of this part of the world in many letters but you will have to see it and to live here to realize and to enjoy what they mean to the citizens who love it so much.

Do you like the mountains, Dora? If so, you will like San Diego County. It's full of mountains and valleys. In some ways it seems like the Holy land with the hills and lakes, while the crops they raise here are about what they wrote about in the Bible. (Figs and grapes and Pomegranates etc. are luxuriant here. (and fine roads—There is a drive that borders and parallels the ocean from Oceanside to San Diego which is a link in the largest paved highway in the world. Many tourists from the north pass through Oceanside on their way to San Diego and the Mexican Border. It is a delight to climb into an auto and drive about "50" along the edge of the largest body of water in the world, on perfect highways.

I know that you must tire of this sort of stuff and so I will stop. (I am almost a native son of California now—you know).

We took an inventory of stock in my store yesterday on December 26 and we will use it as a check on the new system which all the stores will adopt, beginning Jan. first.

We had a fine Christmas. Company 'n everything. Fred Barbard came home from school and Bernice is all excited and they are always going some place. He is a tall fellow and is really a first-class boy. He gave Bernice a fine cedar chest for Christmas. They tell us that they are to be married in two years but Fred wants it to happen sooner than that. Dora, everything is going to work out all right for us and then you shall name the day (day is circled). Oh! Oh! Oh!. Sweet lady, what can I do? How can I wait? My heart skips a beat when I think what it will mean.

But at that we do not want to rush into anything too soon.

There is time yet while we are young to think things over. But I have decided that it's a lifetime or none. If I did not think that I could love you when you were older I would not ask you to marry me now. If we can find happiness together, I believe that we should get married as soon as possible. Long engagements are not so good. Besides being such a strain, they are apt to cause considerable anxiety and worry which is not good. But we cannot remain away from each other much longer. I must see you, Dora and know just what you think about a whole lot of things which must be understood. You know how I love you. I'm terribly homesick to see you and to talk to you again as we once did. Don't get worried about anything, life is too short. Write to me and tell me what you think about the ring and how you think we should decide about it. Of course I shall do just what you say, but I think that you should have it. I am dying to have you with me and have you tell me what you think. Letters are so vague at best, even though those of yours are wonderful, they cannot mean so much as a good straight look and a smile or frown from "just you."

My father has today purchased a half interest in a real estate office here in Oceanside. He has been working out of this office but has not had an interest in it. He seems to feel lots better now.

My greatest desire in business is to be a really big land man. Not the common Main St. Real Estate man but a large dealer and promoter. Those "birds" make money and I can do the same thing. (Gee! don't I hate myself?)

Oceanside is quite a center of vegetable shipping and packing from the extensive back country surrounding it on three sides. The depot (Santa-Fe) is an ancient structure (1887) and has its share of glory in the old town. But Oceanside has doubled its population in the last three years and everybody does not know everyone else's business like most small towns. The post office is on the street going down to the pier which is quite sloping, to the water's edge.

Sundays are spent resting and driving and golf, hunting, fishing (there is a deer season here every year) (quails, too and duck) Plenty of sports in the open, especially in summer at the beach. It is my wish and prayer that you and I will be Californians,

Oceansiders, married people and very happy at this time next year. Thanks again and again for the gifts,

Yours Ray.

December 30, 1926
(Wichita, KS to Oceanside, CA)

Dearest Ray,

I have been wanting to write to my best boyfriend, who is so lonesome, for several days, but I haven't had hardly any time to myself, since I have been home. Christmas eve we spent at my brother's home, and Christmas day, we had the whole family here for dinner—afterward Carl took me to a show. Sunday I went to the church services, had company in the afternoon, and stayed all night at a girl friend's home. Last night, I stayed out all night again. This afternoon I am supposed to go to a party, but I am not going, for I promised to take Mother to a show to-night. Mrs. Witt is having a small party for me. I feel like a lady of leisure, but I am hoping to be a working girl soon. I haven't a position yet, but I filled out several applications. Here is hoping that I hear from one of them soon.

    Soon you will be working unusually hard invoicing. I wish that I could be there with you—maybe I could help in some little way. I am hoping that the new system will be better than all expectations.

    Thanks for sending me a special—it came at a fine time on Christmas afternoon at 4 o'clock. A letter from you always makes me happier. I am glad that you sent the pamphlet on Oceanside, for now I have a better idea of what Oceanside is like—I think that I will like it.

    After I wrote to you about being homesick, I was sorry that I did, because I knew that you would worry about me ever being able to live in California away from the folks. I am sure that I won't get as homesick in California as I did in St. Louis. I don't know whether you noticed it or not, but the further East one goes, the less friendly people are. It takes months to really get friendly with anyone. I like to have a lot of friends—I had quite a few there, but they were all older people, and one longs for friends their own age. By the time I was leaving, I was just getting acquainted with some young people. Out West with you, it will be different, and I won't get homesick. Just being with you will keep me from getting homesick, so please don't worry about that, Ray—Promise not to?

Wednesday evening;

Gosh! I was interrupted yesterday and this is the first chance that I have had to continue this letter.

This morning I was out looking for a position, and I got one, so I worked this afternoon. I am now a typist in Mr. Hyde's Mentholatum factory—I think that I will like the place. It is a fine place to work, for they treat their employees wonderfully. Mr. Hyde practices what he preaches. The office hours are from 8:30 to 5 o'clock—I can tell you more about it later.

Was Santa Claus good to you? He treated me wonderfully by giving me the usual things a girl gets besides Carl gave me a beautiful silk scarf to match my coat, and the folks gave me a check, but I like your present best of all—really I do. I cleaned my room to-day, and put my set on the dresser. I am so proud of it. Everyone thinks it is beautiful.

We have also been enjoying the box of fruit. I am glad that you sent that instead of candy, for we can't get such good figs and dates here.

Ray, never will I forget those nights that we spent together—I only regret that we didn't realize sooner that we cared so much for each other. You aren't the only one that feels like going "plain nutty" sometimes—I feel like that once in a while, I guess we had better not do it, for we would be a terrible pain then, wouldn't we?

I received a lovely letter from your Mother. I am glad that she writes to me, and I will answer it soon.

I envy Bernice, for she and Fred are having such a wonderful time together—I wish we were together too.

Keep your wonderful letters coming in this direction.

Here is hoping you an unusually successful and happy New Year, with just as much love as ever

Dora

January 7, 1927
(Wichita, KS to Oceanside, CA)

Dearest Ray,

I expect that the contents of this letter will surprise you especially after what I said in my last letter.

Tonight, I came to the conclusion that you are right—I should have my ring. I am tired of giving excuses and trying to explain to fellows why I don't want to date them. Several fellows have asked me for dates this last week, and I have to think of some crazy excuse or tell them that I am engaged. When I tell them the latter, they want to know where my ring is—again explanations, and still some think that I am spoofing them. I thought that I could handle them, but I fear I can't.

Gee! I did so want you to give me the ring yourself, but I suppose that is impossible. You couldn't come, could you? . . . . just for a little while anyway? If you can't come, could you send the ring real soon. You pick it out, for whatever you like, I know that I will like it, too. I don't know my ring size, but you can try it on Bernice—if it doesn't fit then, I can get it fixed here.

Ray, dear, I do want to see you so much. My sister-in-law said this evening that we two are missing so much, and so many good times by not being together. I know that we are. I am hoping and praying that we can soon be together.

I hate to make you go to the trouble of sending the ring, but I suppose it will have to be that way. Anyway, I am thanking you in advance, and I will thank you for all the rest of my life.

I love you more than ever Ray, and I am still waiting patiently for you.

Here is a big hug and kiss
X O
from "Just Me"
Dora

January 12, 1927
(San Diego, CA to Wichita, KS via Western Union Telegram)

DORA I KULLMANN
616 NORTH LAWRENCE AVE WICHITA KANS EXCHANGING RING IN LOS ANGELES FOR LARGER STONE FROM WHOLESALE IMPORTERS WILL SEND SOON TO ONLY GIRL IN THE WORLD FOR ME ONLY REGRET THAT I CANNOT BE THERE TO PLACE IT UPON YOUR FINGER WILL EXPLAIN IN LETTER LOVE AND BEST WISHES
RAY A WILCOX.

January 14, 1926
(Wichita, KS to Oceanside, CA)

My dearest Ray:

News has been coming so fast and frequently from California, that I can hardly keep up with it, but Gee! I like it. Friday I received your letter, and Saturday the papers, and Tuesday another letter, and Wednesday morning your telegram came, while I was still lying in bed trying to decide whether to sleep a few minutes longer or get up. I didn't have to decide—the telegram did that for me. I don't quite understand the telegram, but I know I will get a letter soon with explanations. There is one thing that I am certain of, that is, the finest fellow on earth, and absolutely the only one for me is soon sending me a ring. It all seems so unreal—sometimes I am afraid that I am dreaming,—but if it is a dream, isn't it a wonderful one?

Thanks for the San Diego papers, Ray. I don't think that it would be so hard to live near a place like that.

Ray, do you really think that we will be able to see each other in three or four months? Oh! but I am hoping and praying that we will. Then won't we have a lot of talking and planning to do (and maybe a little loving?).

You really want to see Wichita once again, don't you, before we go to California and settle down? I hope that you do come.

I like work real well—everyone treats me so lovely. Did I have to go to work so soon? If I wasn't working now, I would expect that I would nearly go crazy. There isn't anything to do here at home, for mother does what little there is to do. I couldn't sit around doing nothing all day long, for the days are so long without you anyway. As it is, working makes the day fly a little faster, and that only leaves the lonely evenings. Sometimes I embroider, or read, or play—or just sit and think of you and the evenings that we have spent together, and those that we will spend together again. The days pass in some way, but some are mighty long.

Another reason for working was finances. After Christmas shopping and my car fare home, I was nearly broke—"not broke but badly bent" that is, my checking account was very low. Since I am paying all my own expenses, it seemed necessary for me to work. Don't worry about it ruining my health, for it isn't, and it is doing me a lot of good in many ways.

I only wish that we were working in the same place, too—then we could look forward to seeing each other in the evenings. It will all come out all right soon, though.

Good for you, Ray, for venturing into real estate. Now you will find out if you like it or not. The first plunge is always the hardest, but after that it becomes good fun, don't you think? Here is wishing you success in it!

Ray, I will write you anything that you want to know—just ask the question and you will get an answer. I want to be frank with you in my letters, but it seems as though I can't say anything in writing. I will write in a day or so again.

Remember, I am waiting and will continue waiting for you and you only.

As ever

Just "Me" sending you lots & lots of love and kisses.

January 14, 1927
(Oceanside, CA to Wichita, KS)

Dearest Dora,

This is rather late but darling, I have not forgotten you for an hour. I wired you from San Diego Tuesday night when I was there at a managers meeting. I hope that you received it all okay. The ring that I was going to send you was not what I wanted after I thought it over a long time. In my new position I feel that you are entitled to as good as I can now afford. Not that I am getting rich or anything but just because I have been advanced somewhat.

There is only one engagement ring in a lifetime and by everything that's good a girl should have that one as fine as the man can afford. I know that it must mean a lot to a girl to have a good ring.

I have a friend here in the jewelry business who is handling diamonds from a Los Angeles firm who imports them directly. The representative of the Diamond Company will be in Oceanside soon with his samples and I am going to make a selection while he is here. He should be here any day now, in fact is due now. and just as soon as I can get it will send it to you Dora. Please don't worry about it. I am waiting by the hour here and it surely won't be long now. If he does not come soon I shall do the next best thing, get one here or in San Diego.

There is an epidemic of flu in this county now and I have had my share. Gee, I have felt bad the last few days. Can't seem to get anything done right. Make a mess of most everything I tackle. Isn't it the bunk to feel bad when you want to do so much?

I have felt better today. I just could not write you the last few days.

Reading the paper this morning and saw where there was a terrible storm over the west and upper Mississippi valley. Cold and snow 'N everything. I hope that you are well and happy Dora. I could hardly stand it if I heard you were sick or unhappy.

Night before last I could not sleep and I just thought and thought and thought some more. Did you ever do that? Well in this case I kept thinking of you far away and wondered what you were doing and how you were. And just a million other things that I cannot now recall. But one thing that stuck in my mind was this: I am coming to you in the summer and if you are not already here I think that I will drive there in a car. Maybe you will want to come back with me to California. If things work out all right and plans go true to form I will be able to buy a car next summer. Not an expensive one perhaps but something like a Chrysler, etc. I like to think of us spending our honeymoon on a tour in a car and not on a train. What do you think? Write me everything dearest. Say anything you like and write soon and often.

It is awful to be apart and I can hardly stand it. But someday when we are together we can love and love and love and without fear of separation again.

With worlds of love, from your love sick boyfriend.

Ray

January 18, 1927
(Oceanside, CA to Wichita, KS)

Dearest of all,

By intuition last night I went back to the post office to get a letter from you. Sure enough there was one and how happy it made me feel. My only girl, how I wish that I could only kiss you in return for every time your letters have cheered me. My heart beat rapidly last night, Sunday night, when I was reading your wonderful letter, I had been out of town almost all day and after the evening meal had gone back to the store to write up an order for more merchandise. After finishing I walked up to the highway and helped get a doctor for some auto accident victims. I met Homer, (Ray's brother) and started walking home. Here is the strange thing. I stopped and remarked to Homer that I knew I had a letter down at the post-office. He was skeptical but we did turn around and I got the letter. What do you make of that?

Well Dora you certainly have the right kind of determination. I could not help but love you if I tried not to. Many times, I have to swell out my chest every day when I think how fine and good you are and also so lovely. I have always been trying since our engagement, to better myself and to correct faults that I have and which I know you would not like. Sometimes I may be a better acting and thinking man. I know that I am trying. You cannot know how much you have inspired me. I want to live and find enjoyment and happiness.

For the only girl that I have truly loved I cannot hope to do enough. You are the one, Dora, whom I shall always love.

The holidays are gone and we are well on our way on a new year. I have never spent quite so lonely holidays. I have felt lost without you. I want to be ever true and you know there are temptations to go out and have a good time. I know that you have them (temptations) and they are natural when we are so far apart and don't see each other very often. But dearest sweetheart I will be true and we shall both be happy when we are married. I love you and I feel like coming there to you tonight. It is impossible now but next summer it will not be the same way.

I was pleased more than ever when you answered my questions about the money that I ought to have when we start out. I am in love with you more every time I get a letter. I need somebody that is practical and saving. You are both and consequently I am doing myself a great deal of good when I marry you. If I can make your life happier by anything, then I shall be happy too. When I have proved to you my love then I can talk in a more profound way than now. In empty words I seek to express somehow how much you mean to me. But Dora my sweetheart, be true to me and we shall go down through the ages a happy man and woman if God so wills. I am satisfied that you mean more to me than any girl I ever met. I love music, reading, good sensible judgment, wholesome pleasures, etc. and you do, too. I feel ashamed when I am in bad company and I know what is right if I always do not do it. But when I see you Dora and know in my heart that you are the only girl for me, I do not hesitate to make it known.

Oh gosh! Gee! Heck!! I cannot write anything that sounds reasonable. Words fail me.

How are the folks? How is the old town? I never want to go back to live—maybe only to visit. But I might have to sometime. Never can tell.

California has meant a great deal more to me than Kansas. Truly it is a golden state of opportunity. There is so much more doing here that one can find back home.

Last night I went out to a ranch out in the hills with a boy and Bernice and a catholic friend of Bernice's. While the girls prepared the meal and Allan (Kelly) and I milked some cows we watched the sun set. The hills are multicolored and have pastel shades intermingled with the golden shafts of the sinking sun. One color after another in quick succession. It's wonderful. You have to see it before you can enjoy it.

Work is fine—pretty hard but I like it that way. I have been told by some people that "distance lends enchantment" and that maybe we did not know just how we feel toward each other. But I know myself and that's quite enough for me. I Love you, Dora and I want the world to know it.

Will write better the next time—tear this misdemeanor up.

Yours always, Ray

FIFTY-TWO YEARS, SIX MONTHS, AND TWENTY-TWO DAYS

Sometime in 2020 I first considered venturing out to visit the regions where Ray and Dora lived during their early years. This idea was part of a quest to better understand why they left and *what* they left in the Midwest. After many long conversations with myself, I began to realize the importance of the simple yet unspoken truth—Ray was forced to leave, and Dora *chose* to leave.

Full disclosure: Kansas and Oklahoma were not on the top of my "wish list" of exciting or picturesque states to visit. But I thought it might help provide new information or create insights about Ray's and Dora's journeys that could be shared with others. My tentative plan included visiting Wichita and Dodge City, Kansas; Woodward, Oklahoma; and the Plains Indians & Pioneers Museum. Sadly, it took the unexpected death of Ray's beloved nephew, Rusty Wilcox Grosse (Bernice's son and my first cousin once removed), to get me to fully commit and complete the journey. Rusty had been my last living link to the Wilcox family and their lives in Oklahoma and Kansas, but he passed before we got to discuss this in more detail.

Driving alone proved longer and more challenging than expected, and while I was grateful that my travel wasn't dependent on a horse or a train, as it was for Ray and Dora, it seemed like I wasn't moving quickly enough, and I wanted to feel like a man in a man's country. So, I devised ways to entertain myself. I contemplated what it would take to become a cowboy. I could trade in my boring, foreign-made, fuel-efficient vehicle for a larger and more powerful "heavy-duty" truck. Ideally a reliable and rugged Ford pickup. After all, this was the vehicle Dora had secretly learned to drive as a nineteen-year-old in 1925.

Unfortunately, most of my time in Kansas and Oklahoma was uneventful. To be fair, much of this was due to the fact that many places were closed because of government-related COVID pandemic restrictions. Heck, some of our minds and attitudes were almost shut down and closed then too. I'm not saying my trip was dull, but as I think back, some of my clearest memories of that time include understaffed and affordable hotel rooms, long train tracks, lots of land and open country, and the Comanche drive-through liquor store.

The only thing that seems noteworthy is that I celebrated Rusty Grosse in a personal way after I searched most of the town and tracked down a living human being, who provided me with directions to the tiny Ingalls-Logan Cemetery in Gray County, Kansas. There I was in my ridiculously out-of-place hybrid vehicle as I drove carefully down a dirt road to locate the grave of our shared ancestor, Israel Egbert (Rusty's great-grandfather and Ray's grandfather). I found not only Israel's grave but also his wife's. I was alone in the cemetery, and it provided a moment of prayerful reflection and quiet celebration of these people and their lives. It is a fact that some of Rusty's recommended Buffalo Trace bourbon was moderately, righteously, and religiously consumed during that visit. May Israel's wife, Mary Elizabeth Egbert, and all the departed resting there, please forgive me.

My next stop was Woodward, Oklahoma (Ray's early hometown), and after a lovely, green, and uncrowded stretch of a drive, I reached my hotel and quickly unpacked my bags. Lots of things were going on in my head, including concerns about how this "hurried Californian" might be perceived by the nice people at the Plains Indians & Pioneers Museum the next morning. I sat in a small chair by a small desk in my room, and my mind wandered a bit. It finally settled on young Ray and Dora and what living in the Midwest was like for them. I was also slightly obsessed with how much they dreamed about each other during their time apart. Tired from driving, I took a shower, crawled into the queen-sized bed, and turned my phone and laptop computer off. My thoughts floated around me and then arrived at another place.

•••

Now I am the one dreaming. My point of view is from high above the blue planet Earth. Like a diving hawk I scream straight down. My speed is radically fast, and it quickly brings me level with the clouds. The beautiful blue Pacific is now an algae-colored green. I am not sure if it is day or night, and the sky is gunmetal gray, and the only thing below me is a sea of moving sagebrush. The brush is running far and wide and stretches all the way to the horizon. This place is a vast living landscape, and I glide down a little more and float above it. A red-tailed hawk is flying near me and trying to balance her wings in the wind. She rights herself and leads me to a dilapidated wooden structure in a valley.

What looks like a small white wooden cross is lying broken and flat in the dirt. Then, after a quick wingbeat, it disappears. The wind is creating waves and currents, and the sagebrush sways and shifts with the tug of it. I keep looking and eventually find Ray Wilcox sitting in the broken-down building, which looks like the ruins of an old church. He is with the gray-eyed pioneer and trial lawyer Mr. Temple Houston, the man with the same mystical eyes as Ray's sister, Bernice Wilcox. His eyes are otherworldly and full of moonlight and stardust. He speaks to Ray in an ancient language I don't understand. I smell the soil, burning sage, and old wooden things.

It is cold, and both men are wearing long overcoats. Ray is reflecting on his life with this wise companion. He talks about his parents and how hard it was to lose two of his brothers when they were just young men. Dora is gone, and Ray is giving a prayer of thanks that his sister, Bernice, is alive and happy and surrounded by family in Carlsbad, California. Ray's remaining brother, Homer, is also alive and living in Oceanside. Ray looks after Homer and his wife, Rose.

I see that Ray is very old. He looks at me with his kind eyes and asks, "Johnny, when can I go home?" The wind is screeching through the shoddy walls, and I hear the sound of distant chimes. I can feel his pain and sadness. It is overwhelming.

Mr. Houston stands up and slowly walks out of the crumbling man-made structure and returns to nature. I hear wingbeats near me and I look up and see the hawk again and I hear her call. For centuries birds have delivered messages, and I come to realize that this hawk has been guiding Ray on his journey. My niece, Jordan, once told me that many American Indians believe that if a hawk flies above you or across your path, they are blessing you. Within seconds the hawk stretches upward, spreads her wings, and flies over us. Ray and I are blessed together.

Ray looks at me, and with a determined face he says, "Fifty-two years, six months, and twenty-two days." He says it again. I ask what it means. He says, "That is how long Dora and I were together. My heart hurts so that I can hardly stand it. I miss her every moment of every day."

• • •

I slowly awakened, realizing that I was alone and alive in a hotel room in Oklahoma. The unusual dream made me think back to my last visit with Ray when he was in a hospital in California. He was nearing the end of his life, and it was my last chance to talk with him. I desperately scrambled and hunted for ways to gather his wisdom and learn from him. He spoke of the poor and said, "Even when you are walking on a narrow street, there is still room for a few more steps." He added that there are many ways a person can make a living, and he referred to the "many people" in other countries who often had more challenges than we faced.

He said, "Johnny, there are a lot of good things in the world, but there's also the bad side. And if you start gambling, drinking, and chasing women . . . no matter how big a man you are . . . you're gonna lose."

Ray's suggestions seemed like a page from a personal handbook in which he paired "clean living" with a positive vision. His faith in God, himself, and California was profound and powerful. It reminded me of the unseen depth of the oceans, the Earth, and the universe. He clearly knew the distractions that we could fall prey to, and he also knew there were important things he would do in his life. Perhaps the hawks that visit us in life and in dreams are symbolic. They call out and encourage us to rise above these empty temptations to see the deep beauty of new places and things in the distance.

❖❖❖

Ray wrote these "forward-thinking" and encouraging words to Dora about their future life together in California: "We shall have everything to look forward to when we come back here to live. Golden hours, day and night. This is the land of opportunity. Health and happiness on every face..."

As they fell more in love with one another, they envisioned new possibilities and shaped their plans for the future. They began to look at marriage and their life together as a partnership. In addition to going to the gym in the evenings at the Elks Lodge, Dora was also exercising her business mind, and she asked Ray what the average house and rental prices were in the area. In February 1927 she wrote, "It oughtn't to take so much for you and me to live on, so we can save quite a bit from your salary. Let's make a rule right now—whoever takes care of the checks... [they] must put a certain amount of it into the savings account each month. Is it agreed? I will do my darndest to help you save and get ahead."

Ray firmly believed that San Diego County would grow and that he would become a first-rate land man. He benefited from his journey to Florida, where he had witnessed the rapid growth of business and successful real-estate developments. He wrote about his vision for California and shared his desires and expectations with Dora.

Ray's efforts included an extra-large investment of time and energy in community service and also in small yet important matters, like improving his public-speaking skills by participating in Toastmasters meetings as well as studying books and developing new ideas at night. His self-study also taught him how to create large things, like the 130-acre Eternal Hills Memorial Park in 1947; the community-based West Coast National Bank in 1952; and the Oceanside Boys Club in 1952. This engagement and self-improvement with an emphasis on community service made a large difference and was part of the backbone of his success. His gratitude for and upbeat attitude about California was contagious. "I am strong for California," Ray would say in his distinctive phrasing. And he couldn't stop himself from preaching about the natural beauty and opportunities available in Southern California.

In January 1927, Ray shared this vision directly with Dora using these words: "My ambition is to make a good real estate man out of myself. It's hard to stick with a game [the grocery business] like I do and not like it so well. But judgment and experience tell me to stay with something sure until such time as I can cut loose and do better ... My 'dream' is to start and pay out on a lot [of land] and then finance the building of a home just like we want it to be. I know that we will be happy if you will be content to start in a small way. If everything goes right we have many years ahead of us to build up a competence and we can do it. I feel sure that the next few years will be better than the past few years." Roughly thirty years later, at the peak of his working life, he owned, controlled, and syndicated more than one thousand acres of prime land in coastal San Diego County.

For her part, Dora began to share some deeper feelings with Ray as she wrote, "I have also heard that same expression that 'distance lends enchantment' from a couple of people—this comes from people who have never known you. When one hears that expression a couple of times, it makes one wonder, but I always come to the same conclusion that I would have loved you just the same if we had always been together and not parted. I have always loved you, Ray, but when you left I thought that now I will find out if it is real love or just the so-called 'puppy love.' Real love never dies, but the other kind soon forgets. I have never forgotten you since you left."

January 20, 1927
(Wichita, KS to Oceanside, CA)

Ray Dearest,

What has happened? I intended to write sooner, but every day I thought that I would get a letter from you, but every day I have been disappointed. I am hoping that tomorrow night there will be a letter here for me. You haven't had "heart failure" since my last letter, have you?

Nothing exciting has happened around here. We have had quite a bit of cold weather, but that is to be expected. Oh yes, Aimee

Semple McPherson is speaking here today, which has given quite a few people a thrill, but not me.

The folks and I have just been discussing some things about marriage—a good subject, you know. A boy, whom we know, who is only 20 years old, has just gotten married, so I thought that this would be a good time to get their opinion of people marrying young. In most cases they feel that it is a pretty good idea. That agrees with our idea quite well, doesn't it?

Every once in a while Mother talks about table linens and such things that she must get me, so that makes me feel as if something quite important is going to happen in the near future. It seems so much like a dream to me, but the folks seem to realize how real it is. Ray, I can hardly wait until I see you—it surely won't be much longer.

Ray, I had a date last night—you don't mind, do you? Yes sir, I had a date with Mother for a show. Now, does that sound better?

Dear, I must close now, and get some sleep, so this little "Mentholatum Girl" can go to work tomorrow.

I am sending a lot of kisses and love that I hope will cure all your troubles even better than Mentholatum. (now laugh)

As Always Your's . . . . "Dora"

January 20, 1927
(Oceanside, CA to Wichita, KS)

My Dora,

This is Sunday night and I just came home from Escondido, a small town about 25 miles from Oceanside. My hands are still cold and I can hardly write as you can notice. But I feel that I must write to you before I can go to bed.

I worked at the store last night until 11:30 and was up fairly early this morning and have had a busy day. Riding and walking and talking—and thinking of you. My mind is almost always working and you are the cause of about 60% of the effort. Isn't it "funny" to be in love? I simply cannot think of anything now-a-days except in terms of how you would like this and that. There was a time when I thought mostly of myself and how each act would apply to just me. But now it's us.

I wonder how you are now? Happy? I hope so. I want you to always be happy and feeling fit. Your last letter came as a surprise before I could answer the other one and this one is going to be mailed before I have the answer to the one I mailed early this week. You said that you and the rest of the family were still okay. and how glad I am that you are well and with your own family.

My flu has left me and I am feeling fine again. One week ago, today we were down at the beach and snapped some pictures about 4:20 in the afternoon. They are clear—they surprised me because they were taken so late. You can see now what a hard looking "boyfriend" you have on your hands. I'm wondering how you will ever get along with such a "guy" as these "snaps" expose. Don't get shocked at them but send me some of yourself when you have some on hand. I would like a few of you Dora, any kind shape or form. Just wrap up some old ones if you haven't any late ones and send them out. Be a good girl and do as Papa says and write a letter when you send them.

My heart is with you, Dora, and you will bring it here when you come. I am weary of the hours and days that will have to pass before you can come. A young couple from Oceanside were married out at the old mission today and they were "serenaded" through the streets.

I sat in the drug store on the corner and thought of you so much. Maybe about five or six months more and we would be going through the same thing.

My father has taken an office by himself now and thinks he will do better in the future. He has done well as far as that goes but believes that he has a chance to make more money by himself.

My ambition is to make a good real estate man out of myself. It's hard to stick with a game like I do and not like it so well. But judgment and experience tells me to stay with something sure until such time as I can cut loose and do better.

Just as soon as I can get some cash I am going to put it into a small home or lot and have something of a start when you come out.

If you do not like the selection we can change later. My "dream" is to start and pay out on a lot and then finance the building of a home just like we want it to be. I know that we will be happy if you will be content to start in a small way. If everything goes right we have many years ahead of us to build up a competence and we can do it. I feel sure that the next few years will be better than the past few years.

I miss you so much and I love you truly. With each succeeding day I find more to love you about. Your letters reveal your character and I have simply to try to be worthy of your wonderful love. The world is bad in lots of ways but with a girl like you with faith in me, it looks like a better "deal." I love these words in this song:

It seems like a year since I've seen you, dear. Yet, I know it's been only a day. But the hours seem long and the world goes wrong for it's empty with you away. And I dream of your lips and your eyes so true and I wonder if your heart is dreaming, too. For my own heart is crying this whole day through. I'm lonesome; I guess that's all.

The faces I see don't appeal to me, for it's your face I long for today, with its dear little smile that makes life worthwhile for it drives all my cares away. And I wake from each dream of your loveliness just to sink once again into loneliness. I'd give all the world for just one caress, I'm lonesome for you, that's all.

It almost makes me break down and "you know" when I think of living without you. Tears won't help a situation like this—it requires everything a man has to stand and battle for the one he loves best. "Keep on keeping on" is my watchword.

It's late now and I must cease.

Be a good girl—February, March, April, May, June, 5 months—count 'em. Let's fool everybody who says it can't be done.

With oceans of love, a kiss on every wave. Let's hope for a rough season.

Ray

January 23, 1927

(Wichita, KS to Oceanside, CA)

Dearest, dearest Ray,

I am in love with you more than ever, and I am as happy as it is possible for me to be, and still be away from you. You don't think that anyone is really happy on earth—maybe not, but if you had been here today, I know one person that would have been really happy— that would have been me. I guess that you know what happened. Your ring for me arrived this morning. Ray, I think that it is just beautiful, and the thought that goes with it, so more beautiful.

Also, it just fits perfectly. I am so proud of it, and the person that gave it to me. Thanks a million, million times, Ray. Some day, not so very far off, I can thank you in a much better way. You don't know how much this ring means to me. One date that I will never forget is the 22nd of January of 1927.

The next day that I am living for is the day when we will see each other—that will be only four or five months away.

Ray, if you don't feel that you can come here this summer, I am quite sure that I can come there. When I told the folks of your plan to come here for a visit, Daddy said that you were most welcome here, but he hated to see you give up your business and spend so much of your hard-earned money to come, so he thought that he had just better send me out to California. He said that it didn't make much difference, for if you came here we would get married, and if I went there, we would do the same. He says that he knows us too well. So, you see, dear, we will get to see each other soon, and have our wishes come true.

It would be great though wouldn't it, if you could drive out, and then we could take our honeymoon trip back to California? Everything can be decided later, but I can hardly wait until we really know what we are going to do.

I did appreciate your last two letters so much, although I was so sorry to hear of you being ill. I hope that you are over it by this time. I knew that something was wrong when you didn't write for nearly a week.

Ray, I do have some terrible temptations sometimes—I wouldn't blame you in the least for going out and having a good time. Every time that I am tempted, I just get out one of your letters and read it, and this gives me courage not to yield, for I know that my lonesome boyfriend is being true to me. I want to be true to him.

Again, dearest, I want to thank you for the ring, for I realize what it means, and I put it on with these words in my heart—"Ray, I Love you."

Just "Me"
Dora

January 26, 1927
(Oceanside, CA to Wichita, KS)

My Dora,

You are not in love with me any more than I am with you. I truly love you, Dora, and every waking hour finds me thinking of you and wondering how you are. Your wonderful letter came today—the one that I have been waiting for, for days it seems. One thing that I cannot understand is (crossed out word, "that") a girl like you being in love with a fellow like me. I feel so unworthy when I think of our approaching marriage. I know that I shall always love and cherish you—always.

There's a surging feeling of well-being that sweeps over me when I think of the prize that I have won in the battle of life. Whenever I feel just a little blue and things don't break exactly right, I think of you and your love for me and the world looks better immediately. After all is said and done there is always this thought that I like to think of. Someday I will get the chance to make you completely happy and give you everything that your heart longs for in this world. Isn't that enough to look forward to? I think that it's enough for me—I know it is. I am striving day by day to attain this end and make myself a little more deserving of success which I know will be mine in the years to come.

You cannot know how pleased I am to know that the ring fits your finger. Who said I was not a good guesser?

I know that you do appreciate what that ring means dear little girl. We are becoming quite grown up—what say? We are leaving our childhood behind and are about to embark on the happiest period in life. It is a time when we should be the happiest two people in the world. This waiting is a severe strain on us both and if we live through it without mishap we shall be lucky indeed.

About the trip that I mentioned in my last letter and which you write about. You are right about the expense which would be great if I drove a car through. And that was the only reason in the world for my coming to Wichita to see you, so, if you can come about June or July, we could save a lot of money. Your old Dad is a wise old bird isn't he? Pardon the English. He guessed or knew just what was on my mind about marriage. I certainly want to get married just the moment when I get enough money ahead to make the grade. I love you, Dora, and want you here with me by my side. Isn't it terrible that I can't see you often now?

But if you can come this summer we can make our "dream home" out here in the Golden West. We can tour around in the West on our honeymoon can't we?

There's opportunity out here on the coast. More in a day than in a month back there. There are so many new industries springing up that a fellow can get into. And as a place to live there is "none such" in the United States. Happy days and nights outdoors when it's enjoyable. Golden hours of sunshine that peps one up. Glorious sunsets that make a person marvel at their splendor. And the mountains and desert in the background to retreat to when one feels inclined that way. I am thoroughly "sold" on this Western Coast and hope that you will like it as well.

I want you to write and tell. me how much money you think I should have on hand after I "pay the preacher" I want your idea so that I may know how long we shall have to wait.

Remember that I have insurance and a good position for a comparatively young man. If everything goes right I should make $250 every thirty days. After the first of April I can really tell more about the business. It is possible that I can make $350 a month in a year more, that is if plans work out. I am telling you the facts as I know them and when the figures are gone over on the first of April for the first inventory under this new system I can tell how it will work out. In the meantime, I am keeping up on the Real Estate game so that I may switch over if I think best.

There are a host of things and details that must be worked out before we can become married but one by one I am fixing them as I get to them. The main thing is to keep up your spirit and courage and know that everything is O.K. We shall make it and I know we can. San Diego City and San Diego County is teeming with activity now and will continue to increase as the years roll by.

Am I too serious, Dora? I talk of wages and salaries and business, etc. because I have always worked hard and they mean a great deal to me. But I never want to bore you with shop talk. I write what I think and want to be frank with you.

If you can help me save the first year or so and get ahead for the start everything will be lovely. If we get a small house around here and go easy on expenses we shall both have a lot of pleasure in making the salary "do its stuff." Just the two of us for the first year at least don't you think?

I have decided that I had better turn the old pay check over to "Momma" and let her run the home and give me my five cents a week for luxuries, etc.

Write "queek,' answer soon and reply immediately or pretty "Pronto."

Your Californian, you know
Ray.

January 26, 1927
(Wichita, KS to Oceanside, CA)

Dearest Ray,

I really haven't much to write about, but I just feel like writing to you, so I am doing it.

I have been trying to entertain myself all evening—doing a bit of everything and not much of anything. One certainly has to entertain herself here. Once in a while I get so disgusted at Wichita, for it is so hard to find any amusement here. One can go to a show and that is about all—and there really is only one good show left: the Miller. Oh well, such is life in the Middle West. I know that life in the far West must be a little more entertaining and exciting—I shall see for myself someday.

None of the people at the Mentholatum Company (there are only 25 employees) knew that I was engaged or even thinking of it, so Monday I wore my ring. No one noticed it until about one minute to twelve o'clock but by twelve everyone in the office knew it, and I was just "stormed." All during lunch I seemed to be the center of attraction; everyone was "kidding" me. I don't know how I lived through it all, but I did. It was a big surprise to everyone out there.

Everyone thinks that the ring is beautiful. I do too. Now if the man that bought the ring was only here, I could wish for nothing more.

We are having our variation of weather again. In the morning it is all icy, and in the evenings, all slushy. Every morning I wonder if I will reach work safely without sitting down several times on the icy pavement or walk—so far I have had no accidents.

Write me about your latest plans. I am as always, yours for always.

Love and Kisses Dora

February 2, 1927
(Wichita, KS to Oceanside, CA)

Dearest Ray,

I don't know whether to answer "quick," immediately, or "pronto," so I guess that I will do all those.

Your letter just "pepped" me up. Your letters always do. Honestly Ray, I don't know what I would do if I didn't hear from you often. None of your letters bore me, and really you aren't too serious. All the things that you mentioned in your letter must be talked about sometime, and it is better to know how we stand on each question, before we marry instead of finding out afterward.

About how much money you should have, I don't know much about how much is necessary so I asked Dad. He said "the more the better," but he also said that he thought if we started out in life together without so much, and we work hard together, then in years to come when we have more money, and can afford nicer things, that we will appreciate them much more than if we start out with everything. He thought that maybe $500 would be enough, but it might be better to plan on a little more, don't you think? Again, the amount necessary depends on what we are going to do. Shall we buy a little home right away, or rent one a while until we see if we are going to stay there for some time to come? Also, we must have money to get furniture. How much does it cost to buy a house or rent one? We don't need a large one, just a small one.

One of my girlfriends was married Saturday, and as they don't have so much money, she said that they are having a lot of fun deciding on what they can and can't have. We will have to do the same, but I won't mind it, so long as I have you.

How much do you have saved up already? It oughtn't to take so much for you and me to live on, so we can save quite a bit from your salary. Let's make a rule right now—whoever takes care of the checks, whether "mama" or "papa," must put a certain amount of it into the savings account each month. Is it agreed? I will do my darndest to help you save and get ahead. I think that you are right in saying that there should be only the two of us for a year or two— maybe longer (until we can afford more)?

Today is the first of February. How glad I am that one month of this year has passed, for that just makes us one month closer together. I am quite sure that I can come this summer. Oh! I can hardly wait—I just dream of it all the time.

Yesterday I got a picture for our home. Mr. Fischer, who used to be my music teacher, gave it to me. He brought it from Europe for me, so you see we can have at least one picture to decorate the house with.

Ray dear, I know that you are the only one that can make me happy, and I hope that I can add a great deal of happiness to your life. I think that I can, for I love you!!

Now just keep on writing what you think to your "Soon-to-be-a-Californian also."

Just "Me"
Dora

February 7, 1927
(Oceanside, CA to Wichita, KS)

Dearest,

It is Monday night and all is well. Tried to find time to answer your letter last night but was unable to stay awake long enough to write intelligently. Worked hard until late Saturday night and spent a busy Sunday. Thought so much of you on Sunday that I was worried a little about how you were and whether you were thinking of me. Somewhere I have read about people thinking of each other at the same time and I wondered if this was the case. Were you thinking any more of me on Sunday the 6th than any other day? Have you ever felt that way Dora?

Maybe there is something to this mental telepathy stuff after all. I surely thought of you so much all day. I planned and dreamed and thought of how we would like to live in Oceanside. There surely are a lot of fine people living here now. The friendliest people I ever met. They are almost all newcomers and are invariably longing for friends.

Last Friday we had a joint dinner and dance of the Oceanside Rotary and Kiwanis Club. I took Bernice and we had a dandy time. I have danced a lot since coming out here. I can hardly wait until we, you and I can, dance together again. I want you to be a Kiwanette and then we can have the best of times together. The term Kiwanette comes from being the wife of a Kiwanis Club member.

Oh, Dora the time is slowly coming when you can come out and live here and enjoy the best the old earth has to offer. Every minute brings closed the time when we shall see each other and talk over so much of our love. The people out here are mostly all plain and substantial and resting solely on his or her merits here and not what they used to be back home. Each man and woman is sized up according to what he is doing for the good of the country and how much happiness he or she finds in doing it.

In San Diego there are men who are directors of huge corporations in the East and are practically unknown out here. Except to just a few who know him he is passed by on the streets like any common man. Many of the prominent world figures have homes out here. But the West is too big to kowtow to any one man or a dozen. There are so many notables that they are hardly noticed anymore. Douglas Fairbanks and Mary Pickford are building their "dream" home out in the hills about 19 or 20 miles from Oceanside, directly back of the coastal town Del Mar. They are going to spend over a million dollars on it and are having a parlor bus with sleeping accommodations built so they can make the run down from Hollywood and not miss any sleep.

We have company here tonight and the radio is going full blast. If this letter is not in the least intelligent, you have the reason.

Yesterday Allan Kelly and I drove over to a little town called Escondido. We were discussing a hundred subjects, among them women and love and happiness and many other things. We came to the ultimate conclusion that real happiness comes in unselfish giving. We agreed that nobody was really happy on earth. But we can be happy in giving of ourselves in an unselfish way.

Sunday is the day when life is best here for me in California. It means rest and relaxation. "Plenty of Sunshine." We went swimming the Sunday before last. Awfully cold but really invigorating when it's over.

I suppose that you have been reading about the Catalina Island swim. We had it over the radio almost stroke for stroke. I was listening when the race was ending. Almost 2:30 when I retired for the night. It was a superhuman feat when you know how hard the water was to "buck." This George Young, the winner, is some kid, no foolin'.

Dora, when you and I settle down here in this glorious land to make our home we shall take many trips up and down the Pacific Coast. There are so many places to go to and to see that we can never see them all, but we shall see all we have time and money for. Gosh, that is terrible grammar!!

I want to wait 'til you are with me to go to Catalina. We will enjoy it together won't we?

Last night Allan [Kelly] and I drove down to the water's edge at the beach to watch the Western Sunset. It was truly wonderful. Great golden disc slowly dropping into the great Pacific. Orange and purple and bright colors playing on the rolling water. What a site to inspire. After the sunset we turned around to see the moon. It was coming up "full" and soon was flooding the land in a beautiful light that made me wish with all my heart for "just you."

I cannot believe myself sometimes when I read your darling letters. They are so girlish and womanly! Oh, gee!! I cannot begin to tell you how I miss you. Miss you, Miss you, Miss you.

We shall have everything to look forward to when we come back here to live. Golden hours, day and night. This is the land of opportunity. Health and happiness on every face that looks honest.

I am glad that you like the picture of San Diego. We are so close to it here. I am watching it closely and perhaps shall move there when you come.

I am crazy waiting for the ring but I know what I want so a day or two can't disturb me now.

It is my plan now to drive to Wichita in the Summer and see you. I'll come back and make some more money and then get married in the late fall. Maybe sooner if you say the word. I want you to say when and be the "judge."

I love you,

Ray

February 14, 1927
(Wichita, KS to Oceanside, CA)

Dearest Ray:

I did think a lot of you last Sunday, but as far as that goes I am always thinking of you. It seems as though everything that I do or say makes me think of you.

People are the same the world over, I guess. There are some that think our marrying is just wonderful, and give me the most encouragement, and then there are a few who love to be the joy killers.

I have also heard that same expression that "distance lends enchantment" from a couple of people—this comes from people who have never known you. When one hears that expression a couple of times, it makes one wonder, but I always come to the same conclusion that I would have loved you just the same if we had always been together and not parted.

I have always loved you, Ray, but when you left I thought that now I will find out if it is real love or just the so-called "puppy love." Real love never dies, but the other kind soon forgets. I have never forgotten you since you left.

Since you left I have gone out with quite a few boys, and I have liked them all as friends, but just as soon as we would part, I would forget them. You have always seemed more to me than just a friend, Ray, and the longer we are separated the more dear you become to me, so I am sure that I love you, and that no other person could take your place in my heart.

I was playing some old songs today, one of them was "lonesome, I guess, that's all,"—the song that you wrote in one of your last letters to me. Here is another one that I like:

> You told me, dear, to wait for you, and keep
>   smiling!
> You told me to recall the past, and all its hours
>   beguiling!
> I hear the birds a-caroling,

and all day, too, I try to sing, but seems to me
> most ev'rything
Is mighty lonesome!

For all my world and all my life and all my
> longing
Belong to you and you alone,
and memories all come thronging!

Dear memories of a golden past,
of twilight hours, too short to last! ah, yes! there's
> lots of folks 'round here who try to make my
> world less drear;
But just the same, without you, dear
It's mighty lonesome!

This little song expresses a great deal of my feelings.

I would love to become a Kiwanette and dance with a certain Kiwanian that I know. I have danced quite a bit lately too, although I haven't gone to any real dances. I went to a couple of "showers" for some girlfriends, and each time the hostess invited as many boys as girls (although we didn't have dates), so we should dance. The last one that I went to, I danced from 9 to 12 o'clock without missing a dance. At noon's after lunch sometimes some of us girls dance, and there is one young fellow at work who dances really well, so whenever he has time at noon we dance together. He is engaged also, so we get along famously. I don't know whether I have improved or not, but at least I am getting practice.

Wichita is the same old town—as dull as ever. I don't blame you for not wanting to come back here to live. The more I see of other towns, the less I like Wichita.

I went to church tonight with a bunch, and Randolph McCluggage was afraid that I wouldn't arrive home safely, so he escorted me home. He sends his greetings to you.

Well, Ray dear, if I don't stop now, I never will, for I feel like raving on and on, and it is too late to do that. Besides you couldn't stand it, so I am closing now with a goodnight kiss and hug.

Signing off,
Station DORA
Operator
Just "Me"

P.S. I will see you in July.
February is half gone—Hooray!

February 15, 1927
(Oceanside, CA to Wichita, KS)

Dearest,

It's raining tonight and has been raining for four days. I just came home and I am plenty wet but will write to a little cheerful girlfriend of mine whom I am acquainted with in Wichita. Her name will someday be Wilcox I hope.
 This country is naturally semi-arid but the "dope" is mixed some way and we are having a deluge. If it keeps it up much longer there will be rowboats and canoes in service that will resemble Venice Italy. Rain, Rain, Rain—will it never cease? Roads are washed out and traffic is tied upon the railroads and highways. I was downtown tonight and the Philharmonic Orchestra of Los Angeles is stranded in Oceanside. They were on their way to San Diego for their annual mid-winter concert. There were about 150 people in the party and of all the foreign looking people in the world—they simply are the worst. Long hair and curly hair and mustaches etc. Black eyes and hair and musician looking actions that are quite out of place in this small place. The cafes were crowded with stranded motorists.
 The ocean was raging today. I went down with the folks today to see how it looked. Big waves tearing around like a wildfire. White caps out as far as the eye could see. The skies were leaden and the water gray with white foam flecked waves dancing and swirling everywhere. If there is anything in the world that will give you a kick it is to see a storm at sea. I want to live with you near the

mighty Pacific Ocean where we can watch and catch the spirit of its beauty and tremendous power. My Darling, when I think of the years ahead and of how we can make them wonderful joy and great adventure it thrills me to the point of almost talking out loud when I should be quiet and resting. Have you ever thought so much on a certain subject that you almost could not contain yourself? Well you probably know how I feel, the years that are to come mean everything to both of us. The past is to be forgotten except for the happy times and we are to live for the future. To know you better as the days come and go will be happiness enough.

We worked 14 hours Sunday the 13th and with a crew of eight men moved the fixtures in my store and re-modeled the shelving. I now have a regulation Skaggs store and they certainly have the real system. I heard the other day that the Safeway Store was going into Wichita pretty soon to open up stores there. So be prepared to see some nice new stores someday. They mean business and they are business-like. They are the largest grocery chain west of Cincinnati Ohio. Maybe someday I can come back to my old "stomping" grounds and run a store or several of them. I know that there are already operating some stores in Nebraska and Kansas now and they are marching ever Eastward.

Dora, I took an option on some lots on the hill here in Oceanside last week. They are well located and have a fine view of the Ocean. I believe that I will make some money on them and this will be only the start. I will know within thirty days whether I shall lose or make money. But nothing risked is nothing gained so there is no use of working at the same old job day in and day out without making a try at something else. I will write to you if I make any money on these lots. It may be that I can make the $500.00 for our wedding. Let's hope so. I am going to have that much money by July or my name is not Wilcox.

I think that we should take a two-week honeymoon trip after the wedding bells have rung. I have a plan to present to "mama" that might interest you and if you like it, let's stick to it and do it.

There is a steamship here that has regular sailings from San Diego up the coast to Seattle, Washington and Vancouver B.C. Now a sea trip for us landlubbers would be in order and we could enjoy ourselves to the fullest on the boat. With the service they provide and the dancing and other things with side trips at the terminal we could have our share of happiness. I have always wanted to take a sea trip and especially a trip with you as a companion; could anything be better?

But that is all up to you, Mama, let's have your ideas on the subject.

But best of all is the fact that I am going to see you this summer. My little sweetheart, dearest girl in the world, how I want you by my side.

I can't think of a thing tonight except that I am constantly wanting (could read waiting) to express my love and appreciation to you, Dora, in terms which may sound not so good but come from a heart that longs for you. Truly I do.

Will write again this week.

Ray

February 21, 1927
(Wichita, KS to Oceanside, CA)

Dearest Ray,

How are you? I have been wondering and worrying about you all week; especially since the newspapers have published all the news about the storm out there.

Every morning I get up just in time to dress and walk to work. The other morning, Dad said that I had better read the paper. I was so surprised when I read of the storm, so I read the headlines, then I bought a paper downtown and read the rest of it as I was walking along. I have watched every day for a report about Oceanside, but have seen none, although it told of the terrible rainfall in all the towns around there. Were you affected so much by it? Please write me all about it, and about yourself—if you are all right.

I am feeling pretty well, only I have just a little cold. Nothing to worry about, but it is just aggravating enough to make everything go wrong. At least that is the way it seemed for about an hour today, and I was so cranky. If you could have seen me then, you would have said "Deliver me from such a person." After a little while it became funny, and I had to laugh at myself for becoming angry at nothing at all. I feel better now.

We have been having some of your California temperature most of the week, except one afternoon, it turned cold, snowed and sleeted most of the evening, but the next day, our lovely weather was back again.

Ray dear, I am unusually lonesome for you this evening—I am just counting the days until July. Only one week more in February.

How can I wait? At the end of each day I think, "Gee! another day closer to Ray."

Thanks for the valentine telegram, Ray. I wanted to send one to you, but I can never think of a thing to say in a telegram. Anyway, you know that I want you to be my valentine, and I want to be yours.

Write real soon to your valentine so she won't worry.

A flood of kisses and a rain of kisses

From Just "Me" Dora

February 23, 1927
(Oceanside, CA to Wichita, KS)

Dearest Dora,

Your anxious letter came today and I can truthfully say that I am still alive and kicking. But we have had some real weather. The old-fashioned Kansas kind. You know how that is—rain and blow and rain some more. I suppose that all the eastern papers made an awful fuss about this part of the country.

I wrote you about the persistent rain that we have had. Well, that was not the half of it. Oceanside has been isolated as far as the Coast Route was concerned. The highway was washed out north and south and a Santa Fe bridge 5 miles north went out and the

Santa Fe Railroad is transferring passengers by motor stage. At this time things are getting along fine. I seized the opportunity here in Oceanside for selling groceries to the crews of workmen who are rebuilding the train bridge. Some of the young married fellows here put me in touch with the buyers and since then I have done considerable business with them. After all is said and done the only thing we get out of life is the association and fellowship with our friends. It is certainly a source of satisfaction to have lots of friends who are pulling for you and who will speak up for you when you need a word at the right time.

I have made some friends here Dora who will be so glad to welcome you and call you their friend. Every day in some way I have cause to feel happy because of an act or thought of someone whom I know here. It's a small town, to be true but there are some brave spirits here who have worthwhile ideas.

And the town is attracting some worthy people. Hardly a week goes by that does not bring new faces. Just think, only two years ago it was half as large as now.

While we are on that subject I will tell you some more news that may interest you. I have closed a deal today on two lots on the ridge here in Oceanside that overlook the town and ocean. There were four lots in the deal originally but I let a man have two of them because the proposition was too large for me to handle alone. It is my belief that I can make $500.00 on these two lots if all goes well. It will be a nest egg for us if I can make the grade. We can marry on that if we are careful. And I love you, Dora, and would marry you tonight if you said the word. Every minute we come closer together and that is the way to think of it. I am not perfect and am but an average boy but I am ambitious and always will be. If this can make your life a happy one I will be happy and that's all that I can expect. After all, it's happiness that we are all seeking. When we can live together and go down through the years a happy man and wife, with maybe some children to honor our name—what more is there to life than that? Don't suppose that I should mention these little intimate things but they are part of what we call life. I want to always be frank with you, Dora, and have no secrets to withhold. Then, if ever comes happiness and pleasure. To contemplate the glorious years ahead for us is enough to cause a surge of joy to last throughout the day.

I love that song that you wrote in the other letter. The words are wonderful and they express so much of how I feel toward you. Our love has been tested for many months. My deepest regret is that we did not know how much we cared before I went away. Here's the way I feel:

"IF WE CAN be together"

I don't care if it's raining I won't care if it snows, you'll find me uncomplaining Tho' fortune comes or goes.

I'll have no fear Tho clouds appear

and stormy be the weather; The sun must shine, the world is mine

If we can be together,

side margin: All the beautiful lines in the world cannot express the real feeling for you that is in my heart. I can only say that if you will be happy now while we are waiting for each other it will help me so much. You know why!

I have worked hard lately, especially today and that may account for the way this is written—and the bad English, etc.

Will write again soon with all the latest "dope" about everything. Kiss me good-night—With love—

Ray

February 25, 1927
(Wichita, KS to Oceanside, CA)

Dearest one,

I just simply must write a letter to my best boyfriend, who is out in the rain. He will get just what I have if he doesn't quit running around in it.

My little cold continued to grow a little worse each day, so by this time, I ache all over. The folks just made me take a hot bath, "greased" me, gave me a big glass of hot lemonade, and made me go to bed, so I am writing this lying down with one arm sticking out of the covers. Between all this grease and heat, I know that something is going to happen—either burn up or get well.

It seems like an age since I heard from you. Your letter that was mailed a week ago Wednesday just came yesterday. The railroad service must have been tied up there. I doubt if you got mine in time. It made me so happy to know that you were safe and well. The folks seemed as anxious as I was to hear how you were, for we have been getting such terrible reports of the storm. Both coasts seem to be having their share of it, don't they?

About our honeymoon trip—"Mama"' rather likes your suggestion. Everything will be so new to me, that any trip would give me pleasure, but I do think that to take a trip with you that is new to you would be far nicer. Of course, I have never been near the ocean, but one of my ambitions has been to see it. Wouldn't we have a lot of fun? Let's do it!

I am coming to see you. Is it possible? I am counting the months now, soon it will be weeks, then days, hours and minutes until our meeting. Oh, Oh, Oh! Isn't it a grand and glorious feeling?

Ray, I must stop now and get some sleep, so I will be rarin' to go in the morning. I promise you a longer letter within a few days.

Darling, your love for me means more to me than anything else in this world, so I am

Yours Forever
Just "me"

Dora

March 2, 1927
(Oceanside, CA to Wichita, KS)

Dearest,

Since receiving your last letter, I have been worried about you. I had an idea to wire you from San Diego but thought that that might not be so good. I have been kept up late each night for the last week and I haven't had a minute to call my own. But Dearest of All, I am thinking of you all the time. I am building my dream of happiness day by day upon the girl that you are. I know how you feel when you write that I mean more to you than anything else in this world. I would not have the heart to keep on if I should lose you. Dora you have become a part of my life and really the biggest part. I know that I shall love and cherish you as long as I live and after that if possible.

I am so sorry that you have to be sick at this time. It is my prayer and hope that this letter finds you up and well. Colds are the bunk! Please be careful Dora, old girl. Don't let anything worry you. I am all right out here. Working harder than any time in my life. I enjoy it. Soon we shall be together never again to part. I shall hold you in my arms and love you. Moonlight nights shall be ours and California in all its glory will offer us a home. This is a lovely place and we shall be happy.

I love the way that you answer my letters Dora; they are so like you. I believe that you are the finest letter answerer in the world. Darling the days are passing and the time is coming along when we shall be one. I have never been in love before and don't know how it would feel but I can say this. "Ain't love Grand."

The honeymoon on the Pacific "suits" me and I hope that we shall enjoy it as much as we anticipate. There is only one honeymoon trip in a lifetime. It will cost some money but I am trying to make it up now by hard work and effort. As soon as I think best I will change over into the Real Estate Business for good.

Please forgive this short letter and wait for a longer one soon.

I work straight through for eleven hours and the evenings are all taken up on business of some kind. Also play practice—will tell you more about that too.

With all my love—

Yours Ray.

March 6, 1927
(Oceanside, CA to Wichita, KS)

Dearest Dora,

Here it is Sunday night and after ten o'clock. Your letter came Friday but the opportunity to answer it did not come until now. Saturday was the busiest day yet. We had plenty of business—I worked from 7AM to 11:30PM on the run all the time. The District Manager was up from San Diego helping us and he surely got in and worked. I like him and although he is rather cold to the customers he is a pretty good scout after you get acquainted with him.

Our sales on the grocery side was $643.25 for the day. We are out to make it $800.00 and some day we will get it. There seems to be plenty of opportunity to build up the business here and it is up to me to do it. Oceanside is supporting the Safeway Stores in great shape. We have the largest store in town in terms of sales. Worst part of the business is the long hours. Last night after I came home and went to bed I found it impossible to sleep and rest. Too much nervous strain.

It is my hope that I can arrange it so that I won't have it so hard before long. More clerks is the only solution I think. That's enough about business at this time.

Dora, you cannot know how happy I am that you are feeling better now. I know how you hate to feel bad. Life is almost a hardship when we are in health but when we have to keep on when we get sick it's the bunk. Please be very careful little girl for my sake. I love you so. If I had to live without you the world would never be the same. There is joy in life when we realize that we shall soon be together. The time passes so slowly now. But every minute brings us that much nearer. Dora, do you realize that you are coming out to the Western Coast where the sun shines and the flowers bloom the year 'round? It is certainly delightful even in mid-winter. Flowers everywhere you look. We have some big rose bushes in the yard and an especially attractive one is climbing up the side of the house. Near the eaves there is a bud bursting out as large as a man's fist. Pretty soon it will be about 5 inches across like some more we have. I have never seen such roses, even in Florida.

Dora, I was thinking about your coming out here and I thought maybe you could come in June instead of July. Things look pretty good now and unless they change I will have made enough money to get married on. But I am not sure as yet but think that we can just as well move up the time a month if you want it. Tell me, what do you think?

There is one thing that I want to do before you come and that is catch up on my sleep. Just seems that every night brings something to take me out. When you come I want to be in the best of spirits and health. There will be some things that come up that I can't afford to miss but most of them will be left out if I have to lose some more sleep.

How are all your folks? Haven't heard about Carl for a long time. Tell me what he is doing, etc. Does your father intend to operate his mill at Towanda again this summer? How is your mother now? I'm a regular question box but I am interested in your family. I have always liked your folks and feel that through Carl and your father I met and knew you.

We went out driving this afternoon and went out to where the Santa Fe Railroad is putting in a bridge that was swept out by the recent flood. There were quite a bunch of onlookers there—people who have nothing to occupy their time except to watch others work. I got an idea from that crowd that maybe I can use in a scheme of mine to make some money. There are so many people in Southern California who have no way to amuse themselves. They drive around on Sundays and try to kill time but they are mostly miserable. If I can find a way to help them kill time in an innocent way and not cost them too much I can make plenty of money. My idea would be to provide something that would interest old and young together. I am keeping in mind all the objections that might arise from the religious fanatics who might scream some.

You know there are a lot of kill-joys who go through life with a long face and expect all the rest of us to do the same. But I believe that anything to give people a way to find happiness instead of restlessness and inactivity would be service in a high sense.

My darling sweetheart. I wish that you were here now so that I could see you often and kiss your pretty lips. My heart is yearning for your love and something tells me that you love me—and I know that I love you.

Ray

March 7, 1927
(Wichita, KS to Oceanside, CA)

Dearest Ray,

By tonight, I am a full believer in mental telepathy or whatever you wish to call it. (1.) This morning I got the "wicked" idea that I wouldn't go to Sunday School or Church, but about 9 O'clock something told me that they were going to need me to play for the intermediate department (I substitute sometimes). Just then the phone rang and the superintendent asked me to play. (2.) I was sitting in church, and I started thinking about how long it was since I had a letter from you, and just believed that I would get a special this morning. Sure enough! At home there was one waiting for me from my "bestest" boyfriend. (3.) After Endeavor the "kids" begged me to stay for church but again something told me that we had company at home. We did. (4) Right now, I believe that you are thinking of me. Right or wrong?

Ray, if you don't stop worrying about me, I am going to come right out there and . . . . kiss you, I guess. That reminds me of an incident that happened some time ago. I was out to my brother's house one evening, and I was writing and talking to my nephews and nieces, when suddenly one nephew (12-years-old), just to tease me, turned off the light, I would have to cross the room, and perhaps stumble over a few chairs. I wouldn't do that, so I coaxed, threatened and made promises to him if he would turn on the light—no good—darkness still prevailed. Suddenly it dawned on me that all boys at that age hate to be kissed, so in a real threatening tone I said, "Junior, if you don't turn on that light, I am coming over and kissing you!" Immediately, the room was flooded with light. My niece (14-years-old) chimed, "Well, I bet, if that had been Ray, we would have had to sit in the dark all night." Terrible reputation you have, isn't it? Right or wrong again?

I am feeling fine now, my cold has gone, but I am terribly

hoarse. When I talk, it sounds as though I am "growling." I have been that way for several days, but it can't last much longer.

For some reason, this last week has passed so quickly. That makes me happy, for the faster the weeks go, the sooner we meet. Won't I be happy then? Uh. Huh!

We really have had wonderful weather today, and this night is so inspiring. Yes, it inspires one to run for shelter—It is raining, raining, raining!

I can't find any news to tell you, for you know how exciting Wichita is. About all I have done all week is go to work, come home and go to bed, and dream of nearly getting married (but never arriving). One night I nearly married a girl from work, the next night, it was the old book keeper, and the next night my victim was the young painter. Can you beat it? I wouldn't have any of them.

I want only you, dear! Don't wait so long to write the next time, please. Love from yours—now & forever

"Me" Dora.

Also enclosed on a small slip of paper;

MY CABIN

Could I have a cabin, Beside a country lane.
Near meadows sweet with clover, And fields of
    golden grain

Where I'd hear the forest whisper When evening
    winds were low,
And tell to me the story of the days of long ago.

With bird songs in the day time, And crickets in
    the night.
And the brooks unceasing music, In the stars
    reflected light.

I'd say farewell to cities, and live where life is

true;
Could I have just one companion, And that companion, YOU.

March 13, 1927
(Oceanside, CA to Wichita, KS)

My Darling,

This is Sunday night and I just came home from play practice. We are practicing on a 3 act Comedy—put on by local talent. I had to work all day today, Sunday, at a little town called Encinitas. We were putting in new store fixtures there. It seems like every minute is taken up with something and I am constantly being rushed from one thing to another. But perhaps it takes my mind off my lonesomeness.

I am terribly lonesome for you Dora. Just you. All the time I am thinking of the fine times I have had with you and dreaming of our pleasures to come. Never have I worked so hard on any position. But when you come I will take a two-week layoff and we shall see what we shall see.

Your last letter was certainly enjoyed to the fullest and I am glad that the cold is better. It is my hope and prayer that all the hoarseness will be gone when this note reaches you. Deary, you are so good to be faithful and so encouraging. You mean so much to me now Dora. My life is not whole without you. I need you and want you here. I shall never forget the wonderful words of love that have inspired me and kept me on the road to success. When I say success, I mean success. I know that with you to help and with your faith I will succeed. I am determined to get ahead. All these years I have worked to build a foundation upon which I might stand and round out a lifetime of happiness. To be successful one must be happy.

When driving down to Encinitas today I followed the coast route along the water's edge. And Dora, I could not keep from noticing how inviting the water in the sea is now at this time of year. During and after the big rain the beach and surf were muddy for some distance out (we got about 15-20 inches of rain and some flood!) This was on account of the unusually large run-off of the rivers and creeks carrying silt to the sea. Now the ocean is clear and blue again. I am wondering if you have any desire to swim and paddle around in the ocean? The water is plenty cold but it leaves you with a tingle that is invigorating, etc.

The Oceanside pier is being constructed as fast as possible and when you come it will possibly be finished. Here is where we can have lots of fun in fishing if you take a liking to that kind of sport. And someday when we get enough money I will buy a motor boat that we can tie to the end of the pier when not in use. Of course, that is all talk and dreams but why not?

Really Dora, you should see how pretty everything is here now. The grass in the hills is thick and green and beautiful. The trees are all as green and full of foliage as possible.

Some of the fellows around town know that I am engaged and they keep kidding me about marriage, etc. But I laugh with them and then let them go on about their business. They don't know that I have the best little girl in the world for a sweetheart. We shall be sweethearts after we are married just the same. Won't we?

Gee! Dora, you are a dear to write to me and tell me what you think about children. I agree with you in every respect. I think that life is not complete without children of our own. We cannot always say that we can have children but if God in his wisdom grants to us any children then we will have them.

The only thing that we should worry about is to not have them until we are ready to take care of them. Personally, I would rather wait until we had a year or more of married life before we take on this added responsibility. Anyway, we can do as we please when you come, eh!

Dora I love you and I think that I understand you. Days are passing and soon I can hold you close again.—Why not tonight?

The typed poem was a dandy. More of them, please! I was thinking of you at the time you mentioned—mental telepathy—uh-huh? You bet!

As ever, Your Ray A.

March 17, 1927
(Wichita, KS to Oceanside, CA)

Dearest Ray,

It hardly seemed like Sunday, because I didn't get to write to you, but about a dozen of us went from Christian Endeavor to church together, and then the "bunch" came over here and "played around" until quite late. Monday evening my niece came and spent the evening practicing her voice lesson. She always makes me play for her. She is entering a contest Friday, so we practiced extra-long and hard. Last night we had company, so tonight has been my first chance to write to you.

 What have you been doing? Working as hard as ever for your wife and family? You must be busy, for an old fellow, your letters are rather scarce around here. Can't you drop me just a line a little oftener, for you know you won't have to write so many letters—only 3 1/2 months yet and then you can talk instead of writing. It will be easier on everyone concerned; don't you think?

 Spring has come, which simply makes me want to get out and chase a tennis ball around the court. I can't play, but I have a lot of fun thinking that I can. Have you learned to play yet, or don't you play out there very much?

 Another sign of spring: one of the girls called me this evening and invited me to a steak fry Saturday evening. A bunch of the boys and girls are going together—no one is going to have a date. The folks don't care much about having me go, for they don't think that you would want me to go. But, gee, I get so tired of sitting at home. I like to go out with young people and have a good time, and since this isn't a "date" affair, I can't see any harm in me going, can you? Or do you think that I shouldn't go to such affairs? Please, let me know your opinion. I wouldn't have a date for anything, Ray, for I want to be just as true to you as if you were here. It is a lot harder, but I don't mind doing it for someone I love. Tell me what you think.

(Excuse the blots, but I just dropped my pen) Work is just the same. I like the people that I work with, for they are all so jolly. I am only hoping that my job lasts until nearly July. When I took it, they couldn't promise it to be a permanent position—only a temporary one, so I don't know how long it will last. It will last for at least 3 or 4 more weeks yet, I know for I have that much work ahead of me to do.

Darling, it won't be long now, until things will be bright all the time, for I will soon be with you and we can enjoy the best of life together, enjoy it so much more, for we have been apart so long.

I am closing now with a kiss and hug for each day that we have been apart.

"Me"
Dora.

March 20, 1927
(Wichita, KS to Oceanside, CA)

Dearest One,

The morning paper stated that this was to be one of the most romantic nights of the year, for the full moon comes up at seven o'clock and it would be unusually bright. Since I can't be out with my sweetheart tonight, I will do the only thing possible—that is to write to you, my only sweetheart.

Are we going to have an actor in our family? That's good! What play are you practicing on, and what part do you take? I wish that I could see it, when you give it.

Ray, you aren't the only one who is kidded about marriage. All day long at work I am kidded and teased, but I do the same to them, so we have a lot of fun. So many of the women in the office are "old maids," but they are the best sports that I have ever seen.

You should hear all the advice they give me, and they do believe in marriage. You would think they had tried it out.

What does your friend, Allan, say about our marriage? Is he engaged?

I think that marriage will be wonderful. Just think of having a companion all through life. One who likes nearly all the things that I do, and one who is as wonderful and loving as you are.

I most certainly do have a desire to paddle around in the ocean—"paddle" is the right word for I expect that I have forgotten how to swim—I never have known very much about it. Will you teach me though?

I like to fish, too, but I can't stand to put a "wriggly, slippery worm" on the hook. Someone always had to bait my hook for me. Will "someone" do it for me when we go fishing?

Ray, I don't see how we are going to have time to do everything that we want to do—we will have to make some extra time, I guess.

I am getting so I ask about as many questions as you do. I had better close before I think of some more.

As ever
Love and kisses
from

"Me" Dora.

P.S. Read the article "On Marriage" in the April number of the American.

March 20, 1927
(Oceanside, CA to Wichita, KS)

Dora, Darling,

You are a darling to me and always shall be. It seems like many ages since you and I were together but I know that your love is true and that someday in the not too distant future I shall have the privilege of just being with you. Many times, I wonder to myself just how I could be worthy of you, that you could love me. But now that you have said that you will be mine I am trying to make myself better fit to the end that maybe your faith and love is not wasted.

You said in your last letter that the hours and days were moving so slowly—well they may seem that way to you—but to me they are endless. Sometimes at night when I think about your coming—which is practically all the time—I wonder how time can possibly move so slowly. California is calling to you—and the Old Man of the family needs his wife.

Dora, you write like you were bored with Wichita! How come? Is the old town going to the dumps? I remember when it was a pretty fair little place—especially the parks!

I think the Middle West is waking up to the fact that it is just a place to make a living and not a place to live. Many people are coming to the west coast to make their permanent homes this winter. Every time a new family moves out here, it is one less for back there. They come because there is more here for them than drudgery and hard grinding. People out here are finding many, many ways to get out of that kind of a rut. Perhaps they all can't make a living here but what of it. There are some folks that can't make a decent living anywhere.

You ask whether I think you should go out and have a date or a good time. I want you to know Dora that while you are engaged to me—it doesn't mean that you cannot see other fellows and enjoy yourself. I want you to have a good time—always. I am not narrow minded enough to say to a girl that she shouldn't have other dates when we are so far apart. I have plenty of chances to have dates but I am saving all of them for the girl I love best. And besides, I can't afford to spend money on anybody but the only girl for me. But do as you think best, darling, your own judgment suits me fine. It's okay.

I enjoyed your answers to all my questions. They were fine. I was wondering about Carl and how he was making it. It's too bad that he cannot be what he wants to be. A lot of young fellows are like him. But they will find a place where they can fit in and make the world pay them a good living.

Today we all took a ride after the noon meal and drove over to a town called Vista in the irrigation district. Things are picking up wonderfully over there. Lots of opportunity and chances to make a lot of money, if you have money. The crops were green and flourishing. We could look over to the northeast and see the range of mountains that separate the desert and the fine part of Southern Calif. The taller peaks have a great topping of snow and it contrasted so much with the hot sunshine and tropical setting where we were standing. We turned around and looked west and saw the Pacific—glistening in the sunshine. Truly it is marvelous—it makes one feel romantic.

When you come out we can take these little trips and enjoy them. Then there are so many places that I haven't seen which are quite interesting. We can take them one at a time and fill our lives with the beauty that surrounds us.

One good thing—we are close to two fine cities—San Diego and Los Angeles. When we tire of rural life, perhaps we can spend some time in Los Angeles. There is one big place: Hollywood and all. Did you know that the city limits of Los Angeles includes 400 square miles? That is the largest city in point of area in the world. And the city is filling up all the time. People are coming there and industries are building up which will make it the New York of the Pacific Coast.

They say that it takes a man coming here two years before he can place himself in a position equal to the one he held in the East. California has been good to us; that's why I am strong for it.

I am getting a little more sleep now that things are eased up a bit, and on April the first we take a company inventory to determine the profits of each store for the three months they have operated under the Skaggs plan. I don't expect much this time for many good reasons they don't either but on July the first I should have 3 or 4 hundred dollars in commissions due me. But I am not depending on that to get married on. Dora I will have $500 and a position. That is little enough and I wish it were $500 but at this time it is impossible. But I love you Dora more than ever—every day.

Only about 3 months more.
Your Ray

March 27, 1927
(Oceanside, CA to Wichita, KS)

Dora, Dear,

Again, it is Sunday and another week has passed and only one letter from my sweetheart! If you have been as busy as I have I will excuse you on good reasons but you simply must, (see I have said it) write a little more often. It's so awful now. It seems like a bit of heaven when one of your letters finds its way into my box.

When you get over the shock of seeing this stationary (it is written on corporate stationary which reads; Wilcox Investment Company, Licensed Real Estate Broker) I will tell you how it happened that I am using it. We just came home after a church and family picnic party and I went down after the mail and then came over to the office to write where it was quiet, for a change. No other paper in sight so I concluded to use this stuff. Please don't think I am growing careless of you—it's simply because I felt like writing—right now.

This has been a fine day in most respects but I am telling you now that it's almost more than I can stand to be away from the girl I love. It's terrible and the pain cannot be eased in any way except by your coming here. I see the young fellows drive out and pick up their girls and get out in this glorious sunshine and air and it simply makes me wonder why it has to be that you and I are not together. There's a yearning in my heart for your companionship that I cannot explain. Do you remember that time when I came over for you and we went out to take some pictures? Well, today was such a day as that. The air is full of springtime oxygen, and it gets into your blood. The trees are green and the orange and lemon trees are loaded with wonderful fruit. Buds and flowers are springing up and the hills are a riot of color and foliage. The meadow larks are singing that cute little warble that puts joy in your system. Every time I hear one of them I think of spring time in Oklahoma. But with you away I only have to think of the happiness that might be ours instead of living it.

There is this consolation: You have promised to be mine and

there will be other springs and other wonderful days when we can live and love as much as we care to. With our youth and vitality and health to enjoy it we shall drink deeply of the romance of California.

On soft moonlit nights when the sea wind is blowing ever so softly we can sit among the bowers of flowers and I shall hold you close and whisper that I love you. We can spend hours and hours out of doors and make of life what it should be: happiness, instead of worry and drudgery.

When we are married and I make some more money it is my plan to learn to play some games like golf, tennis etc. I want you to hike with me and learn to hunt and fish and camp out. Do you like it? Out here it's so different than you would- imagine. There is fishing out on a barge in the ocean and deer hunting in the backcountry. Can you beat that combination? Of course, I am not losing my head. I know that I will have to accumulate some more money before we can have all these things but why not have some of them while we are young and passing through?

But we can plan and dream of the good things that are in life. The main things are to have the right kind of friends and not have to worry about getting into trouble. I hate troubles. Don't you? When I hear somebody grumbling about his misfortunes I turn away and get out of hearing distance. I have plenty of my own to contend with. I have had so many that I feel that the good things are due now.

So that is that, Dora. I get to writing away and tell you all that I think of you and you have to read it to finish the letter. There is one other thing that I want to say: we both have mouths that turn up at the corners and I hope that somebody shoots us both when they begin to droop and turn down. No matter what life holds for us, we can make it easier if we have optimism and courage and a sense of humor. What do you say?

My darling, this letter must have an end so I will start stopping. My brakes are on the blink.

The town is coming along fine. We will have a new gas plant soon so we will be quite modern. The new pier will be finished by the middle of June. A big celebration is planned for the fourth of

July to dedicate it. You must be here by then. I am working plenty hard—inventory on 4th of April.

The lots that I bought haven't sold yet but I still have hopes. It's a cinch they won't get any cheaper so I will make money eventually.

Please write to the old man; he's signing off with a big kiss.

Ray

March 31, 1927
(Wichita, KS to Oceanside, CA)

Dearest Ray,

Your letter came just at the right time, and it cheered me up. When I came home this evening, I felt so blue and low, that a grain of sand looked like a mountain. You made me feel 100% better.

I hate to tell you all my troubles, but I know that you want to know what I am doing. This morning I was informed that soon I will be out of a job. I have known all the time that I would soon hear that, but it was a shock anyway when it did come. At the beginning the office manager couldn't promise me a permanent position—only a temporary one lasting for several months, until the "teachers work" (that is what I have been doing—sending letters to teachers) was finished. I have nearly finished it, so soon I will be leaving there. It is such a lovely place to work, and I made so many friends there that I simply hate to leave. The office manager said that she wanted to keep me until July, but she doesn't find it possible, for the work has slacked down, so that they can hardly keep the regular office force busy. That is true too, for several have had so little work to do, that they have had to help me in order to keep busy.

I hate the job of looking for a new position, for jobs are so scarce here. Everything happens for the best, although often we can't see it until sometime later.

To continue, everything went wrong at the office today, so that accounts for the blues, but the corners of my mouth are still up, for

I am afraid of "getting shot." I shouldn't grumble, because I am so much better off than a lot of people; a fine home, wonderful friends and you.

Rotten weather though! It has rained for three days. No sunshine. I am glad that California has a lot of sunshine, for good sunshiny days and the right companions makes life seem so different.

My heart aches too, Ray, when I see the other girls going out with their sweethearts. It won't be so long now until I can go out with my sweetheart, and then we'll be "sitting on top of the world." The train will never arrive quick enough to suit me. When it does arrive, look out! If anyone gets in my way, I will just run them down—that's all. Yes, I must get there by the 4th of July to help celebrate the dedication. It doesn't happen to be the pier that I want to see, but it is you!

Ray, I don't care what kind of paper that you use—even if it is wrapping paper—just so you write and write often. Don't scold "mama" for not writing often, for she uses "papa" as an example. It isn't that I don't want to write, for I do, but something is always happening which takes up my time.

Excuse this letter and all its troubles, but I feel that "papa" will understand and forgive.

Love and kisses

From Yours—Dora.

April 5, 1927
(Wichita, KS to Oceanside, CA)

Dearest Ray,

I know that you have worked unusually hard today. I wish that I were there to greet you as you come home, but since I am not, I am writing to you. Did the inventory encourage or discourage you?

I am hoping that it was much more successful than you expected. I am anxiously waiting for the result. You know a good job means so much to a young fellow and . . . more to a young couple.

I am still working, but how much longer it will last—I am not certain. I believe that I still have enough work to keep me busy this week. I can't help but wonder what will happen after I leave there. I am not worrying though, for something will turn up at the right moment.

Did you ever see the play called *Apple Sauce*? It is funny and clever, yet it is full of good psychology—a lot of it is for young people expecting to marry and after they are married. See it, if you get a chance. One fellow in the play compared happiness to a kiss—the more you give, the more you get in return. A good comparison don't you think?

The days and weeks are as long as ever, but I try to keep busy to forget how many hours there are in a day, days in a week, weeks in a month, and how many months until our dreams come true.

Tomorrow I am invited out to a dinner; afterwards I am going to Friends University to hear the glee club concert. I haven't been to school since I have been back—but I expect it is the same as usual.

Ray, my ring is a great help to me in these lonely days. It brightens up the hours so, and all day long it sparkles in my face, the more I see of it, the prettier it becomes. The other day, a man asked me if my ring meant anything to me. I answered "Absolutely, it means everything." He walked away without another word. My ring does stand for the whole future life, and people needn't think that I am joking when I wear it. Don't forget to write to "mama" and tell me the news. Love and kisses from "Me."

I Love you, Ray

Undated/Monday evening
(Wichita, KS to Oceanside, CA)

Dearest Ray,

This is a wonderful spring night, and you aren't here! I made Mother go out walking with me tonight, but if you had been here you would have been the "victim." Aren't you glad that you are in California?

This letter is late again, so I will soon be getting a letter from Mr. Ray A. Wilcox scolding me. Is that right? He scolds rather nicely though so I don't mind much.

My Sunday night letter wasn't written last night, for I couldn't come down to earth long enough to do it after church. A group of Wichita singers rendered the "Messiah" at the church last night. The church was filled by 7:15 and 2,000 were turned away. The program was to begin at 8 o'clock, but a girlfriend and I went at 7:15 and there wasn't a seat in sight but finally someone graciously made a little room in one of the pews and we both squeezed into it. The music was wonderful. It made one forget every earthly care and gave one a new outlook on life. I could have sat there several more hours listening to it. I thoroughly enjoyed it, and I would have been in a "Heaven on Earth" if you had been sitting at my side like you used to.

Do you still go to church once in a while on Sunday nights?

For the first time this year, I played some tennis Saturday morning—two hours of it, and it was cold too, so early in the morning. I played rotten, but had lots of fun anyway.

We are still housecleaning, so Mother is keeping me busy. I have been cleaning out desks, tables and dressers trying to get rid of all my old junk. So many things that I have kept are worthless only for the memories that cling to them. I hate to throw them away, but Mother doesn't want them, and I am not going to drag them across the U.S.

Don't you hate to give up your school day papers, books, pictures, etc. Everything is going as per usual here.

Oh yes, did you know that Lew Lauterbach is our delivery boy now? Do you ever write to him? Honestly, I am getting as bad as you are for asking questions, aren't I?

I must close before I think of some more. All my love and kisses are yours!!

Just "Me"
Dora

ROSES, ROMANCE, AND HEAVEN IN CALIFORNIA

July 21, 2022
Me: I want to quit the book.
Editor: What??!!
Me: I feel like Syphilis pushing a boulder of dull content up the mountain for readers.
Editor: It's not dull. Stay on course. And . . . it's not Syphilis. It's Sissypuss. Damn spell-check. It's Syphilis.
Me: Hello Syphilis!
Me: We need to insert content about Ray and Dora's wonderful life in the '50s—it's the best part of the love story, and we need to do it now before we lose readers from sheer boredom. I also want to become a brand ambassador for Patagonia and sell plant-based beef jerky out of my environmentally friendly hybrid vehicle.
Editor: It's too soon. The story will be out of order.
Me: You're out of order! And you married a musician! Our readers are smart. They will like the plot twist.
Editor: This isn't helping. If you do shift things here, we'll need a transition explaining why you jumped from the '20s to the '50s. It's out of sequence and too early. Dora hasn't even arrived in California yet!
Me: But—the '50s were California's best era evuh, brah.
Me: You know what?

Editor: What?
Me: I can't quit the book . . . or you. ;) ;)
Editor: Good night.

• • •

As I revisited Ray and Dora's world in the 1950s through some of the documents and pictures they left behind, I could see the fabulous life they made together. In fact, on Sunday, May 16, 1954, *The San Diego Union-Tribune* ran a feature story about their new home in Oceanside titled "Hilltop Living." The article noted, "Low rolling hills that rise along the eastern half of [the city] offer wonderful opportunities. The hilltops here command a sweeping overlook of the ocean and its beaches, the city business districts, the new freeway, the lagoons, the farm valleys and the mountains in the east." The story described the house enthusiastically. "The interior arrangement is fascinating," it read. "Actually the kitchen, the den and the big living room are all one central living area, divided only by an angular construction of half walls. An exposed beam, gabled ceiling is open over the entire area. It adds tremendously to the open feeling of living space." The article added other details, like: "In the kitchen is a split brick wall with barbecue, hooded with copper. There is a giant flagstone fireplace in the living room and another fireplace of red brick on the terrace. Large picture windows catch the view on three sides of the living room—a view of the ocean, the valleys and the mountains."

And always, as I well knew, there were the roses. Fresh-cut roses were a fixture in the Wilcox house. Ray and Dora's stunning rose garden could have given Pasadena's Huntington Rose Garden a run for its money. The rose garden created wonderful childhood memories. Moments there became even more meaningful when Grandad would take me by the hand to talk about, examine, identify, and smell each blooming bush in the yard. The palette of colors and scents produced a deep sensory memory that lingers to this day. What is special and important, too, is that this garden was another promise Ray fulfilled for Dora as he enticed her to join him in the miraculous and growing land of sunshine and heart's desire.

I still wonder about these moments in their garden and Ray's playful personality as he taught me the name of each rose, such as Peace, Mister Lincoln, Blue Girl, and Double Delight. I thought that he was making the names up, but after growing my own roses I now believe he knew them all by heart, and the simplicity and innocence of it all makes me want to cry. I am not sure why, but all this reflection and reminiscence conjures up some deep sadness for me, like the image of a coyote left to die in the road after being hit by a speeding car. How careless and hurried we have become in our increased effort to transcend space and time, so hurried that we lose sight of the beauty right in front of us and easily dismiss it when it dies.

Ray was a handsome gentleman, and to me he looked like a Hollywood film star or a male model who could have been the subject of a *Vanity Fair* photo shoot. I recall that most of the time he would be dressed in a suit or a sport coat with gray slacks, a fashionable tie, and black dress shoes. And if he wasn't wearing a jacket, he would be sporting a slightly more casual tie selected to match an upscale golfing sweater. I swear he must have had twenty different shades of front-buttoned long-sleeved sweaters, ranging from cream to avocado green, periwinkle, fuchsia, sea green, mustard yellow, scarlet, and lavender. I'm not sure which—Ray or the rosebushes—provided a more colorful attraction for both guests and family alike. F. Scott Fitzgerald may have created an imaginary character named Jay Gatsby whose love interest, Daisy Buchanan, wept when he tossed around his fancy shirts, but we got to see the real deal with Ray Wilcox wearing white dress shoes and violet socks while sweeping the patio in his backyard oasis. And . . . it's funny, too, the things you remember as a child—Ray always smelled almost as unique as one of their hybrid tea roses. All seven of us grandkids could never figure out what soap or cologne he used, and only after he died did we discover the origin of his manly scent. It came from a bottle of Aqua Net hair spray we found hiding under his bathroom sink! It seems a case could be made that Ray was a bit of a dandy.

Dora's personal style wasn't as easy to pin down. My sister Robin remembered our grandmother as typically being simply but fashionably attired. She wore dresses and skirts and ensembles of the era—but during special occasions, like Christmas, she would add heels and lipstick.

Robin also shared details about Dora's kind and loving side. Our mother, Bobbie (Dora and Ray's daughter), was a much more casual "jeans and beans" type of dresser and really didn't place much emphasis on contemporary clothing. Dora was sensitive to the fact that Robin occasionally received some hand-me-down dresses from another family in town. So, Dora would take her clothes shopping once a year for her birthday and buy her a new dress. One year, when Robin couldn't decide between two, Dora surprised her and generously bought her both.

Dora came from tough German stock, though, and became even more direct as the years moved along. So it was often hard for me to understand her—for example, sometimes she would say things about people like "They should be shot," and it seemed like a joke, but I couldn't really be sure. Maybe she was just sending a message to us grandkids so that we knew she meant business. My cousin David Wilcox compared Ray and Dora to the legendary business partners Walt and Roy Disney. He said Ray was the big-vision, likable public-relations front man (Walt), and Dora was the back-room deal closer and operations and contracting person (Roy).

Just as Walt and Roy Disney first created their commercial playground on 160 acres in Anaheim, California, in 1955, the Wilcox property began in 1952 as 160 acres of open land in Oceanside. Ray and Dora designed their home as the centerpiece, and throughout the years added other components, like a woodworking shop, a rock-grinding and -polishing station, the "Attitude Adjustment Center," and an exotic-plant greenhouse to delight their friends and visitors. In addition to all the free entertainment that these areas provided, there was all-you-can-eat Baskin-Robbins "31 flavors" ice cream as well as nonstop wildlife tours. By the mid-1960s, when I was a child, the place felt like a private Disneyland for grandkids.

If you stepped inside their home, you would have immediately seen the progressive architectural design. The house was noteworthy at the time, and local media clearly recognized this. The *Blade-Tribune* also published a feature story with photos on October 15, 1954, with the headline "A Country Home Within the City." Ray was quoted as calling it "a ranch house on a big patch of ground with a patio and view." The news writer played upon Ray's quote and wrote, "The big patch of ground is 160 acres in the San Luis Rey Valley, away from neighbors and street noises. The view from the living room picture windows extends from Palomar [Mountain] to Catalina [Island] and the loudest sound is the ticking of a grandfather clock." However grand the house was, Ray quipped, "The patio is the best room in the house."

The layout included a great room that you could enter from both the front door and the rear of the house, which forked and opened into the kitchen, with a breakfast nook on one side. On the other side was an additional sitting area bordered by Ray's gorgeous library of hardbound books. There was also a well-appointed bar that was hidden behind double wooden doors near the library. President Kennedy's 1961 inaugural invitation was placed proudly inside the bar, along with a portrait of Ray with a cheap name tag stuck on it reading: "Ray A. Wilcox, Bartender on Duty."

When we would gather in their sitting area beyond the library, Ray would be positioned in a comfortable reclining type of chair and Dora would be seated on an aging leather sofa to his right. Dora was tiny and lightweight, but she sank up to her neck on the left edge of that sofa. Some days it appeared as if all that we could see was the top of her head and right arm, cradling a cocktail, and left arm, holding a cigarette skyward like a lantern or a torchlight. It seemed like she was treading water. The smoke from her cigarettes would float above and around us. My sister Robin said that she once visited Grandma and Grandad, and just the three of them sat and talked together. During that visit Dora's cigarette consumption hit an all-time high, which created a roaming blanket of smoke that circulated throughout the house like a living, breathing fogbank. After a few minutes it set off the smoke alarm in the master bedroom. Dora didn't flinch as the annoying alarm continued. She just casually kept smoking, raising her voice just a touch to say, "RAY . . ." (Long pause.) "GET THE GUN."

Ray and Dora built a unique curving hallway that connected the kitchen and library area to the bedrooms. This makes me wonder how it might have felt walking through it and leaning into the curves if they had had a few too many "snorts" of bourbon. The house had three fireplaces, including one in the kitchen. Ray and Dora both had excellent taste, and in the great room you would find Dora's polished grand piano made with dark-brown tiger-striped walnut wood. Their furniture included two handcrafted pieces created by a talented but obscure craftsman named Joseph Sauer. The first was a china cabinet, and the second was a ten-foot-tall three-piece grandfather clock. They were both signed and dated "1905" by Mr. Sauer. One technician with whom I contracted to examine the clock said he had only seen one like it west of the Mississippi, and another technician marveled at the handmade mechanisms inside it. He said he had never seen anything like it and asked if he could photograph it for his fellow antique-clock enthusiasts. It was fun to learn these things, and for some silly, childlike reason I liked the idea of someday telling someone, "I'd like you to see my grandfather's grandfather clock."

Grandma Dora didn't always fit the stereotypical mold of the loving, kind, good-natured grandmother. Yet some of my distinct memories of her include kissing her goodbye at their front door, and her cheek was so soft that it felt like an oversized marshmallow. Being with her at that time, we made an odd pair . . . we could have been two cartoon characters, since my voice at this time was near the pitch of a frog's, and she smoked so much that her voice had dropped a couple of octaves and edged closer to that of a crabby man.

And while most grandmothers welcome grandchildren, at times this didn't feel like the case with Dora. My Catholic father told me that he once survived a surreal moment standing alone with Dora in her kitchen as she casually and expertly used a large knife to gut (remove the entrails) and clean a turkey for Thanksgiving while she lectured him about the benefits of new birth-control products. Perhaps the pinnacle of Dora's sarcastic humor occurred when my mom excitedly told her she was pregnant with her fifth child and Dora quickly responded, "Well, something always happens to spoil my Christmas."

There were other stories too. Ray was a long-term member of the Elks Lodge in Oceanside. My brother Randy told me a story about Grandad once playing cards at a small table with friends there. Suddenly, the bartender shouted out, "Ray. You have a phone call . . . It's Dora." The game stopped, and his friends grew quiet and alert like bird dogs when a covey of quail is near. Ray casually walked over to the bar and picked up the phone. During the course of the brief conversation everyone in the room could hear him say, "Yes, dear. Yes, Dora. Yes, dear." No one was really counting, but there may have been something like twenty-four "Yes, dears" whispered into the receiver. Ray eventually hung up the phone and slowly walked back to the table. He leisurely picked up his cards and said, "Well, I guess I told her."

My brother Randy also told me that once, while visiting Ray and Dora when he was a young man, he gathered the courage and asked Grandad Ray if he believed there was an afterlife or such a thing as heaven. Ray didn't hesitate with his reply and said, "Well, of course there is, boy. There has got to be something better than this!!" This moment remains significant and seared into our collective memories. Our perception of Ray was that his life, including his success and achievements, his house and garden, was so exceptional and remarkable that the idea of something "better than this" didn't seem possible.

What a wonderful gift life can be when you have the time to reflect and think deeply about fond moments like this—moments about yourself and your relationships and experiences. Author Wayne Dyer once said, "Change the way you look at things, and the things you look at change." And now, in the fourth quarter of my life, my vision and the things I look at are changing. And when it comes down to it, as we move toward the finish line, it's not money, success, or things we desire; all we really want is more time.

• • •

I remember being in my midtwenties, sitting peacefully alone in the great room of the Wilcox house on the hill with its vaulted ceiling and exposed wooden beams. There were two small light-colored, cheerful-looking sofas in the space. The sofas had a floral rose pattern and faced each other in front of a large fireplace. I recall sitting with my back against one of these sofas for hours and hours on weekends and evenings as I typed up Ray and Dora's original handwritten letters. During the process I occasionally felt a strange sense of calm and serenity there. While alone and transcribing their words, my mind and heart became full and overflowed with love and gratitude for my grandparents. They were gone, but not completely gone, and I found myself daydreaming.

I began slowly gliding on a gentle ocean wave of appreciation. The wave was generated by warm Pacific winds around me, mixed with

Ray and Dora's loving presence. Several times the ocean started to churn and I needed to cut back as we sailed over and through the rip currents in life. I kept going and surfed through a spinning timeless vortex . . . as we pushed through the challenges and opportunities in life together. We navigated the deep holes and sandbars to eventually seek safety and solace on the warm sand and land.

As I complete this book, it appears that I have transcended space and time anew, because my grandfather's grandfather clock has started ticking again. Suddenly I am a child, and I find myself playing the role of the young prince of the castle on the hill. I am free to rule and walk alone. I am on foot and searching for subjects to praise me and animals to capture and bring back to the kingdom to impress the queen and king. I begin circling the territory. I steadfastly walk the well-worn paths within the glimmering gardens of this treasured, free, and open land. I sneak around corners and look in every single brick planter and flower box. I am completely and absolutely immersed in the full-body sensory excitement and hope of finding and catching the elusive fire-breathing dragon—which fortunately exists in the much smaller form of a fast-moving blue-bellied lizard. Before I wake up and leave this hilltop citadel, one perfect word rises above all the others I have ever seen or heard to describe it. And my heart clings to this word and this special place where time still stands still . . . SANCTUARY.

• • •

With the last batch of Ray and Dora's letters we'll (finally!) experience their long-time-coming reunion. Both knew that it was close, and a sense of romanticism seemed to be in the air.

On the evening of April 12, 1927, Ray wrote, "The moon is silvery bright and soft white fleecy clouds are floating in from the open sea that roars its greeting or warning—as you like it or not. The fireplace feels good and we have a giant vase of red, red roses on the dining room table that perfume the house. They grew along the side of our house and I have stopped many a night and inhaled their beauty when returning late. I always like to think of you when I have a fresh bud of a rose that's especially pretty."

That same month, Dora attended an evening church service, then wrote to Ray that the only thing missing in her life was her future husband. "The music was wonderful. It made one forget every earthly care and gave one a new outlook on life," she said. "I could have sat there several more hours listening to it . . . I would have been in a 'Heaven on Earth' if you had been sitting at my side like you used to."

The letters stopped when she finally made her way to California by train in June of that year, but their love story certainly did not. It was just the beginning of decades of their fuller "California love story."

•••

April 9, 1927
(Oceanside, CA to Wichita, KS)

Dearest Dora,

It is Saturday morning and I haven't had a chance to write all week. I am going over for the mail right now and hope to find a letter from my "sweetie."

Yesterday a Safeway Store in Carlsbad burned to the ground. It was a total loss. Carlsbad is three miles south of Oceanside. Today, they have bought out another store and will continue to operate. You have to hand it to them—they are fast workers.

The play that I was in was put on the night before last—to a large crowd. Everything went okay. I had the part of a married man who had been around quite a lot and had seen the world. In one scene I had to kiss my wife after coming home from a convention. I didn't put much action into it. So today and every day I am being "kidded" about that scene. Probably will never hear the last of it.

Now that the play is over, maybe I can find time to sleep some. But there was an election of officers the other night at the Moose Lodge. I was elected Vice Dictator beginning the 28th of this month. I have never seen a place where a person can assume work as easily as in California and there never was a place in the world where individual effort counts for more than on the West Coast. Where a man's money hardly counts—it's the man—himself.

This note was the one I promised this week. Tomorrow being Sunday, I will find time to write a long sweetheart letter.

I received your sweet letter the day before yesterday. Could use many more just like it. How about it, can you ship out some more if they were ordered?

Darling I am more than ever in love with you and every moment means just that much less time before we can meet. I am sorry that you will not keep your position with the Mentholatum Company. It must be nice to work with them.

Truly yours,
Ray
P.S. Excuse shortness this time. This is Saturday.

April 10, 1927
(Wichita, KS To Oceanside, CA)

Dearest One,

Now, please don't scold me, for I know that I should have written sooner, but every day I expected a letter from you, and finally one came yesterday. I couldn't answer it last night, for I went to a surprise party for one of the girls, and I got home late as usual. This morning, I worked; this afternoon I did some baking for Mother, and tonight I took her to the show. At last, I am in my room alone—with you.

I suppose that I really should be blue today, for this was my last day of work at the Mentholatum Company but for some reason I am as happy as I can be.

Perhaps there is a reason—our dreams may come true sooner than we had planned. The other evening a cousin of Dad's whose home is in Whittier, California, came to see us. We see him quite often for he travels back and forth about every 2 or 3 months. He said that he thought he would be back here again about the last of

May or first of June and stay a week or two, then go back, and he wants me to go back with him. The folks like the idea because they would rather that I traveled with someone I knew then go alone. He said that if you didn't want me until the 1st of July that I could stay with them until then, but I hardly think that is necessary, do you?

Anyway, he told the folks that he would watch us and see that we get along all right. Anyway, we have been invited to spend some weekends at his home in Whittier. This isn't so far from you, is it? By the way, he told us of a land proposition that might interest you. His name is Mike Orban. Have you ever met him?

I am hoping that things turn out all right, and I get to come in June, if that is alright with you?

By this time another worry is off your mind; your play is over. You didn't get stage fright, did you?

I don't think that you read my last letter right, for I never said that anyone had won your title of 'arm twitching champion' for I don't know of anyone that can twitch their arm the least little bit—not even to the extent of one twitch!

What is your sister Bernice doing? Is she going to school?

How are your radishes growing?

Do your folks like it in California as well as here?

You had better watch your step in Tia Juana, for from things that I hear, it is not very tame. Ray, you will know so much about this country that I won't be able to talk to you intelligently.

I must stop now if I expect to get my "forty winks" tonight, for it lacks only a few minutes of being midnight. I will be looking for that record-breaking letter, but I don't believe that I would use the whole box of stationary for one letter—leave at least one sheet for Bernice. Please tell Bernice "hello" for me.

With love,
Dora

April 12, 1927
(Oceanside, CA to Wichita, KS)

My Darling,

Saturday night, the district manager called up from San Diego and asked if I would come in Sunday and help fix up some special advertising that we are going to put on. I told him I would come in so Sunday morning I took the stage (bus) into San Diego and we worked and talked until 5 o'clock in the afternoon. The stage back to Oceanside did not leave until 7 o'clock but I wanted to see some of the town while I was there. I looked around for a while and finally went to the Pantages theater and came out at 7:30. The show was too good to leave. The next stage left at 10:30 so I was alone and wanted entertainment and went to another show. This time I came out about 9:30 and waited in the stage depot for the stage to start up the coast.

When we finally got about half way home it was so wet and sloppy that a big moving van had skidded across the highway and was blocking the traffic. The traffic up and down the coast is pretty heavy on Sundays and we were two hours tied up waiting and working to get through. You should have seen the number of cars that were lined up waiting for the road to be cleared. To make the long story short, it was 2AM when I got to Oceanside. So, you see Dora it was then too late to write on that day as I had promised you. Next time I go to San Diego I will have our car or I will try walking or swimming.

I have some news that might interest you, darling. The lots that I bought some time ago will soon be paid for and then they will be ours. They have not traded or sold yet but then someday they will be entirely ours and will be a fine place to build if we decide to build. They are high up and have a fine view of the ocean. I believe that they are worth $18,000 or $20,000 and I owe about $6,850 altogether on them now. Perhaps I can trade them for a nice house that we would like to live in. Anyway, it goes, I cannot possibly lose money on them and it is a splendid way to save money.

Tonight is a wonderful night. The rain has cleared away and the moon is as pretty as a picture. The air is invigorating as it blows in off the restless sea.

Work is about the same. Competition is very keen and I have to keep stepping or these birds around here will steal my stuff. We have to keep originating something new all the time. Beginning Thursday, we're going to do some of the best kind of advertising, namely "Dodgers" with the stamp of approval of the home office (Safeway Stores) in Los Angeles. I am anxious to see the results. This business is certainly interesting and it keeps you on your toes all the time. Right now, we are the biggest store in Oceanside in point of sales grocery stores. I mean, maybe the others are not doing any more I don't know. I know that the time is coming when the Safeway Stores will dominate this field in their line. I may not be with them then but they will do it anyway. Our business in Southern California has increased by 21% since the first of the year. Since the consolidation of the two companies everybody has had so much "pep." It's wonderful to see it work.

But Dora, dear, I am still thinking seriously of the real estate business and if I can do better it will be best for us. Especially if the business picks up as it has the last 30 days. But I will never leave a sure job at good wages for an uncertain proposition. If I cannot see far ahead enough to justify the taking of the chance. As long as I keep fit and on my toes, I feel that I can undertake anything.

I would like to try the real estate game before we are married so if it does not prove out like I expect the loss would not be serious. It might be that I could clean up quite a lot of money and then again it would be bad luck if I did not make a thing. But, dearest of all girls, have faith in me and hope for the best. I shall love you through good and bad years and through everything that comes up. When we are together and married we can live, really live, as we want to. You have strength of character and a goodwill and with determination to make a success of life we can go down through the years in pursuit of happiness and contentment. I firmly believe that we can find all that is best right out here in sunny California.

I have read everything I can find time and energy to read on marriage. Although so many writers are writing of the failure and breaking down of the marriage pact, I still believe in it and have come to love you even more deeply than ever before, I cared for you,

Dora, and ever since the first I have felt that if you liked me I would like you a lot- well everything has gone so far and we cannot see each other now but I have not let that worry me much.

I remember about you and what you were and how good you were to me n' everything. And that's how I came to love you Dora. I do not admire girls who talk all the time and who flirt a lot. They only cheapen themselves when they do these things and you are not that kind.

You are the kind who will stick and help a man save his money and then help him enjoy it. And help enjoy the companionship of the man while the years pass by. I love you for these and many other things that I will tell you about when I hold you in my arms again. Life will be so real and so good when you come and we can take two weeks of honeymooning and have all that's fine and good. My heart beats faster and I feel a twinge of exhilaration when I bring to mind the thought that you are to be mine to love and to protect and to safeguard. Surely there is no other thing I can think of that would bring me more happiness.

The time is slowly passing and we are just that much closer at the end of each day. When April passes it will be but 60 days until I can greet you here. Many things can happen in that time but I am hoping and praying that you will get here o.k. Then it's up to me to convince you that we should get married. I could do it tonight if you were here. The moon is silvery bright and soft white fleecy clouds are floating in from the open sea that roars its greeting or warning as you like it or not. The fireplace feels good and we have a giant vase of red, red roses on the dining room table that perfume the house. They grew along the side of our house and I have stopped many a night and inhaled their beauty when returning late. I always like to think of you when I have a fresh bud of a rose that's especially pretty.

There's something romantic about the nights here in Southern California. Here is where the Indians made their homes and camped and hunted before the Spaniards chased them away or killed them. In San Diego county was the first mission established by the Franciscan Fathers and here also was the birthplace of California. Here is where the gay young Spanish fellows made love to their Senoritas. And here is where I will take you as my wedded wife—never again to part—if you say the word and like it here.

Nights are mysterious and carefree and the flowers blossom so luxuriantly and the sea speaks a language all its own. Oh! I want you to know it all and love it so even as I do. We will find out all the dope about the past and a lot about the present and very much of the future. Ha! Ha! When you step off the train and see how the "old man" has been making it out here away from his sweetheart.

"When I look in the heart of a rose" I love you more than ever.

Ray

April 17, 1927
(Oceanside, CA to Wichita, KS)

Dearest of all,

At last I am all alone to write to my "boss." The folks have all gone to church and I just came home from San Diego in time to have the evening meal with them.

I have had a day of genuine good pleasure. Bernice and I were invited to a weekend party at San Diego, by a family named Shand. They have a beautiful home in the Mission Hills district of the city. With another family of three we went out for a boat ride on the bay. Mr. Shand is a retired businessman who has a hobby of boating. He has a palatial little boat all fitted up and equipped for sea travel. It is one of the finest small boats I have ever seen. We sailed up the bay and past Coronado to a point about sixteen miles from our starting place. There we anchored and had the finest lunch you can imagine. Mrs. Shand prepared it on the boat and served it in real style. By the way, he is a former St. Louis man and has plenty of money but he is a Scotchman and comes in for a lot of good-natured kidding. He showed me all over the boat and explained to me how much this and that cost him when he had the boat built.

But Darling that is not what I am writing to you tonight to tell you. I want to tell you that I have read your letter about coming out to Whittier earlier than you expected and I want to say this; you cannot come any too soon to suit me. I want you as soon as you can possibly get here. I may not be in shape, financially to get married as soon as you come but I want you just the same. You can come here and stay with us and get to know us all better. We all love you, Dora, and want you so much.

If you can come in May or June, do so. You cannot know how much I want to see you and talk to you again. And I know that you want to come, too, Dora. I know that we will be happy. I know that I can make you happy. We have reached the age of reality and understanding. We are no longer children in the sense of life's values. We are ready for larger undertakings. I have not minimized the hardships of married life and I do not think that everything will be lovely all through life. It has never been that way and I don't expect it to be in the future.

Life is not that way. But I love you, Dora and truly believe that you love me enough to take a chance with me through life. You realize that I am only human, and apt to do things that might not please you so much, but never-the-less we have it in our minds to get married and I am strong for it. I know that you are the one girl in the world for me. Every time I meet a new girl I compare her with the Standard of Comparison (you). But they always fall short. They have something wrong with them that I don't like. I suppose that they all think the same way about me. I have known and half-loved lots of girls—I suppose that every fellow has but until I knew you, I was always looking ahead. Somehow, Dora, I love you more every letter and letters express a great deal of how one feels.

This letter is full of ("I's")—but for one reason, "I" concerns mainly (You and I). I am not writing about Jim Jones or Mary Lou. It's about you and me! Ain't that egotism for you?

(an arrow points to the word egotism) that's a 90¢ word!!

Many days are slipping away and my lovely little Kansas girl will soon be out by the Rolling Pacific. Roses are blooming and the flowers are beautiful to see. Spring is here and summer will soon be turning the plants and flowers brown and June will find everything like October in Kansas. Our winter comes in the fall and late summer, Spring is in January and February and March. The hills have given off their first harvest of wild oats. "Wild oats" are natural here in the backcountry and the farmers mow them and use them for hay. I passed a field today that had been cut and stacked to cure—already. I am raring to tell you all about your future home. And whisper words of love to you and tell you of my plans, etc. There is so much that I can tell you that I can hardly wait. But mainly I want to talk to you about our love and future happiness. We have both lived cleanly and come from fine families and should be entitled to some of life's better things. Most of them come through hard work and I know that I am ready to do that.

This has been a fine Easter day and I hope that you have had a good day too. I think that I was at Church one Easter morning with you. How about it? Easter is a wonderful day and it means much to all Christians, or should at any rate, don't you think? Saturday was a good day at the store. We had a good week. $13,550 altogether. The inventory has not yet been reported. However, I am not expecting much of a profit on our first three months under the new system. But from now on we can show some nice profit. And I will let you know just how it came out even if it's nothing or less.

Oceanside is still going ahead. My father has made a little money lately. He seems much improved in health when business picks up. Isn't that natural though? The last few years have been hard for him and I want to see him do well. There is lots of news that I should tell you but I will have to write later in the week. I can't think of it now.

Affectionately—
Ray

April 24, 1927
(Oceanside, CA to Wichita, KS)

Dearest,

Enclosed you will find orders and written instructions as to the best ways and means to manufacture and ship "letters."
However, I am not particularly concerned about the texture and finish of the product but would respectfully urge that quantity

production begin at once and machinery be kept going until such time as the manager sees fit to come in person.

Please feel that we are interested at all times and any suggestion that might help speed up the output and help in any other way will be forthcoming if you say the word. As our interests seem to be in common, a free discussion of our problems would help to bring about a better understanding between us, the same discussion to be held at this place and on the date set by yourself. And . . . . That's enough of that!!

Dear darling Dora, you simply must come as soon as possible and keep company with the "old man." All this week I have been thinking and dreaming of you. If it was not for your picture above the fireplace on the mantle I could not stand it as well as I do. Some nights when everyone is in bed I sit down by the fireplace and hold your picture before me and wonder and think of you and the future. Darling, I am not worthy of such a person as you. I feel like I am getting so much and have so little to offer. But, dearest of all, somehow I feel that I can make you supremely happy when we are married. I know that I can and will do my best and that's all any man can do. One thing that I have that I want to keep is ambition. With you to work for and to love and to cherish I know that I can succeed. Success in a material way too. It may be that I will never know what it means to be rich with money. But real riches of life are not always found in computing the amount of any man's money. Good friends and neighbors, a happy wife and children and a clean life count for more than mere dollars. The west is a good place to test out this because here they measure a man by what he is instead of what he has. Of course, this is not always the case but there is no 'kowtowing' after the rich people like there is in the East.

What is the latest on the trip out here? Do you plan on the auto trip or will you wait and come on the train? I want you to come the first chance you have. If you can come sooner than the last of June, please do. Don't wait because that time happened to be mentioned. We can and Mama would love to have you with us. I want you here before the summer is over. My folks suggested that you come out and stay with us and then if you and I still feel the same way toward each other we could get married. But Dora, I want you to be the judge of everything. Anything that suits you suits me too. But I want to be fair with you. You should have time after you come to know me better and then if you want to get married at once—let's do. Things will look strange to you probably but you will recover I'm sure. I am older and a little taller than when we were together last. Bernice says that I have improved in some ways since we left Wichita. I am just dying to see you Dora—I know that you must be lovelier than ever. I always thought that you were one of the nicest dressers style and everything—and I know that I shall love you more when we meet and come to an understanding. This marriage business is fine but it means so much to both of us. After not having seen each other for almost two years it will be the happiest day in my life when you arrive.

We are both so young and more or less care free but we both realize the responsibility of married life. But real love overcomes all things and is the most beautiful thing in the world. Surely we shall be fitted for each other and marry.

Yesterday was a busy day at the store—(we took in $601.00 at the store Saturday) we had a lot of specials on sale and people were eager to buy and then we tried to sell all we could. My store is steadily building up to the mark I have set. Of course, we have poor business some weeks and then again some fine ones. But on the average, business is good. The inventory has not yet been reported.

Today my father asked me how I would like to take over the insurance end of the office. I am undecided as yet but feel that I could make it go if I had time and money to carry me over the lean days. You see the business I am now in is 'sure pay' and as long as they are satisfied with my work, I can depend on a steady salary. Now if I should stop and go into the real estate game in earnest, I might not make any real money at first and we would have to postpone the wedding—what do you advise me to do? If you say take the chance before we are married I could see how it came out and it would not be so hard. You see, Dora, I am up against a problem. If business should get really good in the real estate game I would plunge into it and make it sure, I know. But if things get quiet, maybe it would not be so good.

We have made so many friends since coming here that it's a

marvel. Many of them are looking forward to the day when you can be here. There is a young, married set here who seem to be really nice and they have many good times together.

The other day when I was in the bank signing up some papers on that lot deal, I came across the words, the party of the second part one, "Ray A. Wilcox, a bachelor—does hereby and herewith . . ." etc. (Gee, it made me feel really old.) Wonder how long I shall remain in that state? Not very long if you were here I'll bet!

These last few days were regular California days—warm and sun shiny. Summer is upon us and already the hills are beginning to turn the least bit brown because it never rains here in the summer.

Be a good girl- keep up the old pep and just a few more days I shall hold you close and say that I love you. Truly I do.

Ray

April 29, 1927
(Wichita, KS to Oceanside, CA)

Dearest Ray,

After reading your instructions about the manufacturing and shipping of "Letters," I have decided to take your advice. In doing so, I expect to increase the quantity and also the quality, providing you, as the second party, promises to fulfill your share of the work by complying with my orders.

In order to increase our production, we must have a reason and also an incentive for such an act. If the second party sees that letters to be answered are increased in number each week, we will see that they are answered. As an incentive, your signature is enough for us at any time.

If there are any problems which you wish to discuss more freely, just state them in your natural style, and submit any questions that you wish to be answered. An effort on our part will be made to give you all information desired even to the smallest detail. Thus, our standard of our quality may be raised.

As I expect to be in your excellent city soon, I will call on you and we will discuss everything in detail. Personal contact is much more enlightening than written words.

When I am certain of my plans, I shall let you know, and I hope that you will be as good as to allow me a few moments of your precious time.

Sincerely Yours.

Etc.

'Ats too much o' that."

If you can't understand the first part of this letter, don't pay any attention to it. It really is nothing, Darling. I don't know much more about the time of my departure from here than I did. If I do go with this relative, we will go on the train. I heard from him the other day, and he expects to come at the time he stated. He and his wife want me to come and stay with them a couple weeks or longer before I go on to Oceanside, for they also want to show me a good time. How can I ever do that—be that close to you and not see you for a week or so—I can't do it! We shall see how things turn out, but I would much rather come right on down to you. If I do have to stay there a while, you will have to come there to see me, that's all there is to it.

Gee, Ray, you are a dear! Of course, you can make me happy. If only I can give you something which will make your life less dreary, I will be satisfied. With your love and understanding, I feel that I could do anything. We may never have lots of money, but who cares? We can be rich in many other ways, rich in love, and friends, and we will be more happy than those rich in money.

Someone sounds as if he were getting a little nervous already. I am just kidding, but really, Ray, when one does think about marriage and all the things it concerns, it does rather alarm one, doesn't it? I think of you all the time, and often I wonder how it will all end.

Of course, we won't get married as soon as I arrive, for you must have a chance to see me "as is" and to see if you would really want me for life. It wouldn't be fair otherwise. When we are sure, then we can get married. If you have changed, I know that it is for the best, so my opinion of you will only increase in a better way. You say that you are a little taller? Another ambition realized. I remember very distinctly several times when you mentioned how you would like to be taller.

I don't know if I have changed much or not. You can be the judge and pronounce the sentence "guilty or not guilty."

Darling, please do as you think best about going into the real estate business—I don't know how to advise you. If you want to go into it, and we would have to postpone the wedding we most certainly would do so, or I don't want to marry until you feel able to do so. Do as you want to do.

Dear, I must close, otherwise I might ruin the "old bachelor's" eyesight by letting him try to decipher a longer letter. Also, it is midnight, and this "old maid" must be able to work in the morning. I am working at the Salvation Army Office for a few days again.

I am trying to be a good girl—for your sake. Don't you do anything that I wouldn't do either.

Soon I can be in your arms and whisper to you those three small words which mean so much "I love you."

Dora

Undated Friday evening

(Wichita, KS to Oceanside, CA)

Dearest Ray,

What is there about your letters that always warn me that there will be one at home waiting for me? Wednesday evening, coming from work, I felt that there would be one there, but I also doubted it because usually your letter that you write on Sunday gets here on Thursday. Anyway, there was your letter. Daddy said that the Post office must have thought it very important, because it arrived at the Post office at 5 o'clock, and they brought it to the house at 5:15. Usually they wait 4 or 5 hours before delivering them. I guess it was important—all of them are!

I started a letter to you yesterday noon and one to-day, but the girls at work wouldn't leave me alone long enough to finish it, so I hope that this attempt will be successful, because I expect that "Daddy" would like to have a letter—even if it is from his "wife"!?)

Last night a bunch of us girls (about 20) had a waffle supper (Gee! the waffles were good too!), and then we got really "wild" and went to the Crawford Theater. In fact, we spent a lovely evening and had a fine time.

I suppose that I am bored with Wichita, Ray. It isn't going to the dumps, but it is still the same as when you left it, only a few more buildings. The parks are fine, if you have the right company. I lack the right company—and that is you.

Ray, did you read my last letter correctly? I didn't ask you if I could have dates—for I don't want any dates. I don't see anyone around here that I would date, and another thing—if I can't have dates with you, I don't want any. I'm stubborn, aren't I? I'm saving mine too for the finest fellow in the world, and the only one for me. I just merely wondered if it wasn't all right for me to go out with a big bunch, that's all. If I do go out with a bunch, you know that I will be perfectly safe for I can take care of myself.

While we are on this subject, I didn't go on the steak fry—none of us did. For it rained Friday night and all-day Saturday.

I dreamed about you the other night. You and I were running along the shore and playing in the ocean water, and having the "best us" time. That dream might come true in about 3 months, mightn't it?

Anyway the "old man" is going to get to see his wife. She needs and wants him so much, too.

With more love than ever,
Dora

May 2, 1927

(Oceanside, CA to Wichita, KS)

My Darling,

Tonight is a bad time to start writing to my sweetheart but I want you to know that I have been thinking of you and that I received a fine and wonderful letter from you on Sunday night when I came home from a long day's trip into the desert. We were gone from six in the morning until dark on Sunday and had a hard and enjoyable trip. I can not tell you all about it here but in another letter that will follow probably tomorrow night, you will find all the dope on the trip in writing.

We had a busy Monday and tonight my father and I went down to a Chamber of Commerce meeting down the coast to a small town called Encinitas. We just came back. It's late and everyone else has gone to bed but I just had to sit down and write to my honey girl who cheers me so much with her love and letters. Dora, I know that I shall love you more and more as the years go by. You mean more than all else to me now. If all else should disappear and fade away and I could have you, I could stand it and face the world.

Many things have happened here lately. I can hardly wait until you arrive. This town and country are undergoing a remarkable change as I think I told you before when we first came out. I saw the possibilities and can still see them and I am proud of the fact that I can still live here and take advantage of all that comes my way. Last week I took out a membership in the Oceanside Golf club even though I don't play now. Golf attracts the people who have money and are willing to spend it. A town or city without a golf course is doomed as far as the tourists and travelers are concerned. So, I am investing a small sum each month with that feeling that I will be more than repaid in time to come.

Honey, I am looking forward to the time when we can meet again. Surely we shall be one happy couple. You may be sure that if you come to Whittier, I will come there. But really I want you to come to Oceanside or San Diego first. It will thrill me beyond description to see you get off the train. All I need to know is the time you will arrive and I will certainly do the rest. My mother wants to take care of you and my father is more than anxious to see the girl his young son has chosen. We all want you to come. Bernice and Fred are still engaged and happy and he will be "hers" about the middle of June. Oh, yes!! I am going to answer a lot of questions in my next letter. "Signing off" now about midnight on May 3rd. Station R.A.W. loves station D.I.K. very much.

As ever,

Ray

May 3, 1927
(Wichita, KS to Oceanside, CA)

Ray Dear,

If you have fully recovered from my last letter, you may read this one. Otherwise don't attempt it.

Our output has not increased yet, since the second party has not complied with our terms yet. Anyway, our output is steady, although soon it is expecting a big rush in business. How about it?

You wish me to be a judge of your penmanship. Well, I must receive several copies of it each week, so I can see if there is any improvement. You know "practice makes perfect"—at least it is supposed to. My penmanship is getting terrible too—simply because I write too much on the typewriter.

I am still typing as usual at the Salvation Army Campaign Office. This is a very interesting job for one gets so much inside "dope" on people. Since working there, I have received different impressions and opinions of many people than I held before. Every day since I have been in the business world, I have learned something new. I wouldn't give up my experience in the business world for anything.

Of course, I have been teased about our engagement in the office. The head of this campaign, a Kansas City fellow, was talking to me the other morning and he said that he knew that you were going to succeed in life (he doesn't know you) because (the rest was just a little "apple sauce" which he handed me)—Isn't it fine to have a stranger believing in you, too?

You know that I believe in you and nobody in the world could shake my faith. I just think of you continually. Soon it won't be a case of just thinking of you, but I can also be with you to hear you talk and laugh and to love you. It seems too good to be true, dear, but it is. May has already arrived and it is on its way so June can come—and you.

I can't think of anything to-night but that I love you and want you.

Write real, real soon.

Love and kisses and lots of them from "Me"—"mama"

May 3, 1927
(Oceanside, CA to Wichita, KS)

Bernice Wilcox to Dora Kullman

My dearest Dora,

The days have slipped by without accomplishing the things I wanted to do most—writing to you. Every day I have planned to write and to tell you all of the interesting news but I know Ray has kept you well informed.

It doesn't seem possible that another school year has passed and June is just a few days off. Ray and I have just been existing until June.

Dearest Dora, we all hope you will find it possible to come to Oceanside and to us in June. Every trip or every beautiful scene Ray sees he says, "Gee! I wish Dora could see that." He is so sincerely in love with you that he is getting absent minded. Honest. You must hurry up before Ray loses complete control of his mental facilities.

Last Sunday we drove to San Jacinto, the setting for the story of Ramona. You would have enjoyed seeing the different kinds of country we passed over to reach the beautiful valley. We drove through mountains, valleys and deserts and long shady pepper tree lanes. Although this trip is one of the longest and most interesting, we have planned trips and weekend parties in the mountains for you that I hope will prove to be much more interesting to you.

Fred will come home from school about June 15th. And if you could be here we would like to go to Baldy (mountain and resort) for an overnight party. You will love Baldy and you will hold its beauty dear to your heart. Just we four will go with our mother or someone for a chaperone. It does seem that engaged couples shouldn't have to be chaperoned, doesn't it?

Because Fred feels the urge to go to work soon after getting home from school we will have to take our trip during the middle and last of June. Of course, I know Ray will want to keep you all to himself, and he certainly shall. But not all the time 'cause we are almost as anxious to have you come out as badly as he.

I wish it was possible to tell you about all of the things Ray has planned for you but since this is the only kind of stationery I have at the office I won't have enough.

I hope this little note finds you well and happy.

Hope there will only be a few more days before we can be together.

Love, Bernice

May 7, 1927
(Wichita, KS to Oceanside, CA)

Darling,

I failed to get my usual letter yesterday, and I didn't like it one bit. It gives me the blues when I don't hear from you at least once a week. I watched for the postman this morning and he did bring me what I wanted. Anyway, it made me dream of you last night. I dreamed that we were expecting you home (here) on a certain day and you didn't come and we didn't hear from you. Finally, in the evening the telephone rang and mother answered it, and she called me to the phone. I thought, "Oh gee! That's Ray." Just then I awoke with a start (at 7 o'clock this morning) and mother was really calling me to go down and answer the phone. At first I didn't realize where I was and for a moment I thought that maybe you were calling. No such luck! Only a girlfriend inviting me to a party.

I enjoyed Bernice's letter so much too and I am glad that she is so happy. I know that we four kids are going to have a wonderful time when we get together.

So, you are a golfer now, although you don't play! I hope that you learn, for every one that knows the game seems to enjoy it so much. Several years ago, I tried the game two times, but I did so rotten and lost so many balls that I have never had the nerve to try again. I wish I could play it though.

You say that your mother wants to take care of me. She doesn't realize what a job that will be. Some time ago, my mother told me that if I didn't pay attention to your mother and do as she says, that she would come out and spank me. 'Nuff said! I want to do as you and your folks think best, and whenever I need advice and help, I want your mother to help me. I hope that your mother approves of me.

It makes me jealous of you when you take all those wonderful trips. Here one sees the same old thing all the time. I won't have to look at it much longer though—For I am coming out to look at you. (Should I wear my glasses, or will there be any danger of eye trouble?)

A good night hug and kiss
From Your "Mama"

May 9, 1927
(Oceanside, CA to Wichita, KS)

My Sweetheart,

Your fine letter came today and although I waited all day for it, it was certainly welcome today, Monday. You cannot know how much I enjoy your letters, darling. They mean so much to me now that the time is here—or nearly here for you to start. Everyone is a classic in itself.

I finally heard from the inventory and the results were "punk." I found that I have been working for wages the first period. It was tough news but I hardly expected much of a showing on the first three months operation. The district manager was not disappointed and we have a good volume of business worked up now and it really means more in the long run for me. We can begin to raise the prices now and take the profits due me. We have increased and made more of a showing than most of the stores in Southern California. But Dora, darling. I feel like doing something definite soon that will change my whole course.

By the time you are out here I will know just what I will do and maybe sooner. Sometimes I wonder if I could not do much better in some other line than groceries. One of the things I feel I can do is to go with my father and eventually have a business of my own. I will have to eventually but I want to get ahead soon. There is a big field out here for insurance and real estate. The country is filling up so rapidly and there's much building on all sides that a young and aggressive salesman can corner a lot of business. The only thing that keeps me with the company is the guaranteed wage and perhaps a future. I have done well with them and they have treated me very well indeed. But the years are likely to go on and find me only a store manager with the job of six days a week and a couple of nights, too. Wouldn't that be a hard thing for you to face? Me, too. So, that will not happen in this case. I would rather go back to Kansas and sell Western Kansas Farms.

I made a talk last Thursday night at the quarterly meeting and today at the Kiwanis Club. It gives me a great deal of pleasure to be able to stand on my feet and address a meeting. In my mind, public speaking is an art. If I can face a crowd and say something at the right time that will benefit anybody it would be quite a satisfaction.

Personally, I admire the man or woman who can sway a crowd or move an audience. If perhaps a few times on my feet helps me to overcome the great fault of mine- self-consciousness—I can well afford the time spent in the play and at the church socials, etc.

Sunday, Bernice and I drove up to Los Angeles and on over to Santa Monica where we went down to Ocean Park. There we went to an entertainment given at the Gables club for the Mississippi flood Relief. There were many of the movie people on the program. Also Jack Dempsey gave an exhibition and the Duncan Sisters did their stuff. But the biggest thing on the trip was the Hollywood and Beverly Hills sight-seeing we did on the way back home; we came by the Fox Studios and the United Artists and many others. Los Angeles is overcrowded and I would not like to live there or work there.

You just can't imagine the traffic that is handled on the city thoroughfares—even 20 miles out from the heart of the city. To see it makes you dizzy but to drive it makes you a nut. Think of the number of people who have cars in California and then imagine seeing them all at once in one city, that's Los Angeles. There is a car in California for every two people according to reports and there are 1 million 250-thousand people in Los Angeles and they all get out on Sunday in the sunshine. When we finally came back to Oceanside I was a wreck and had a real headache. Dora there is no other place in the world like Los Angeles. At one place 25 miles from the center of town they have a traffic officer at the intersection and the road is wide enough to allow 8 autos abreast and surely it is exciting to go through that and much worse on downtown. There is no such thing as city limits of any town out here. It's all one big city, Southern California.

Out in Arizona, across the desert from L.A., there is a tiny filling station which caters to the traveling public and on a sign board, close by there is this sign. (A road sign is drawn here that reads "Los Angeles, City Limits, 250 Miles") Only the 250 miles are written so small you can hardly make them out. That's enough about Los Angeles.

Dora, my sweetheart, what is the latest about the time you will start? Have you made any further plans?

One of my friends got married secretly in Santa Barbara last week. He is the son of a well to do meat market man here. The couple are trying to keep it quiet for a while and he has not even told his mother, but his father knew it because the old man had to finance it. He wanted his sons—there are three boys in the family—to get married and settle down. This makes the second in the family now and the third is taking a wife this winter. She lives in Orange, up the coast by Santa Ana.

There is some talk of forming a newlywed's club here and having good times together. There is one over at Escondido and they have the best times imaginable.

My darling, the hours drag and days stand still and you are not here. Oh Dora, this all has been a terrible strain on us both and the twenty months that we have not seen each other are past. Now the glad times are coming. I want you so much and I know I shall love you even more deeply when you come. The days have come and gone and faith alone has carried us through. Many times, I have been tempted to step out and do something that would not be right and then I think that it would not be just and fair to the girl I love. Your faith in me has held me steady and I could never leave the path with the thought of shattering this faith. And I love you Dora . . . . that is all.

True love will sacrifice and give in while the profane seeks only self-satisfaction. That's the difference between sacred and profane love and that's also the difference between love and passion.

The world goes "stale" for the person who lives only for enjoyment and pleasure. Bored by everything that takes thought and action and work the idlers gradually sink to a lower level and finally land in the lowest depths. It takes an interest in life and lots of work to make the living worthwhile. When a person loses interest, it's time to look up the phone number of a good "Mortician." Even if a person is old and feeble, if there is still a spark of interest, then life is still worth living.

That's the reason life is best when we are in love. We are so interested. Isn't it the truth?

Write soon and many of them! Anything of importance that develops here will be broadcast to you as soon as it happens.

THE OLD MAN.

May 10, 1927
(Wichita, KS to Oceanside, CA)

Darling,

Since I gave special attention to "Mothers" yesterday, I feel that I must give some attention to "Papa" today, for he must not be neglected." "Papas" are quite important people, at least I think so. I know one that is.

Just as I was leaving Saturday evening for a party, your special [letter] came. I felt like answering it at that moment, but some of the girls were waiting for me, so I had to postpone the business of writing. That isn't good business to delay filling a special order, is it?

We were having a good time at the party, when about 11 o'clock one of the fellows came after his girl, and instead of coming right in, he tried to scare us. As far as I was concerned he was successful to the Nth degree. The kids had more fun watching me than over the scare, for they said I turned as white as a sheet. I really surprised myself. Then they all wished that you could have seen me—I'm glad that you didn't for you would have said "So that is the kind of girl she is!" It was funny, though!

I really fulfilled your request, before you ever asked it, Ray. Some more mental telepathy must have been passing between you and me, for the first part of last week, I decided that I must read "Ramona" before I go to California. At the first opportunity, I went to the library for it, but it was out (someone else must have a sweetheart in Southern California), so I will try again tomorrow. I will also read "The Pride of Palomar." It will give me a better understanding and appreciation of what I will soon see. I also want to read them again after I get out there, for then I will have read it from two different viewpoints. The first time I will not be able to enjoy it as much as the second, after I have become acquainted with the country.

You have already made me like the country by your description of it. I may be prejudiced, but I doubt it, but you know, dearest Ray, that you could make me like just about anything.

Although I have never had very much of an opportunity to be outdoors a great deal, I like it, and as the years go by, I long more and more to spend hours outdoors doing interesting things such as hiking, fishing, riding etc. I don't like spending hours in an office every day and then spending one's evening inside also. Let's you and I go out and enjoy nature and the fresh air as much as possible, shall we?

Speaking of fresh air, I would like to breathe a little right now. The air is so full of dust and sand that it nearly chokes one. It was this way yesterday too.

Dear, this is May 9th already. Soon comes June 9th and then it won't be long until the "choo-choo" will be carrying one more passenger headed for the wild west where "men are men, and women are wild."

Ray, I dream continually of you, not only daytime but also at nights. Just everything reminds me of you. I do love you so, Ray, more than I can tell you!

There won't be many more weeks of this separation and then we will be happy.

A carload of love and kisses until then.

Yours for happiness
Dora

May 13, 1927
(Wichita, KS to Oceanside, CA)

Dearest One,

I am so sorry to hear the results of your inventory. I know that you didn't expect much, but even at that you expected more than you got. When such disappointments happen, it makes one feel that there isn't much joy in living, doesn't it? In my life I have only had a very few disappointments and I know how hard they are to take. You have had more than your share of troubles, but things won't be that way always—already things are looking brighter, aren't they? Everything is for the best. Perhaps this does mean that you should change your business. I don't think, Ray, that you will ever be satisfied until you have gotten into the real estate business, will you? For deep down in your heart you like the real estate business better than any other, always you are dreaming of it. It must have been born into you.

Remember you will always succeed better at anything you like than at any other trade. I know that you will succeed in the grocery business, for you are that kind. You will do good in any business, but will you ever be satisfied to stay with it? Why don't you try the real estate business? You can win in it, and the sooner you start, the better.

I know that you are terribly uncertain as to what to do, for you think that if you don't have steady wages you can never get married. If you feel that way, Ray, I can wait, for I will wait for you, dear, until you are ready. One great philosopher has said, "the best thing for a man to do when he is out of a job and poor, is to get married." Often marriage is the only thing needed to help a man to success. You can decide for yourself, Ray, and we will do whatever you think best. Don't think and reason too much, but go out and do whatever your heart tells you to do.

I have been thinking all day of your experiences, and I do want to help you so much. Can I do anything in any way?

I am proud of you for talking before clubs. You will soon lose your self consciousness. When you get up to talk, never feel yourself inferior to anyone, even the president! Just think that you know as much as the rest of them do and your ideas are as good or even superior to theirs. It helps a lot. I can't make speeches but once in a while I like to get up and express my own ideas. It takes a lot of courage to do it sometimes, but I don't mind it as much as I used to.

Dear, don't drive in Los Angeles if it is going to make you a nut. Something might happen to you or . . . don't you have squirrels in California? (Ha, Ha)

I don't know any more than I did about when I will be out to California. sometime in June. Nearly half of May is gone, so soon I will be bidding dear old Wichita good-bye, and then greeting the one I love.

Dear, I must close for mother wants me to go to a show with her (I am not working now). Since I won't be here so long, I like to go out with her as much as possible.

Write me soon.

I can't hold steady, so hurry up and kiss me! There—that's a good boy!

Love, Dora

May 19, 1927
(Oceanside, CA to Wichita, KS)

From Ray's Mother; Dessie Egbert Wilcox

Dear Dora—

We are looking forward to your coming to us with keen pleasure.

I just feel you will never regret it. It is all so raw and new and beautiful that you and Ray can grow and build together. We love it more and more here. Of course, Ray is working long hours but he has assumed obligations that he feels he must not quit just now for light work or hours. But things are going our way and the prospects are brighter and any day we hope to have good news to send you. It has been a wonderful education for work and business combined that I doubt a college could have given him. It has given a business standing that no one need be ashamed but proud to have. I feel you two can work in thought together so harmoniously that nothing but happy results will be gained. I don't think we could stand to have you go somewhere else when you land in California. Dear Dora, don't be afraid to come right here, you are as welcome as one of our blood which we will always feel you are from now on.

If I can really be a mother to you, nothing would make me happier. And your own dear mother, my heart goes out to her in having to let you go so far away, but tell her I shall try with all my love and devotion to make you happy. I wish you could have been here for all this past month. I never saw such a wonderful lot of flowers in my life. Roses so big, so beautiful it brings tears, it brings one so near to God. Ray has a wonderful view from the lots he is buying and on one of the finest streets. Won't it be fun to plan a home for such a view? Dora, hurry and get here.

We are poor but happy. Ray will be very, very much happier when he has you. I was that way and so was Dad. We have been married thirty-two years and . . . well come see for yourself. Such is life honey and God made us to be happy and do his will.

Your loving, shall I say Mother, Mrs. W H Wilcox

May 20, 1927
(Oceanside, CA to Wichita, KS via Western Union Telegram)

```
MISS DORA KULLMANN
616 NORTH LAWRENCE AVE WICHITA KANS
RECEIVED BOTH LETTERS BUT HAVE BEEN AWAY FROM HOME
EVERY NIGHT UNTIL TONIGHT VERY BUSY LATELY WRITE AS
USUAL SUNDAY EVERYTHING OK THINKING OF YOU ALWAYS AM
SENDING YOU THIS MESSAGE AND MY LOVE BECAUSE THE MAIL
IS TOO SLOW DON'T WORRY SWEETHEART. KEEP WRITING
RAY.
```


May 20, 1927
(Wichita, KS to Oceanside, CA)

Dearest Ray,

I was beginning to wonder this morning what was the matter with you after the mailman had passed and not a letter from you. At noon your nice letter came. I nearly didn't get it at all, for they had the address as 6116 N. Lawrence. It was thoughtful of you to send it, Ray, and I really appreciate it.

What are you doing all the time with yourself? You aren't trying to work at night too, are you? I wish that I had some of your work to do, for I feel so terribly lazy, doing nothing except fooling around home and going out once in a while.

Last night Mr. Alex Hyde entertained the employees of the Mentholatum Company at a picnic on his farm about 28 miles west and south of here on the Ninnescah. They asked me to go. We fished, walked for miles, and then he had the tenants on his farm serve us a wonderful fried chicken and fried fish dinner down by the river. There were huge pans of food—everything imaginable and it tasted delicious. Afterward we played some ball, and walked and talked some more, and finally we went to the farmhouse and danced for an hour. We had a wonderful time. That's all. The more I see of the Hydes, the more I think of them. They are always trying to do something to make someone happy. They make their life worth living.

Tonight, a girlfriend has invited me to a show and to stay all night with her and play tennis in the morning.

Tomorrow my niece wants me to stay with her and go to a show. Shows, shows, shows, shows! Sometimes I get so tired of them, but there isn't much else to do here. I am glad that there are other things than shows to see in California. My plans are as indefinite as ever. I hate such uncertain plans, but I have to wait and find out what these relatives in California decide to do, before I can do anything.

I am getting more impatient to see you as the days go by. The folks won't be able to live with me pretty soon. I know that I will be madly in love with you, dear, and maybe you can love me just a little bit. We will be happy, but we have a right to be for we have waited long enough for it. Haven't we?

I am sending you more love and more kisses in this letter.

Although these kind don't satisfy one very much, it is the best that I can do now.

Lovingly
Dora.

P.S. On these cool nights when I am sitting in the porch swing, I do miss you so much. It seems as if you should be there with me. Write me real soon.

May 23, 1927
(Oceanside, CA to Wichita, KS)

My Sweetheart,

I am really ashamed of myself for not writing any sooner, Dora. I know that you have looked for letters until there seems that someone is deliberately keeping my letters from you. I have felt that way and have gone away from the P.O. with a heavy heart many times. Really Dora I have not forgotten for a minute how much I care for you and it seems that every night when the only chance I have to write to you was already engaged previously. All last week was taken up with meetings both here and San Diego. Except one night and that was a dinner dance given by my Kiwanis Club. Several of the nights I came home after one o'clock and that is too late to do any intelligent letter writing.

    I am so tired of meetings that I could swear. All I want to do now is get off by myself and rest. The guy who invented meetings has a place reserved for him in the lower regions.

    The only thing that I can think of now Dora is you. I'm always thinking of you and oh how much I need you here Dora my sweetheart! The nights are incomplete without you. I am lost without a girl who understands and a girl I can understand. Just to hear you play one sweet song and perhaps sing a little would be joy enough to satisfy me for a whole night. But to hold you in my arms and feel your pulsing heart and just to love you for a night would be incomparable.

When you come out and we get settled in a home of our own we can begin to understand how much we really mean to each other.

Today, Bernice and Mother and I drove down to San Diego. I went on Company business. I wished mightily for you. We came back inland through Escondido and it was really warm away from the coast. Although the business requires my time for 6 day a week, once in a while I have to make an extra effort on Sunday. Yesterday—Saturday—the store sales were $677.00 which was the best day I have had. The profit is coming in now and I should receive a nice check after the inventory on July 1'st. When you come out I can explain to you the reasons why the profit did not come the first period.

My father is making a few deals now and hopes to make some money this summer. He has some nice options on choice property here and probably will move them to advantage. The new pier is out in the ocean a quarter of a mile. Now the railing has to be put on and the 100 ft. square on the end has to be built. The paving on the strand is just starting and will be ready for use in July. I wish that you were here to watch these improvements go in. They are interesting and especially after these many years that the town has been sleeping.

The New York to Paris flight proves that San Diego builds good air planes, doesn't it? I have been out at the flying field many times. I have a big picture of Capt. Lindbergh getting ready to start for St. Louis. When the news came that he had landed safely in Paris, San Diego went wild. Whistles shrieked and sirens and guns added to the noise. They kept this up for an hour; it was like the signing of the Armistice. This shows how the world loves a hero. He is a hero and he has my praise.

My darling, I have been figuring out a way to spend our honeymoon to the best advantage. If we like the boat trip, it shall be a boat trip. But I have been thinking that maybe we would like a car trip better. The parks up north offer some delightful trips. And I would like to see San Francisco. If you know of a better way, please let me know. All I know or care about is how much I love you and how I can make you happy. If we are not happier after we are married than before, it would be a mistake to even get married at all. But I am not worried about that. If you are willing to take a chance with me and you say that you are, then that's all I want to know. I love you and want you.

May is passing, June is almost here and June brings my Dora. The air is full of expectant waiting. Nights are lonely without the one that I love. Roses are wonderful now and the air is laden with the scent of semi-tropical flowers from the flower garden. The folks love to have them in the house and they are so beautiful and perfect. It almost moves one to poetry (if possible).

Sweetheart, you cannot know how much I appreciate your telling me that you will wait until I make good. I love you more for it, if possible. I will make good and justify your faith in me. Surely our love will overcome all obstacles. I know it will—with you here.

Yesterday I scribbled on sales pads in such a rush that today I cannot possibly unlimber my fingers to write decently. All I can say is, if I can't make love any better than I write, then it is no use. Did you ever write all day for 15 hours and write fast and scribble and then try to write clearly. When do you start, honey? Let me know as soon as you know. I will write in a night or two again.

Ray

May 27, 1927
(Wichita, KS to Oceanside, CA)

Dearest One,

It seems as if I am never home long enough anymore to even get a pen in my hand. So many of the girls that have been out of town or teaching school elsewhere have returned, so there has been something going on from morning until night. But through it all, I have been thinking of you most of the time (in fact, all the time) except when I have to answer some questions which requires a great deal of concentration. When you don't get letters, you think that I have forgotten you, don't you? I could never do that, Ray, for you are too big a part of my life.

Last night a bunch of us had a picnic at Sunnydale Springs. One of the girls brought a portable victrola, so we sat around the fire listening to music. With all that bunch around, I felt positively lonesome- lonesome for you. The evening was a lovely one for a Kansas evening. It made me long for you and your love. Love songs seemed to be their favorite. It is the favorite of anyone, don't you think?

We do need each other. I know that I need you. There is an emptiness in my heart, which no one can fill but you, darling Ray. You bet your life that June is going to bring Dora to California. I don't know when I am leaving, but I will let you know the minute I find out.

Dear, we can discuss our honeymoon trip when I get there, but really I would enjoy any kind of trip—land, sea, or air. It is up to you, for I want you to do the thing that will make you the happiest. To see you happy will make me happy too.

I can't write on any other subject except "you and I" tonight, but that subject is as good as any and better than most. My letters are getting worse and worse, but there are so many things that can't be written, but can be said, so I am waiting until I can say them. You will wait until then, won't you?

Love and kisses—all you want
From "Me"
Dora

May 30, 1927
(Oceanside, CA to Wichita, KS)

Darling Dora,

It is Monday night and we just came home from Los Angeles. Real tired and fagged out after seeing so much of Southern.

California. But I know that I can find happiness in writing to my sweetheart.

Your letter was waiting for me when I came home. It is always pleasant to get letters from most everybody but the biggest kick that I know of is to open one of your darling letters and find there the written testimony that you still care for and love me. How it cheers me to know that back there I have a friend who cares and one who understands.

Allan Kelly and Jack Huntoon and myself drove up to Pasadena, Saturday night after work. Jack Huntoon is about 25 or 26 years-old and he is clerking in my store. He has his parents and a brother living in Altadena, a sub-urb of Pasadena, and we were their guests over the weekend. Among the things we did during the time was one trip in particular, the trip up Mt. Lowe by cable car. The Pacific Electric Railway has a cable car all fitted up and they haul passengers up a steep ride of the mountain by means of an end-less cable of steel attached to a three decked passenger car. It's a real thrill because the climb is 1245 ft., at an angle of 60 degrees! When you come out we can take the trip together sometime. We hiked all over the mountains on the trip and then took a trip over the city of Pasadena, also Hollywood and Beverly Hills. I suppose that the most beautiful homes in the West are in Beverly Hills and Hollywood. They are as grand as money and climate can produce. We saw Doug. Fairbanks and Mary Pickford's home, also these others—Charles Ray, Charlie Chaplin, Tom Mix, The Talmadges, James Cruz, Antonio Moresto, William Haines, Pola Negri—also Zane Grey's home and many others too numerous to mention. We visited all the famous show places in and around that district and heard all the usual scandals.

It seems that the majority of the movie people are notoriously immoral. At any rate that is the consensus of opinion of those you meet and seem to know. One of the things that go to produce lawlessness is the money that comes easy. It almost disgusts the sane and sober people who go to the movies and see their favorites, and who know that in their private life they are terrible beyond all decency. Of course we are not all angels and I would not have you get the impression that I am one but the stories and tales that are told about the money mad and jazz mad people of Hollywood are awful. Of course I don't believe all of it and you see articles in the papers and magazines about how really decent Hollywood is. But to go there and see it and learn more about it is the only way to know. We saw enough to make us think that all we heard was not without foundation. It was a new and strange sight to us after all and we came away wondering what it all means and how it will all end. The young fellows are trying to make good under an influence that is the worst of any in the west. If they succeed eventually it will be a triumph over the tawdry, flimsy rotten nightlife that exists there and the girls who become stars pay and pay and pay.

The man we were with is an antique dealer who knows many of the film folk and has furnished lots of homes for them. He showed us a lot of homes he had been in—including Pola Negri's etc. He is rather sophisticated and rarely goes to the movies. But he tells us that the parties that are given and to which he was invited had been plenty rough. But it looks good!

That is enough about Hollywood for now.

Honey, I am waiting for the day to come when I can see you again. Less than a month now and you will be here. I said waiting, but I mean that I am getting ready for you to come. Minutes are passing and I wonder just how you are going to find me. Ready or not.

Update, I haven't sold the lots but have good prospects. If I can move them I will have plenty of small cash to get married with. And they will sell this summer. If you are willing to start housekeeping for a while until the lot money comes in, then we can get married at once. We don't need so very much when we love each other so. Of course, I should have several hundred dollars in the bank but it is not absolutely necessary. I have many friends here and my folks are always glad to help me in every way possible. But I know that I am capable of supporting a wife and the possibility of help is too remote to consider. If I did not think that we could make the grade I would certainly not ask a girl to marry me.

The store is doing fine and when the next check-up comes I know that the result will be gratifying. We have checked up on the old method and consequently we know that we are getting a profit on our merchandise. Some time in the later part of July I will get a good check for all this work and worry. You will be here by then and if you want we shall steal away and take our honeymoon trip.

Won't it be glorious just to have each other? After our days of waiting and sacrifice and worry? Just to have you to love and love and love and keep you always near would be supreme happiness. Cool nights and fragrant breezes, whispering trees and a murmuring sea. Glorious sunsets and happy care free hours with the one— who is coming. I love you, Dora. Please come soon.

This is a bum letter but I have a good one for the next I think. (Dora, write every chance you get until you start)

Ray

May 31, 1927
(Wichita, KS to Oceanside, CA)

Dearest Ray,

I am so excited! At the dinner table this evening the main subject up for discussion was California. We haven't heard from these relatives in California yet, so we do not know if they are coming or not, so Dad said that if we didn't hear from them this week that I may as well get ready and go right away. He thinks that I may as well be having a good time in California as trying to have one here. If we don't get a letter this week, I imagine that I can start about the last of next week. I am not sure but I hope so. That won't be so long from now. Gee, it makes me happy, for I can see you soon, dear, and get to talk to you.

I am going to have company on the train anyway. A girlfriend of mine, she is really a St. Louis girl but she goes to university here, is going to spend the summer in California at the home of her grandparents. She has decided to go when I go, for she goes as far as Long Beach. I know that we will have a good time traveling together, for she is a good sport.

Darling, just as soon as I find out what day I will start, I will telegraph you. I want to go right to San Diego and have you meet me there. Could you do that, or would you prefer to have me come some other way? Tell me what you think is best.

I am feeling quite well, but I did get a "dickens" of a cold from that picnic the other night. One of the girls got poison ivy, and she is having a terrible time with it, so Dad took me out to-day and showed me what poison ivy looked like. Nature lesson, eh?

What are you doing lately that is exciting? Still having meetings? Well, there is one more meeting that you are going to have soon, and that is with me. This is to be a very informal meeting, isn't that right?

Write me often, for soon you won't have to do much more writing.

I Love you, sweetheart. Lots of kisses

From Dora

June 1, 1927
(Wichita, KS to Oceanside, CA)

Dearest Ray,

While I have a few moments to myself, I am going to write a few lines to the one I love best. This may be the last letter that I write to you before I leave, so don't get worried if you don't get any more. You know that there are just so many little things to do before one leaves, and I am leaving here sometime next week. I will give you all the information in some other way than by letter next week about my arrival, etc.

Listen, dear, I am going to ask something of you. Will you try to keep next Sunday (June 12th) open for me? I think that I will be there by that time anyway.

Ray, I have waited months and months for the time when we should meet again. Now that it is really only a few days yet, I feel as if I were dreaming. I am so happy that I can't sit still, or get anything done. Wishes do come true, don't they, for I have been wishing that I could get to California by the middle of June or sooner.

We are having some terrible weather—cold, rainy and dreary, but soon I will be in the land of sunshine, so why should I worry about this weather?

Brother Carl arrives home Friday. One comes and one leaves, which makes it even, I guess.

I may as well close, for I can't seem to write a coherent letter. Ray, I just want to warn you that I am coming. I know that we are going to be a happy couple, and that all our dreams will come true.

Dear, I love you—love you—love you, and I am sending you a kiss—until we meet and I can give you a real one.

Lovingly
"Me"

June 5, 1927
(Oceanside, CA to Wichita, KS via Western Union Telegram)

MISS DORA KULLMANN
161 NORTH LAWRENCE AVE WICHITA KANSAS

BOTH LETTERS CAME AND AM VERY HAPPY HOPE YOU GET AWAY ON TIME MY BEST ADVICE IS YOU LEAVE WICHITA ON SANTA FE NUMBER ONE FRIDAY MORNING SIX TWENTY AND I WILL MEET YOU IN SANTA FE DEPOT EIGHT FIFTEEN SUNDAY MORNING IN LOS ANGELES AND WE WILL DRIVE DOWN TO OCEANSIDE BEST REGARDS TO FOLKS WIRE WHEN YOU START

RAY A. WILCOX

July 19, 1927
Oceanside, CA

Ray and Dora were married in Oceanside, California, on July 19, 1927. One journey had ended, and another had just begun.

TIME AND CHANGES

October 9, 2022
During the meandering journey to complete this story, I often asked myself: What am I missing? The word "missing" and the question itself are filled with melancholy and double meaning. I am missing all the things at Ray and Dora's house on the hill—the roses, the fruit trees and tall sycamore trees, the pheasants, the blue-bellied lizards, rabbits, quail, and coyotes. I miss watching the red-tailed hawks hunting and losing myself in the sagebrush checkerboarding the hillside. I miss the doves flying in at dusk to roost in their trees and the scent of gardenias and orange blossoms lingering in the air, along with the fennel plants whose broken stems smelled like licorice.

I am missing my grandparents' presence, just being with them as we explored their "north forty" together. I miss visiting with them, and their sense of optimism and contentment, and enjoying the powerful scents of each sacred living thing in their glorious garden. This was the house where so many important life events and accomplishments were celebrated. It's where grandchildren ran free. It's where our love for natural things began and grew as we touched the Earth's soil and smelled her fragrant flowers. Being there created great joy and emotions that still linger in my heart.

So, yes, there are many things I'm missing—but also things that I've gained and learned late in life about my relationship with Ray and

Dora. Perhaps the most unusual discovery came in the form of a surprise my mother (their daughter, Bobbie) casually dropped on me as we talked one day at her assisted-living facility before she passed. "It was a shame we had to send you off to go live with Mother and Daddy when you were a baby," she said out of nowhere. If I had "channeled" my inner Ray Wilcox, my reply back then might have been: "That was a shocker for sure, Bobbie!!"

I knew my younger brother's birth had been very difficult and that my mom was in traction for a long period of time afterward, but it seemed strange to learn this fact at this stage in my life. To be fair, Mom was compromised by cognitive decline and Alzheimer's disease during her final years. But my older sister confirmed this event in my early childhood and noted, "I always wondered how it was for you, moved from your home at that stage of life. It was so odd to have our little baby John disappear. 'Where is he?' I kept asking Mom and Dad."

During the last four decades, I have mostly avoided visiting the Wilcox house on the hill. Viewing the changes since my grandparents' passing has created some strong reactions within me, and my thinking was, Why should I even go there? The nice couple who first purchased the Wilcox house from our family transformed it into a part-time platform to display large-scale public art pieces. Suddenly things were out of place, and my family didn't belong there anymore.

I've secretly driven up there a few times, though, with half-hearted hopes of finding something other than the ghost or shadow of Ray and Dora's faded California dream. My mind was always full of anxiety, thinking about seeing the remnants of the once new and happy home they built on the gently rolling hillside. It's hard to look past what's become of the hillside. The Wilcox house is now surrounded by a clutter of 207 homes in the Sea Mesa real estate development, built in the 1980s. Several of these houses block the ocean and valley views that we all enjoyed for so many years. A large, malformed volunteer pepper tree now grows alone on the front lawn where the majestic sycamores and cottonwood trees once stood. Those tall trees, which framed the ranch house, grew like sentinels, protecting Ray and Dora and providing sanctuary for visiting wildlife.

Then one journey to the house was different, and I was rewarded immediately with the good fortune of seeing a beautiful, healthy coyote on the property. She seemed to be surveying her meal options from the advantageous position of the crest of the hill. I was so excited that I could barely get my car parked along the roadside before I hopped out and ran up the road to try and capture a photo of the magnificent animal. All the swirling emotions and distractions in my head suddenly disappeared.

Just then a woman's voice shouted from a window of the home, "Hey!! Hey!! Can I help you?" I could see her inside and noticed she had a white towel on her head. The only thing that this human trespasser could manage to eke out was "I'm sorry" and something awkward like "My grandparents built this house." The woman's demeanor changed. "Are you a Thill?" she asked. "Yes," I said, surprised she knew. She quickly replied, "I'll be right out!"

The young woman (whose head was by then towel-free) was gracious and generous as she invited me to see first the guest cottage and backyard and then the inside of what was once Ray and Dora's home. She described the improvements they were making to the property and directed us to look at the wonder of Ray's now twenty-foot-tall orange tree. It was loaded with fruit from tip to trunk, and it was still producing for a new family nearly fifty years after he had planted it. A partial rose garden still lived, and they were replacing the grass in the backyard that the prior owner had removed. She expressed genuine appreciation and respect for the place. When I told her how grateful I was that she and her husband were restoring parts of it to how Ray and Dora had first designed things, she told me, "It's interesting. We don't really see ourselves so much as owners as we do caretakers of this house."

It didn't seem possible, but at that moment it felt like this special place—a place that was once new and beautiful but had grown old and neglected—was now becoming new again. My head and heart were full. I felt a renewed sense of peace and contentment about the home and my personal connection to it.

•••

During my final look through our Wilcox-related records and keepsakes, two handwritten pieces from Ray stood out as important to share with others. The first related to the city of Oceanside and a speech Ray wrote in 1938 called "The Spirit of Oceanside." He delivered this address to the mayor and city council during the fiftieth anniversary of the city's incorporation.

> *Oceanside this year will witness the culmination of 50 years of physical growth. We have seen a modern city developed from the sagebrush and uninhabited desert waste. In all of Southern California and especially along the coast we have remained the least spoiled from the ruthless hand of spoiled man as far as natural beauty is concerned. And after all, in a world reeking with the spirit of greed and gain, it is a tribute to the people who have so unselfishly guided the community during the past half-century.*
>
> *Our best assets, in my opinion, are our natural geographical location and our climate perfection. If we can develop the true beauty that will correlate these advantages there is no finer future ahead of any other city.*
>
> *There is an attachment to Oceanside that grows on a person. It goes beyond pride in showing strangers our hidden jewel of a beach, our splendid street and water system, and our rapidly growing business and residential section. I believe it is something that makes us really hate to go to the big city and be forced to stay a while. It is that certain something that makes us want to hurry back home. It is a magnet that draws us all back to our city by the sea "where life is worth living." It is also in your neighbor's heart and it is a spirit that amounts almost to fraternalism. May the next succeeding 50 years in Oceanside be eventful, inspiring and tranquil.*

For more of Ray's address please visit: www.johnwthill.com.

The second piece was a note Ray wrote to my parents. It included a progress report on a college fund he and Dora had created to help all seven of their grandchildren pursue a college education. This was significant in that Ray at one point in his own life had clearly hoped to complete a college education, but work and other responsibilities interrupted it. Referencing the fund for us grandkids, he wrote, "It has been a labor of love and I want to see it through. Dora would be happy to know that I followed through in good times and bad, all with love for the finest families in this part of the world."

The last thing to share with you is that Dora and Ray saved many letters and thank-you notes from friends, community members, and all seven of their grandchildren. Reading and holding these heartfelt messages helped me realize that in a small way this book serves as my final thank-you letter to Ray and Dora.

EPILOGUE

A few weeks back I drove out to visit Heritage Park again. It was cold and windy after a surprisingly powerful late-night rain and thunderstorm. The early sunlight was working hard to break through large, fast-moving clouds. As I got closer to the park, I was distracted by a small cemetery that I'd never seen before. It was just west of and almost connected to the park and included a tiny church. I pulled my car over and stopped to look at it more closely. The place was well cared for and so compact that within no time I had walked through all the rows and examined the names and symbols on each of the grave markers.

As I turned to leave, I noticed there was an older man on the edge of the property. He was slowly and carefully cleaning up the grounds, removing the scattered and fallen pieces of nature that had been knocked down by the storm's rain and wind. I watched him work for a while; then he paused and smoked a cigarette. Time passed and the wind continued. Eventually I walked up to the man and thanked him for his effort. I asked if he was the caretaker for the church and cemetery. "No. I am a volunteer," he replied. We didn't have much else to say to each other, and after a silent beat or two I said, "Well, thank you again for your work tending to the place." He didn't respond this time; we simply looked at each other. I paused again and then, to fill the gap, added awkwardly, "May peace be with you."

I stayed a few minutes longer, took some photographs, and reflected on life as I watched a dried-up leaf being tossed around by the wind. The leaf made faint scratching noises as it cartwheeled across a small section of gray concrete. It was moving west, away from the morning sunlight, in the direction of the graves of what I later learned was called the All Saints Church and Cemetery.

I got back into my car and drove only a few hundred yards north to Heritage Park. I parked and walked through the open gates, surprised to see that no one else was there. The aging wooden buildings greeted me, and I found some open space that allowed me to better appreciate all the things around me. I paused to admire Dora's sycamore tree. It stood tall and lovely, and white, tan, and gray bark illuminated its distinctive trunk. The crown of the tree must have been ten feet higher than anything else at the park. I knew that somewhere wrapped in the soil and roots of this living thing was a handcrafted symbol of appreciation from her daughter—Dora's small black marble monument.

These changes can't be seen during a single visit. Sometimes it takes a lifetime to notice and understand the importance of the people and things around you. Ray and Dora's love story was once just a dream, and it may have been written in the past, but it is still alive in these roots that have grown deep and strong in the rich California soil.

ABOUT THE AUTHOR

John W. Thill is a learning and development specialist, adult literacy advocate, and tutor serving people in Southern California. His life experience incorporates over forty years of business and community service work. John's passion and expertise includes assisting people in understanding their strengths to better navigate relationships and lead themselves to places of fulfillment and success. He is a graduate of San Diego State University, a past president of the Rotary Club of Carlsbad, and continues a fifty-year love affair with the Pacific Ocean. For more information, please visit www.johnwthill.com.

Made in the USA
Columbia, SC
29 July 2023